M000251992

"You need to do this. You can do this. I can help." This is what it feels like to work with Kris Putnam-Walkerly. What a delight it is to now have in book form the wisdom, inspiration, and tools of a gifted writer and leader in philanthropy. Thank you, Kris. We need your voice, your encouragement, and your mad skills in this work. You are a gift to the field.

Ellen LaPointe, President & CEO, Northern California Grantmakers

Aristotle once told us that giving well is tougher than you think. *Delusional Altruism* is a welcome guide that shows why he was right and what you can do to get better. Written in practical down-to-earth steps and sensible advice, it's valuable whether you're beginning the journey or wanting to check your current practice. And it even translates well "across the pond!"

Paul Streets, CEO, Lloyds Bank Foundation

Effective philanthropy can elude even the best of intentions. Kris Putnam-Walkerly gets it—and with a page-turning mix of hard truths, good humor, and tough love, she's ready to help you avoid those all-too-common mistakes that prevent your pursuit of the greater good from having its greatest impact. This inspiring and provocative book will change the way you think about changing the world.

Lara A. Kalafatis, Chair, Cleveland Clinic Philanthropy Institute

Kris Putnam-Walkerly brings her visionary gift of change-making philanthropy forward in this book. Not only does she identify many of the common mistaken notions of giving that are found in all types of donors and organizations, but she also clearly shows how to redeem the act of giving with seven strong strategies that lead to better impact.

Tamara Fynan, Executive Director, Community Engagement & Philanthropy, The J.M. Smucker Company

We all know the expression, "The road to hell is paved with good intentions." My years of experience of working with all kinds of donors show that good intentions are not enough, and HOW is probably more important in giving than WHAT. This book is very important because it holds a mirror to donors' common mistakes and gives them a chance to improve and achieve bigger impact.

Maria Chertok, Director, Charities Aid Foundation, Russia

This is a thought-provoking book full of straight talk and practical advice for philanthropists of all shapes and sizes. Putnam's questions and ideas will push funders to think differently about everything—from strategy to mind-sets to time management.

Kristi Kimball, Executive Director, Charles and Helen Schwab Foundation

My father, cofounder of the Sheraton Hotel Chain, told me that the greatest pleasure his money ever gave him was in giving it away. But he also warned about having a full heart and an empty head; philanthropy done badly could make matters worse. Kris Putnam-Walkerly's book is the perfect answer to the problem my father foresaw.

Mitzi Perdue, Philanthropist & Founder, Win This Fight, Stop Human Trafficking

This book will be that voice in my head that says, "You can change the world. You just need to do it differently," and then shows me the way!

Peter Long, Senior Vice President, Blue Shield of California

In her latest book, *Delusional Altruism*, Kris Putnam-Walkerly identifies several key elements to transformational giving alongside the delusions every thoughtful donor should avoid. Readers will gain clear direction on why we all must eliminate the delusions that limit our impact and sharpen our focus to truly transform through our philanthropy.

Wendy H. Steele, Chief Executive, Impact100

Putnam-Walkerly weaves years of successfully guiding leading philanthropists with a straightforward and honest assessment of the field to give us a breath of fresh air in her latest offering, *Delusional Altruism: Why Philanthropists Fail to Achieve Change and What They Can Do to Transform Giving.* If you're a time-tested pro or thoughtful newcomer, Kris's insights and perspective will help you move from simple charity to high-impact giving!

Jed Emerson, Blended Value

Delusional Altruism is a guide book for anyone who wants to gain a better understanding of how to create the biggest impact with their philanthropic investments. Kris Putnam-Walkerly writes with an insider knowledge of the philanthropy world, analyzing our missteps and offering practical tips for examining our grantmaking practices and making simple changes to further our reach and create positive, systemic changes in our world.

Dolores E. Roybal, Executive Director, Con Alma Health Foundation, New Mexico

We all want to change the world, but sometimes our thinking gets in our way. For philanthropists, clouded thinking can hold you back from helping society in big and important ways. In *Delusional Altruism*, Kris Putnam-Walkerly shows you how to sidestep faulty thinking, so your resources create the greatest impact possible. I highly recommend this book!

Daniel H. Pink, New York Times bestselling author of
WHEN* and *DRIVE

All philanthropists can support transformational change—but not without some support of their own! *Delusional Altruism* is a great guidebook to help avoid unnecessary pitfalls on the path to achieve impact. Through her years of experience working with foundations and donors and her passion for making the world a better place, Kris Putnam-Walkerly provides a candid and credible look at why how we give is just as important as what we give.

Kathleen P. Enright, President & CEO, Council on Foundations

Kris Putnam-Walkerly offers insightful observations of the typical misunderstandings that donors and foundations have when they give, as well as useful tools for philanthropists to reflect upon their mind-sets and actions. As a philanthropy practitioner, I can tell the ideas and wisdom shared in her book come from extensive first-hand experiences in the field and continuous reflections. *Delusional Altruism* is definitely worth reading for those who want to make their giving more impactful!

Yanni Peng, CEO, Narada Foundation and Chair, China Social Enterprise and Impact Investment Forum.

I once thought giving away money was easy. I learned the hard way I was wrong. As Kris Putnam-Walkerly makes abundantly clear, we can easily trip over our own good intentions. In *Delusional Altruism*, she identifies the ways we often fool ourselves—at times not even recognizing what we are doing—and then goes on to offer practical advice and guidance on how to transform our giving and increase our impact. Whether you are an experienced philanthropist or just getting started, this should be on your reading list.

Henry L. Berman, CEO, Exponent Philanthropy

In *Delusional Altruism*, Kris Putnam-Walkerly helps us understand that when philanthropists unintentionally restrain ourselves—through fear, a scarcity mentality, or simply asking the wrong questions—we also hold back the change we can make in the world.

Benjamin Bellegy, Executive Director, WINGS—Worldwide Initiatives for Grantmaker Support

A thought-provoking and insightful look at smart giving. Kris scrutinizes the pitfalls that hinder traditional philanthropy, making a compelling case for a more strategic form of 21st-century giving. This is essential reading for anyone who wants to really make an impact.

Emma Turner, Director, Barclays Private Bank Philanthropy Service

It's always a worthwhile endeavor for philanthropists to look at how they can get better with their giving, and Kris Putnam-Walkerly's new book helps them do just that. Her honest assessment of seven *Delusional Altruism* practices is a must-read for all philanthropists, and her seven strategies for "Transformational Giving" can help all of us get out of our own way and make the greatest impact we can with our gifts.

David Biemesderfer, President & CEO, United Philanthropy Forum

Delusional

. . .

Altruism

KRIS PUTNAM-WALKERLY, MSW

Delusional

Altruism

WHY PHILANTHROPISTS FAIL TO
ACHIEVE CHANGE

AND WHAT THEY CAN DO TO
TRANSFORM GIVING

WILEY

Library of Congress Cataloging-in-Publication Data

Names: Putnam-Walkerly, Kris, author.
Title: Delusional altruism : why philanthropists fail to achieve change and
    what they can do to transform giving / Kris Putnam-Walkerly, MSW.
Description: Hoboken, New Jersey : Wiley, [2020] | Includes index.
Identifiers: LCCN 2019057780 (print) | LCCN 2019057781 (ebook) | ISBN
    9781119606062 (hardback) | ISBN 9781119606093 (adobe pdf) | ISBN
    9781119606048 (epub)
Subjects: LCSH: Charity. | Altruism. | Humanitarianism.
Classification: LCC HV48 .P88 2020 (print) | LCC HV48 (ebook) | DDC
    361.7/4—dc23
LC record available at https://lccn.loc.gov/2019057780
LC ebook record available at https://lccn.loc.gov/2019057781

COVER ART & DESIGN: PAUL MCCARTHY

Printed in the United States of America

V10017433_021020

This book is dedicated to my husband, Terry. Thank you for your unwavering support and belief in me. I love you.

Contents

Foreword   *xiii*

Introduction   *xvii*

PART I   **Delusional Altruism**   **1**

Chapter 1   You Save Money on All the Wrong Things   3

Chapter 2   You Are Fearful   21

Chapter 3   You Respond Too Slowly   35

Chapter 4   You Have Too Many Steps   43

Chapter 5   You Are Too Overwhelmed to Take Your
                    Next Step   51

Chapter 6   You Are Fooled by Your Own Efforts   61

Chapter 7   You Ask the Wrong Questions   71

PART II   **Transformational Giving**   **79**

Chapter 8   You Start with the Right Questions   81

Chapter 9   You See and Act Abundantly   109

Chapter 10   You Are Fast   123

Chapter 11   You Transform Lives   141

Chapter 12   You Are Unstoppable   177

Chapter 13   You Found Your North Star   195

Chapter 14   You Do What It Takes   211

Chapter 15   Get Moving: Transform Your Giving and
                 Change the World!   225

Acknowledgments   *231*

About the Author   *235*

Index   *237*

Foreword

It's fitting that I first met Kris Putnam-Walkerly at a Points of Light Foundation Board retreat in the fall 2018, where I was moderating a panel on which she was speaking. Points of Light is a nonprofit that seeks to inspire, mobilize and equip people to effect change through volunteerism and service to others—a description that also fits Kris perfectly. She's been advising as a global philanthropy expert for more than 20 years, sharing her deep domain knowledge to help ultra-high net worth donors, funders using donor-advised funds, foundations and Fortune 500 companies make a significant impact for worthy social causes through charitable giving.

From the start of our relationship, I was impressed with Kris' profound insights on the sector, particularly as they relate to the concepts of *Delusional Altruism* discussed in this book, which commonly plague well-intended philanthropists. These delusional or misleading thoughts and approaches—which often see givers focused on the wrong questions, assigning themselves too many steps or feeling too overwhelmed to even take the next step—hinder their ability to maximize impact in their giving.

Kris' philosophies on overcoming these challenges mirror many of those that I share as president of Fidelity Charitable, an independent public charity that has helped donors support more than 220,000 nonprofit organizations with over $40 billion in grants since 1991. In different capacities, we ultimately strive for the same goal: to drive a higher level of satisfaction and effectiveness in our donors' philanthropy.

One of the biggest hurdles I see hindering this goal in philanthropy, and one of the many provocative ideas that Kris discusses in this book, is the misconception among donors that nonprofit organizations must be frugal in investing in infrastructure. This generally misinformed mindset holds that nonprofits spending the least on overhead deliver the greatest value to the people they serve. That may be the case, but often may not.

As Kris explains, this scarcity mindset is rooted in fear of failure rather than fact. It holds back well-intended people from pursuing their philanthropic goals. Like Kris, Fidelity Charitable subscribes to an abundance mentality when advising donors on worthwhile nonprofits, believing that the more an organization invests into the infrastructure driving their mission, the more long-term, sustainable results they'll generate for their social cause.

Think about it in the context of an organization trying to feed hungry children. A donor operating under a scarcity mindset narrowly focuses on ensuring the funds supporting the organization's infrastructure don't outweigh the funds needed to purchase and distribute food. Thus, if the organization is spending money on administrative overhead, the donor believes it's not properly allocating funds.

In my experience, this is a short-sighted understanding of what it takes to support a truly effective nonprofit organization and create social change. In fact, the organization may be more successful in its objective of aiding hungry children if it is able to attract and retain top talent to aid in its mission, thanks to donor support. Support for state-of-the-art technology could help it deliver more food more efficiently. Support for the nonprofit to advocate for policy changes might give more families the resources they need to feed their children without outside assistance.

Like any successful organization in the private sector, healthy nonprofits also need to invest in people, innovation, systems, and technology to drive productive action, as Kris details. Providing funds to support and train top talent and equipping them with the best tools and resources to do their jobs not only ensures they can effect change in line with the nonprofit's mission—but likely do so more efficiently, and at a greater capacity, than a spartan organization with little means to achieve an end.

I find that this concept of abundance mindset, that you must support an organization itself to support the realization of its mission, is easy to grasp once explained. And yet, comprehension and understanding in the philanthropic sector takes time—the commodity our society seems to be lacking most.

Kris' straightforward, easy-to-read guidance within these pages helps you identify and conquer delusions that may be holding you back from making a measurable social impact through altruistic efforts. These are critical ingredients to making confident, informed decisions to lead a nonprofit or see your charitable contributions put to good use. This book is a rewarding investment for any reader interested in reexamining and changing how you give to accomplish the greatest impact for a cause you're passionate about.

Practical idealists, you must read on.

— Pamela Norley, President, Fidelity Charitable

Introduction

I'd like to introduce you to three philanthropists. Just like you, they want to change the world (or their corner of it). They also share an additional characteristic—let's see if you can spot it.

The Kenya Community Development Foundation Wants to Change the World

A group of Kenyan nonprofit professionals started this community foundation with one aim: shift power to communities. They understood transformational change is possible only when communities can take charge and find their own solutions for development.

So they created a different model for community philanthropy.

Their foundation supports poor and marginalized communities to uplift themselves through their own efforts. It invests in community-led initiatives to meet priority needs. It develops grassroots leadership, builds the capacity of local institutions, and changes policies to ultimately lead to durable, lasting development.

They do this by bringing together a range of local and global donors: philanthropists with considerable wealth; middle-class Kenyans; community residents; and funders such as the Ford Foundation, Wilde Ganzen Foundation, and Comic Relief, among others. Collectively they've allocated more than $22M U.S. to community-led development projects that have benefited more than 2.2 million people.

What does that mean? It means a community dispensary that brings treatment to people's doorsteps, educational access for students threatened by wildlife on their way to school, and renewable energy to improve living standards in local villages.

Social Venture Partners India Wants to Change the World

It wants to do this by changing India, city by city. This venture philanthropy initiative was inspired by Social Venture Partners (SVP) International and launched by a group of Indian CEOs. Since 2012, SVP India has mobilized 180 Indian business leaders, philanthropists, and citizens to raise $460,000 and offer 17,000 volunteer hours to 18 nonprofits, impacting more than 245,000 lives.

SVP India had a goal to improve livelihoods through job creation and vocational training. But its members quickly realized it's not enough to move a few people out of poverty and into jobs by providing small grants. While they benefit from the vast experience and insights of SVP chapters worldwide, they also needed to find an "Indian way" forward that worked effectively in their cultural context.

To tackle massive social problems in India, they needed to mobilize the entrepreneurial spirit of their members, partner with larger nonprofits, and create scalable solutions. Their ambitious new goal? To create a million sustainable jobs over the next five years.

The William and Flora Hewlett Foundation Wants to Change the World

With a mission to advance ideas and support institutions that promote a better world, a staff of 120, and assets of $9.8 billion dollars, the Foundation awards more than $400 million annually to address climate change globally, encourage public engagement in the arts, and equip every student for a lifetime of learning, among other priorities. To give that much money away, they need to make a lot of grants in substantial amounts.

But they realize that to do so, they also need to make it easy for nonprofit organizations to apply. The Foundation, then, did something almost unheard of: They simplified their rules.

Many of their programs allow a nonprofit to simply submit the same proposal to them that it previously submitted to another foundation—without changing a word. What's more, many organizations seeking general operating support can submit a copy of their annual report and an audited financial statement. They don't need to spend precious time writing lengthy proposals and completing cumbersome budget forms.

And that's not all. The foundation can also make grants up to $1 million on a rolling basis with approval from the foundation's president. No waiting for additional board review.

What characteristics do the Kenya Community Development Foundation, Social Venture Partners India, and the William and Flora Hewlett Foundation have in common? They are all philanthropists. Did you guess that additional characteristic I asked you about earlier? It's this: when it comes to changing the world, each one of them knows how to get out of their own way.

We Are All Philanthropists

"Philanthropist" sounds highfalutin, doesn't it? So you might be surprised to learn that "philanthropist" describes most of us. Philanthropists and philanthropic organizations actively promote human welfare. They donate time, money, experience, skills, or talent to help create a better world. They possess a deep desire to solve social problems and help others.

I bet that sounds like you.

You are a philanthropist.

You aren't alone. About half of all Americans and 90% of high-net-worth individuals give to charity.[1] Collectively, Americans donated $427 billion in 2018.[2] In addition to individual giving, this includes giving through 80,144 independent and community foundations, 2,670 corporate foundations, and 3,311 operating foundations.[3]

In 2017 there were 463,622 donor-advised funds in the United States, representing an astonishing 60% increase from 2016. These funds held over $110 billion in assets, and donors used them to contribute $19 billion in grants to qualified charities.[4]

Similarly, about 44% of Europeans donate to charity,[5] and the region houses more than 140,000[6] registered public benefit foundations. The total amount of annual philanthropic contributions in Europe is estimated at $96.5 billion (87.5 euro).[7]

China represents one of the fastest growing philanthropic countries, spurred in part by having the largest number of billionaires in the world—819 of them in 2019.[8] Chinese philanthropy has quadrupled, from $6 billion in philanthropic contributions in 2009 to $23.4 billion in 2017.[9]

These numbers will continue to grow. In fact, over the next 25 years nearly 45 million U.S. households will transfer over $68 trillion in assets to heirs and charity.[10] That's right—trillion with a T. This wealth transfer isn't just happening in the United States; it's happening around the world. India (home to 119 billionaires) will experience a $128 billion (Rs 8.6 lakh crore) intergenerational wealth transfer over the next decade alone.[11]

The portion of these assets used for social good represent an upcoming "philanthropy boom."

And it's not just the countries with the most billionaires who give. According to Charities Aid Foundation (CAF), the world's most generous country in 2018 was Indonesia, followed by Australia and New Zealand. In fact, the top 20 most generous countries (ranked by three aspects of giving behavior: donating money, volunteering, and helping a stranger) include Singapore, United Arab Emirates, and Sierra Leone (the United States ranked fourth).[12]

The world has a lot of philanthropists. This book is for all of them—but especially for those who aren't quite achieving the impact they seek. They come in many forms: ultra-high-net-worth donors, wealthy families, foundations, Fortune 500 companies, donor-advised funds, celebrity activists, professional athletes, family offices, giving circles—individuals and organizations large and small.

Just like you, they want to change the world.

It might not be the whole world. It might be your small corner: You raise your children to become loving and successful individuals. You volunteer at your kids' school because you want all kids to succeed, not just your own. You donate food and money to your local food pantry because you believe no human being should go hungry. You've identified problems in the world and you want your donations to help solve them, whether you are giving $10, $100, $10,000 or $100,000,000. You hope your contribution, large or small, will help discover a cure for cancer, stop human trafficking, or end genocide.

What's more, you aren't looking for bandage solutions. You want transformational change. Lasting change. You want to tackle the problem at its root, so it no longer exists.

So what is the big secret to this transformational change? It's this: How we give is as important as how much we give or which causes we support.

Let me make it as clear as I can: The key word here is *how*.

How.

How we give matters. *How* we give allows us to be transformational.

So when it comes to giving that matters, what stands in our way? The thing between us and that type of transformational giving is something I call Delusional Altruism. Now, by "delusional," I don't mean we're stupid or crazy. I mean we're hindering our impact unnecessarily, because of a handful of deceptive and illogical thoughts we choose to hold dear. These illogical thoughts are making us get in our own way, and we don't even realize it. When we can't get out of our way, we reduce our speed to impact. When we don't realize it, it's difficult for us to change.

Delusional altruism shows up in our lives in different ways. For some of us, it's a scarcity mentality. For others its fear. Many of us ask the wrong questions, which send us down the wrong paths. Or we let ourselves be fooled by our own efforts.

In Part I of this book, we'll examine the seven most common ways we experience Delusional Altruism. Of course, not everyone suffers from all seven, but suffering from even one can derail a program of giving. The good thing is that no matter how many delusional thoughts you suffer from, none of them need be permanent. You can rid yourself not only of the thought but of the effect that thought has on your giving. In other words, you can turn things around—both in your mind and in the world.

In Part II, we'll look at the top seven strategies for Transformational Giving and how you can use them to defeat any of the delusions you or your organization hold. Together, the philosophy behind these strategies constitute a mind-set that will make you unstoppable. It will alter how you see the world and how you can create change in people's lives.

I hope you're ready to begin. After all, the work you're doing is too important to put off or get wrong. We all need what you bring to the table. The planet is waiting for you to up your game and make your giving as powerful as it can possibly be. The world needs you. Let's go!

Notes

1. https://www.privatebank.bankofamerica.com/publish/content/application/pdf/GWMOL/USTp_ARMCGDN7_oct_2017.pdf.
2. https://givingusa.org/giving-usa-2019-americans-gave-427-71-billion-to-charity-in-2018-amid-complex-year-for-charitable-giving/.
3. Foundation Center (Active US Foundations by Foundation Type, 2017) https://candid.org/.
4. https://www.nptrust.org/reports/daf-report/.
5. https://efc.issuelab.org/resource/an-overview-of-philanthropy-in-europe.html.
6. https://www.swissfoundations.ch/sites/default/files/European_Foundation_Sector_Report_2015_0.pdf .
7. https://ernop.eu/giving-in-europe-launched-at-spring-of-philanthropy/.

8. https://www.rockefellerfoundation.org/report/philanthropy-in-china/.

9. Ibid.

10. https://info.cerulli.com/HNW-Transfer-of-Wealth-Cerulli.html? utm_source=CNBC&utm_medium=Press%2520Release&utm_ campaign=1811%2520High%2520Net%2520Worth%2520PR and https://www.cnbc.com/2018/11/20/great-wealth-transfer-is-passing-from-baby-boomers-to-gen-x-millennials.html.

11. https://www.fortuneindia.com/opinion/giving-more-power-to-the-people/102342.

12. https://www.cafonline.org/about-us/publications/2019-publications/caf-world-giving-index-10th-edition.

PART

I

Delusional Altruism

1 | You Save Money on All the Wrong Things

Philanthropists like to save money, but they save it on the wrong things. Let me explain what I mean.

Foundation leaders, donors, professional athletes, corporate executives—all philanthropists—want to be good caretakers of their charitable wealth. They want their assets and profits to grow, so there's more wealth to give. They also want to reduce their charitable costs and save money, so there's more left over to give to the causes they care about.

All of this is well and good.

The trouble is, in their altruistic effort to be frugal, they hold back on investment in important things like talent, strategy development, research, evaluation, technology, relationship building, and even their own personal learning. They hold back investment in their grantees, too.

They do this by setting arbitrary limits on how much money can be spent on nonprofit "overhead," or on when they expect to see grantees' results, but at the same time they refuse to fund evaluation costs.

3

When they do this, they hamstring themselves and the nonprofits they support. They genuinely want their philanthropy to change the world, but they're under a misguided belief that saving leads to impact. They're delusional about the damage caused by their thrift.

Frugality rarely leads to social change.

This type of destructive frugality happens to all types of philan-thropists. Let me give you a few examples:

The CEO of a foundation with more than $200 million in assets refused to allow his staff to take company laptops on business trips. Why? For what he felt was a good reason: He worried his staff would acciden-tally break or lose them, and he didn't want to spend $1,700 for each replacement machine. The problem, though, was that on business trips the staff couldn't get work done.

You might be wondering, "Why couldn't they use their smartphones instead?" This was in the early 2000s. Sure, they had cell phones back then, and even some early versions of smartphones like the BlackBerry. They weren't the powerful, multitasking microcomputers we today call smartphones. The problem for foundation staff was that without laptop computers, they couldn't make productive use of their time on airplanes or in hotel rooms. They couldn't prepare grant recommendations or research funding opportunities. Responding to emails was cumbersome. They certainly couldn't access the foundation's grants management sys-tem to review proposals. In other words, while they might have attended a useful conference, foundation staff got nothing else done for three days every time they made a business trip.

Why? The CEO didn't recognize that the value of investing in his employees' productivity far exceeded the unlikely expense of $1,700. With $200 million in assets and an annual grantmaking budget of $10 million, the laptop expense should not have been a concern.

Here's another example, from the grantee's perspective.

A nonprofit requested a three-year policy advocacy grant from a donor to advance an innovative approach to drug treatment. The donor, however, authorized a grant of only one year. But influencing public policy can require consistent effort over the course of years. Efforts include conducting research, raising public awareness, organizing residents, educating the media, and meeting with policymakers. It takes time.

Because the nonprofit lacked a realistic three-year funding commitment, its CEO couldn't hire top talent. The experienced person she wanted wouldn't leave her current job and risk her family's financial security for a one-year gig. The CEO ended up hiring someone who was less proven.

In the no-laptops-on-trips and one-year-of-money-instead-of-three examples, the funders saved money up front. But they did so at the cost of staff productivity and program expansion. They saved money on the wrong things. They were under the delusion that they were being good stewards of their philanthropic assets. Instead, they were getting in their own way.

Why does this happen? Part of the spell of delusional altruism is a *scarcity mind-set*. Yes, you read that right. Despite access to wealth, philanthropists live, work, and breathe with a scarcity mentality.

The scarcity mind-set happens to all philanthropists. It probably happens to you, too.

A scarcity mind-set is the misguided belief that a Spartan operation equates to delivering more value on the issues funders care about. It's a belief that, by not investing in their own capacity, talent, research, learning, strategy, technology, effectiveness, and infrastructure (or that of their grantees), funders can allocate more money to the causes they support and therefore achieve a greater impact.

Surprisingly, the scarcity mind-set has little to do with money. It has everything to do with belief.

Scarcity-minded donors believe that investment in their own operation is only warranted when the need is urgent. They limit their opportunities based on current capacity, not potential impact. Improvements they make, therefore, are only incremental. They feel they should always do more with less. In fact, they often believe they don't *deserve* what's best, fastest, or most efficient.

After advising ultra-high-net-worth donors and philanthropy leaders for more than 20 years, I believe this scarcity mentality is one of philanthropy's most detrimental self-created restraints.

The problem with a scarcity mentality is that it hinders your talent, stalls your creativity, and hijacks your opportunities to create systemic change. And it seeps into just about every aspect of philanthropic giving.

I realize you don't want to hear this. You don't want to be a glass-half-empty philanthropist! No one does. But read on. Part of what makes "delusional altruism" so delusional is that we get in our own way *without realizing it*. Let's learn about how we inadvertently allow a scarcity mentality to creep into our lives.

It Starts in Your Mind

A scarcity mentality is the lens with which many donors view their philanthropy. It's important to understand that this is a belief system that misguides your thinking. It's a trickster. It fools you into believing that you are saving money. That the less you invest in your talent, infrastructure, and knowledge, the more you can help others.

This is of course ridiculous. The deceptive scarcity mentality is all in your head.

Before we talk about the ways that the scarcity mentality shows up in philanthropists' lack of investment, I want to talk about the guises it takes in your mind.

This happens most often when you don't trust yourself to make a decision, you limit yourself based on your current capacity, you believe you don't deserve something, or you believe you are too small to make a difference.

Not Trusting Yourself to Make a Decision

Too often, funders don't trust themselves to make decisions. Instead, without realizing it, they shroud themselves in a blanket of "more information." Here's how it works: You know (or are pretty darn sure you know) the answer. Then, you waste lots of time and money reassuring yourself you're right.

Here's an example: The leader of a corporate foundation wanted to hire a consultant. Two consultants were recommended highly. Still, she wasn't sure whom to choose, so she cast a wider net. She spent months developing a request for proposals (RFP) to find a consultant and another few weeks disseminating it widely. Next, she spent two months sifting through the dozens of proposals she'd received, scheduling and conducting interviews with finalists, selecting one consultant, and negotiating the contract. Six months later, she is ready to make the hire. Unfortunately, she's now lost half a year of her time, wasted countless hours of dozens of consultants' time, her project is delayed, she's behind in her other work, and the people her company is ultimately trying to help have been forced to wait—again.

What's even worse? After all that time and money she spent to find the consultant, she probably didn't find the best one. Why? Top talent in high demand wouldn't waste that much time applying!

Why do philanthropists do this to themselves? Their scarcity mind-set holds them back. They don't trust themselves to make decisions.

Look, sometimes the people involved genuinely don't know something, and they need to take time to learn. I get it. But in this example, the leader was smart. Think of how much better off everyone would have been had she met with each of the two recommended consultants, plus a couple more she could have easily found by asking trusted colleagues, and simply made a decision.

Limiting Yourself Based on Your Current Capacity

Too often funders say, "I can't" because they look at their current capacity and abilities and simply cannot imagine taking on a new task.

Does this ever happen to you or your colleagues? You postpone a project of strategic importance because you are "too busy" right now.

You decide you can't address the root causes of a problem because you don't have enough funds, so instead you fund projects to address the symptoms. You decide not to fund something because you don't know enough about the issue. You choose not to ask community members to inform your funding strategy because you don't feel equipped to address the issues they might raise.

Here's the thing: You might be busy, lacking information, and ill equipped. You might not have enough funds to adequately address the root cause. Great! Now we know where you stand.

But, then again, so what? Your current capacity, knowledge, ability, and funds shouldn't limit the transformational change you can create. You can increase your capacity, gain new knowledge, equip yourself, and leverage additional dollars. It might not be easy. It might take time. And you will probably experience a few bumps and scrapes along the way. That's just fine.

Believing You Don't Deserve Something

Too often, philanthropists feel they don't *deserve* to [fill in the blank], such as invest in themselves, retain an executive coach, fund a needs assessment, attend a conference, improve their technology, hire top talent, spend time learning with other philanthropists, share their accomplishments publicly, learn how they can advocate for policy change, or fund an evaluation.

Why? Because they have a misguided belief that all their money should go to help others.

This is especially pervasive in family philanthropy, among those who have inherited wealth, and among entrepreneurs who have earned their own wealth. But it's true for most any philanthropist.

Mind you, they might simultaneously be spending $15,000 to graphically design, print, and mail hard copies of their annual report; budgeting $30,000 for new marble kitchen countertops for their third vacation home; spending $100,000 annually to mist the plants at corporate headquarters; or forking over half a million dollars annually on fuel for their private jets.

But when it comes to charitable giving, scarcity rules the roost!

This belief might appear noble. In reality, it is delusional. In order to have the greatest philanthropic impact, you need to be the greatest philanthropist you can be. This involves understanding yourself, understanding the issues and communities you want to help, and investing time and resources to build your philanthropic muscle and know-how.

To help others, you first need to help yourself.

Believing You Are Too Small to Make a Difference

Not every philanthropist is a billionaire. You might be giving away thousands of dollars each year, not hundreds of millions. But a small funder should not limit its aspirations. Even donors with limited means can operate with an abundance mind-set. The world is rife with examples of small funders that created big impact. In fact, Exponent Philanthropy, a U.S.-based network of foundations with few or no staff, philanthropic families, and individual donors, regularly showcases members who achieve "outsized impact" compared to their size.

Too often, however, funders of all sizes believe they are too small to make a difference.

One philanthropy leader had this kind of poverty mind-set when it came to achieving her strategic goals. Her organization organized high-net-worth members to donate to progressive causes. They set specific goals of tripling the number of donor members and dramatically influencing how those donors allocated their funding.

However, she didn't know her baseline. She had no idea how much money her members were already donating to progressive causes. Nor did she know how much influence her organization currently had on her members' giving priorities.

She had a vision for her organization's desired future state, but no idea about its current state. Therefore, it was impossible to create a plan to move forward. When I suggested she conduct research to understand their current baseline, she balked. "No, we're just a small nonprofit. We really can't afford it," she insisted. Instead, she asked her staff—who were already working overtime and lacked research expertise—to figure it out on their own.

In other words, she was unwilling to make an investment in something of strategic importance to the organization, because she felt her organization was "just a small nonprofit."

Remember, her membership organization is comprised of high-net-worth donors who saw the value in this organization's work. They paid to be members! The wealth was sitting right there. But she wasn't willing to ask any of them to support this project. I'm sure one of her members would have been delighted to fund a research project that would help more philanthropists donate to progressive causes. But her scarcity mentality held her back and stifled her organization's philanthropic impact.

Lack of Investment

Now that we've discussed the guises a scarcity mentality takes in your mind, let's look at how it shows up in philanthropists' lack of investment.

Lack of Investment in Your Own Talent

Too often funders refuse to invest in the human capital of philanthropy. They think they're saving money, but they're shooting themselves in the foot.

Philanthropy is comprised of people. Donors are people. Family offices are run by people. Foundations are nonprofit organizations staffed by people. When we need legal, financial, and coaching help, we retain people. And the people we want to help are, well, people!

Given philanthropy's people-centeredness, the lack of investment in people is stunning.

What do I mean by investing in people? I mean investing in *you*. You—the person reading this book. And the people who help you with your giving. This could be your board of directors, your employees, your boss, your kids, or your spouse. I'm referring to bringing on the best talent to help you start, design, grow, manage, assess, and scale your philanthropy to achieve maximum impact. I also mean providing them with the resources and support they need to be their best selves and contribute their talents. After all, you want to change the world.

Sadly, this often does not happen. Most well-intentioned philanthropists don't invest in themselves.

Let me share a few examples.

One former professional football player started a nonprofit foundation to give back to his community. He created football camps and tutoring programs to offer low-income kids an opportunity to learn a sport, gain teamwork skills, have positive role models, and increase their educational opportunities. Although he made significant financial contributions, he knew he needed to raise additional funds to scale and sustain these programs.

Like most people, he lacked fundraising experience. He didn't know the best way to raise money. He and his wife tried, but their efforts didn't result in large contributions. Yet he refused to hire a fundraising consultant or grant writer. Why? It would cost money! You can guess what happened. He was able to maintain terrific camps and tutoring for a small number of kids, but he couldn't realize his vision of helping greater numbers.

In Africa, a multifamily office hired a talented nonprofit leader to serve as its first director of philanthropy. His job was to help the families become more philanthropic. The thing was, though, that while he had excellent leadership skills, he didn't have much knowledge about philanthropy. The family office leadership knew that from the outset, but they just assumed he'd figure it out. They refused to provide him with any professional development or coaching to boost her knowledge and expertise. Without any specialized information and support, the new leader quickly became overwhelmed.

A new health foundation was created following the purchase of a nonprofit hospital by a for-profit hospital. Overnight, the hospital board of directors became the foundation board of directors. The board hired a chief executive officer but refused to allow her to hire any additional staff. The CEO was expected to develop the foundation's strategy, navigate the board through politically charged local issues, create new partnerships, and grow the foundation. But she was also required to personally proof-read, photocopy, and collate meeting materials; find and schedule the caterer; take meeting minutes; and handle the bookkeeping.

Bookkeeping is important. And everyone likes to eat food at meetings. But you want your leaders driving the train, not shoveling coal into the furnace. The problem here is that the board refused to invest in any additional staff—not even a virtual assistant or part-time bookkeeper—to handle the back-office work so that the foundation leader could lead. As a result, the CEO spent nearly three-quarters of her time doing administrative tasks. That's time not spent building relationships, assessing community needs, planning, or thinking. Not surprisingly, she was frustrated. A year later, she was secretly looking for a new job.

Hiring the right talent and positioning that talent for success is critical. Unfortunately, all types of philanthropists fall prey to a scarcity mentality that holds them back. Lisa McLeod, author of *Leading with Noble Purpose*, explains:

> Many corporate leaders make the mistake of not putting a power player in charge of corporate philanthropy. They hire lower-level, less expensive employees for this role. This sends a message that philanthropy is not important. It also results in less effective philanthropic impact. If businesses want to give in meaningful ways, they should invest in philanthropy leaders who have both the positional authority and personal authority to make a difference.[1]

Not every region of the world is equally positioned to invest in philanthropic talent. In Russia, for example, the philanthropic sector has few people with appropriate degrees, and there is no systemic training in the management of nongovernmental organizations. "In general, the [philanthropic] sector offers lower financial remuneration than the business sector," explains Oksana Oracheva, executive director of the Vladimir Potanin Foundation. "Few foundations offer competitive salaries; the best-paid positions (at the program officer level) are within the US\$3,000–US\$5,000 per month salary range."[2] Some effort is under way to offer nonfinancial benefits, such as extra days off, flexible work schedules, conference participation, and special recognition awards, to attract and retain top talent. Unfortunately, these efforts are not used systematically, and it's still difficult to attract people with the right skills.

Lack of Investment in Your Own Capacity

A scarcity mentality holds philanthropists back from investing in themselves in other ways. This includes a lack of investment in research, organizational learning, operations, infrastructure, and innovation.

One couple wanted to spend \$1 million to reform public education across a 12-state region of the United States. On one hand, a million dollars is a lot of money. On the other hand, it would cover the salary of about 16 teachers. For one year. It's hard to reform public education by hiring 16 teachers for a one-year gig.

Unfortunately, this couple was not willing to invest the time and resources necessary to learn about the strengths and challenges of public education, best practices in education reform, or ways it could realistically make an impact with this level of investment. Nor were they interested in exploring how they could leverage their million dollars by partnering with existing education reform efforts. They wanted all their funds to support education. While noble in its intent, this approach would not help them reach their goal.

Lack of Investment in Nonprofit Talent and Capacity

Well-meaning philanthropists just like you have a scarcity mind-set when it comes to investing in the talent and organizational capacity of grantees.

Simply stated, you don't invest enough. And what you do invest is too often tied up in unfair and unnecessary hoops, hurdles, and hoopla.

As you know, your grantees are helping you achieve your philanthropic mission. Chances are high that you, the philanthropist, aren't the person building low-income housing in Philadelphia, installing portable toilets in Ghana, or training the next generation of teachers of color. Your grantees are.

And, as you know, your grantees are comprised of people. Amazing people. These outstanding people rely upon information, training, technology, curriculum, fundraising, financial systems, governance, and a host of other things to do their best work.

Don't you want the most talented people doing their best work to help you fulfill your mission? Of course you do!

Yet time and again, funders withhold investment in grantee talent and infrastructure. Do you want your grantees to have mediocre financial management systems, outdated technology, and lackluster board governance? Of course you do not! Yet philanthropists just like you overlook these real needs all the time.

Instead, you believe all your money should "help people" (or animals, or the environment), without recognizing the needs of the organizations doing the help. You have a scarcity mind-set, and it's undermining your effectiveness. Let me share a few examples.

One donor told me she would not allow grant dollars to pay for personnel costs of their grantees! You read that right. She will fund a program, but not the employees who run the program. She might fund a tutoring program, but funds could not be used to pay the tutors. Or she would support policy advocacy, but her grant could not be spent on the advocates.

How on earth can you expect students to learn without people to teach them, or legislators to vote differently if the policy advocate cannot meet with them? You can't. To think otherwise is delusional.

Not paying for personnel costs is one example of a scarcity mind-set. Another is paying below-market rates. In reflecting on the UK-based

Shell Foundation's 15 years of investment in social entrepreneurs, former Portfolio Director Simon Desjardins explained how underinvestment in talent resulted in poor outcomes:

> Though most recognize the importance of building a world-class team, few are prepared to pay for it. In many quarters, it is still assumed that because an enterprise has a social objective, its compensation levels can and should be below market. . . . In some regions (especially Africa, where there is often a shortage of trained professionals), investors and even some entrepreneurs will balk at the idea of paying . . . a market-related salary and typically opt for someone with a lesser track record. Time and again, we have seen this decision backfire and result in lost time and wasted money.[3]

Increasingly, philanthropists are recognizing that to achieve real outcomes, they must pay the real costs necessary to achieve those outcomes. Philanthropy California, an alliance of three regional associations of grantmakers, and the Nonprofit Finance Fund have come together to create the Full Cost Project. The goal of this initiative is to increase philanthropy's impact by adopting new funding strategies centered on the needs of today's social sector organizations. According to a report issued by this association of grantmakers:

> Real cost funding is not about overhead rates. Rather, it is a holistic approach to grantmaking that starts with the end in mind—what are the outcomes we are looking to achieve and what does it really cost to deliver those outcomes? . . . Simply put, the real cost of outcomes includes all of the necessary costs for a nonprofit organization to deliver on mission and to be sustainable over the long term.[4]

These might include the costs of donation management systems, strategy development, talent recruitment, professional development, fund development, financial management, board development, information technology upgrades, data collection and evaluation, start-up costs, and more.

In an open letter to all U.S. donors, Charity Navigator, GuideStar, and BBB Wise Giving Alliance encouraged all donors to move beyond the myth that low overhead rates mean better nonprofit performance:

> In fact, many charities should spend more on overhead. Overhead costs include important investments charities make to improve their work: investments in training, planning, evaluation, and internal systems—as well as their efforts to raise money so they can operate their programs. These expenses allow a charity to sustain itself (the way a family has to pay the electric bill) or to improve itself (the way a family might invest in college tuition).[5]

Yet most nonprofits continue to feel hamstrung by the philanthropic donations that are supposed to help them. In its 2018 survey of 3,400 U.S. nonprofit leaders, the Nonprofit Finance Fund identified nonprofits' top challenges. These included achieving financial sustainability (62%), raising funding to cover full costs (57%), and offering competitive pay (66%).[6]

This scarcity mind-set isn't limited to philanthropists in the United States. Italy's history and culture have contributed to societal beliefs that social sector organizations do not warrant infrastructure investment, according to Carola Carazzone, secretary general of Assifero, an Italian association of grantmaking foundations and institutional philanthropy. This includes a culture of Catholic voluntary service and a social services system in which for hundreds of years services have been provided free of charge by the church and, for the most part, by women.

"The spiral of producing [and] reporting projects only to match the priorities of calls for proposals launched by public and private funders, together with the perpetuation of a chronic underinvesting in the organizations, skills, and staff has led Italian civil society to the failure to develop its full potential," argues Carazzone. This has resulted in a culture of "low pay, make do, and do without."[7]

Charitable organizations in Kyrgyzstan, a Central Asian country bordering China and Uzbekistan, face even stricter challenges. They are "... obliged by law to spend 98% of their income on a charitable purpose or purposes within a year after receiving a donation, and thus leaving only 2% of this income to cover general overhead costs, including the salaries of personnel," according to Dinara Musabekova, director of the Civil Society Initiative at the University of Central Asia.[8]

How Do You Know If You Have a Scarcity Mind-Set?

Do you suffer from a scarcity mind-set? Don't take this personally, but chances are high that you do. I do, too. We all experience this at some point. I commonly see eight warning signs among philanthropists.

Take this eight-question Scarcity Mind-Set Quiz and see if a scarcity mentality might be holding you back. Give yourself a point for each question you answer affirmatively:

1. You frequently ask, "What's the cheapest way we can do this?" regardless of impact on quality, speed, or your discomfort. For example, you'll take a red-eye flight home to save money on hotel costs, even though it means you are exhausted and unproductive the next day.
2. You don't *regularly* make investments in your talent and infrastructure, or that of your grantees. This might include getting professional development or coaching, upgrading computer systems, attending conferences, evaluating your impact, etc.
3. Your workplace culture values working harder, not smarter. For example, people are expected to work late hours or on weekends, long meetings are the norm, and there are always lengthy processes for strategic planning or budgeting.
4. You hold a belief that every dollar you raise should go to the people and communities in need. You feel guilty investing in yourself.
5. You believe the real problems you want to tackle are impossible to solve with your funding. Instead of figuring out how to leverage your funding for outsized impact, you choose smaller, easier-to-solve problems. You often fund projects that eradicate the symptoms and not the cause.

6. You know something is critical to the success of your endeavor (e.g., a communications plan, developing partnerships, taking time off), but you never feel you have the time or resources to obtain it, do it, or fund it.
7. You don't invest in the people who could help you navigate your philanthropic journey, avoid mistakes, or save time. These could be trusted advisors, professional services (e.g., attorneys, accountants, donor-advised fund sponsors), content experts, consultants, or administrative support professionals.
8. You or your staff feel you don't have time to regularly think, plan, or build relationships because you're always too busy.

How did you do?

Let's first look at the worst-case scenario. If you scored 6–8, you need an intervention. You might even need therapy! In all seriousness, with a score like that, I'd wager that a scarcity mind-set is holding your philanthropy hostage. You could have greater impact, but you thwart yourself at every turn. But don't panic. Remember, a scarcity mind-set is just that—a mind-set. It's your beliefs. Beliefs can be changed. And just as in Alcoholics Anonymous, the first step is to admit you have a problem.

If you scored 3–5, your scarcity mind-set is certainly holding you back, but it's not strangling you. At least, not yet. Take a good look at the statements to which you answered "no." If you embrace an abundance mind-set for those questions, think about how you can transfer that abundance mind-set to all aspects of your giving. (I will tell you more about an abundance mind-set in Chapter 9, "You See and Act Abundantly").

If you answered "yes" to only one or two statements, you are in pretty good shape. But take a hard look at those statements. What's holding you back? Why do you feel scarcity in those areas? What investments in time or resources could unleash your effectiveness?

Now, if you scored a zero, you're likely in denial! Reread this chapter and open yourself up to the possibility that you are holding yourself back in some area of your work or life. In my entire professional career, I can only think of one person who genuinely, consistently, and in all aspects of his life could answer "no" to all of these questions.

Now, if you do truly feel that none of this applies to you, email me at kris@putnam-consulting.com and let me know how you do it! Seriously, I'd love to hear from you.

Why Does This Happen?

What causes a scarcity mind-set? In my experience advising hundreds of wealthy donors, corporate executives, foundation leaders, and everyday givers, it comes down to just one thing: fear. Funders feel fear, and this fear causes them to hold back.

In the next chapter, we'll take a close look at how fear contributes to a scarcity mind-set and the different kinds of fear that cause funders to hold back. Once you face your fears, you can overcome them.

Notes

1. Author interview with Lisa McLeod, August 8, 2019.
2. https://www.alliancemagazine.org/feature/financial-and-non-financial-striking-a-balance/.
3. https://www.alliancemagazine.org/feature/five-lessons-about-human-capital/.
4. "*The Real Cost Project: Increasing the Impact of Philanthropy in California,*" August 2016, https://www.socalgrantmakers.org/sites/default/files/files/pages/Real%20Cost%20PRoject%20Final%20Report%20Full%20Version%20FINAL.pdf.
5. http://s5770.pcdn.co/wp-content/uploads/2014/10/GS_OverheadMyth_Ltr_ONLINE.pdf.
6. https://nff.org/news/nff-survey-nonprofits-are-challenged-creative-unwavering.
7. https://www.alliancemagazine.org/blog/debunking-two-myths-avoid-agony-italian-civil-society/.
8. https://philanthropyinfocus.org/2018/11/26/a-look-inside-central-asian-philanthropy/.

2 | You Are Fearful

I recently spoke to the CEO of a foundation association who wanted to refresh the association's strategic plan. He wanted to start with a "learning tour," on which staff and board members would travel to multiple cities, set up town hall meetings in each, invite funders to attend, and engage in an orchestrated conversation to "learn" in order to inform the strategic plan. I told him he suffered from a scarcity mentality and was wasting time and resources. As you can imagine, he was shocked.

I explained that between his many talented staff, his seasoned board members who represented their entire geographic footprint, research they recently commissioned, and his team's collective learning from attending conferences and talking with members, they already knew 80% of what they needed to know. There were much faster and cheaper ways to gain that missing 20% than spending six months on a "learning tour."

The leadership of this organization suffered from a scarcity mentality because of fear. They didn't trust their own talent. They lacked confidence that they already had most of the knowledge they needed, or that they could quickly gain the rest. They didn't regularly invest time in their own organizational learning to capture and use this knowledge. As a result, they were willing to spend a lot of time and money on the wrong things (the learning tour)—and were willing to hurt themselves by postponing strategy development as a result. They were delusional in their altruism. They thought they were doing the right thing, but they were just getting in their own way.

Fear manifests itself in myriad ways in philanthropy. And it causes loads of problems. Fear wastes money, time, and talent. It prevents you from learning and improving. It results in less impact. And it's no fun! Who wants to be fearful?

Let's talk about some of the most common ways we experience fear in philanthropy. As you read these examples, think about the many ways fear holds funders back and how this contributes to a scarcity mentality. It might result in funders giving less, investing less in their own growth and development, or not openly sharing what they are doing and learning.

Fear of "Coming Out" in Support of a Cause

Many funders fear taking a stand on an issue. They worry that there could be negative repercussions to their reputation. They worry people might no longer fund them, hire them, or like them. This happens frequently with community foundations.

Community foundations are grantmaking public charities that raise money from donors in their community and make grants to nonprofits in that same community. Because they serve the entire community, they often feel compelled to meet everyone's needs. For example, they feel they need to support all issues—from healthcare to the arts to education—and appeal to all donors. As a result, they fear that if they take a leadership role on a particular issue, such as racial equity or education reform, they might alienate some of those donors.

Similarly, celebrities fear "coming out" in support of specific causes because it might alienate fans, cause a backlash, and result in fewer starring roles. In today's polarized world, electrified by social media, this fear is not unwarranted. Actor Tom Selleck learned this when he posed for a print advertisement for the National Rifle Association (NRA). The ad depicted him with a rifle over his shoulder accompanied by the slogan "Shooting teaches young people good things." It came out a month following the 1999 massacre at Columbine High School in Colorado, where two high school students murdered 13 people and injured 21 students.[1] The unfortunate timing of the ad resulted in a public backlash, starting with a challenging televised appearance on *The Rosie O'Donnell Show* where, instead of plugging his new film *The Love Letter* as he had planned, Selleck ended up debating gun control with host O'Donnell for more than seven minutes.

Often families fear they will be deluged by funding requests if they publicly announce the launch of a new foundation or new funding priorities. And in many parts of the world, such as the Netherlands, there is a strong cultural belief that talking about one's philanthropic giving is a form of bragging.

As a result of fear of coming out in support of a cause, or even talking about their charitable giving, many philanthropists inadvertently embrace a scarcity mentality. They hold themselves back. They refrain from fulfilling their philanthropic passion. They give anonymously. Or they don't give at all.

Fear of Being Out and About

Philanthropists also fear exposure. Not exposure that they have done something illicit or unethical—I mean fear of being seen. Fear of being out and about in their community. Fear that others will have access to them. As a result, they stay inside their bubble. They withhold themselves. In the process they suppress their own learning, and they make life harder for the those they want to help.

I understand why this is a real concern for celebrities. You might want to attend your favorite charity's gala, meet with parents to understand opportunities to improve local schools, or just go for a walk in Central Park. But you can't because you will be overwhelmed by fans and photographers. Or you could be someone with a fear of wide open spaces, crowds, or strangers. Attending the charity gala might truly be horrifying!

But chances are, you don't suffer from fears like these and you're not George Clooney.

Yet, like many philanthropists, you might maintain an arms-length relationship with your grantees and communities. Many donors hide behind family offices, wealth advisors, and publicists. They give anonymously through their donor-advised fund. They literally stay inside their offices and mansions. I once worked with a foundation executive who refused to visit nonprofits at their offices, insisting they come to him because it was more convenient (for him).

You might be on the board of directors, though, and guess what? Fear extends there as well. I am constantly amazed at the firewalls that some philanthropies put up around their board members—separating them from staff, from grantees, and even from community. I suppose there are board members who might appreciate that shelter, but if that's the case, I question whether they should serve in the role. Foundation board members should provide a key means of connection with community. Foundations should leverage not just the financial contributions of board members but also their relationships and influence. Board members can make key introductions, act as advocates, give presentations, and make themselves available to community members as representatives of the foundation. Yet too often, they are relegated to the boardroom.

As a funder, it's regrettably easy to stay in a "bubble" of isolation and fear—constrained either mentally by your own assumptions and knowledge, or physically by never leaving the office and venturing out into the community. If you're in a bubble, you probably aren't intentionally undermining your own effectiveness—but you are deluding yourself that you're achieving the impact you'd like to see. For effective grantmaking to really happen, you need to break out of the bubble and make an effort to deeply understand and connect with the communities you serve.

Fear of Failure

Many philanthropists, both new and experienced, frequently ask a universal, fear-based question: "What if it fails?"

For example, they ask, "What if we launch a new funding initiative and it doesn't achieve the desired results?" "What if we invest our money in mission-related investments, but we don't get the same return rate?" "What if I don't have what it takes to be the CEO?"

"Many philanthropists have a mind-set that if it doesn't work, it's a failure. This mind-set holds them back," explains Meredith Shields, managing director at the Sorenson Impact Foundation. "When you don't have a complete guarantee, when you can't rely on a tried-and-true strategy, sometimes you just need to do it and learn."[2]

The fear of failure is real and prevalent. Philanthropists respond to this fear with a scarcity mentality—they hold back themselves and their resources. But at the same time, they invest time, talent, and treasure on the wrong things. They engage in labor-intensive efforts dancing around the question: conducting excessive research and data analysis to unearth every facet of an issue before deciding to launch the initiative. Relentless benchmarking to see how they compare against others. Participating in endless leadership development programs instead of taking the plunge and applying for that CEO role. Or simply never trying.

Fear of Not Being a Good Steward

Most funders, like you, take their role of philanthropic stewardship seriously. This might mean ensuring that your foundation exists in perpetuity, or that monies allocated from your giving circle are aligned with your goals. This is especially true for professional staff of family offices and foundations—people responsible for giving away someone else's money.

This appropriate sense of responsibility can turn into fear when you worry that you aren't being diligent enough. Fear of not being a good steward can spiral into a scarcity mentality.

For example, if you're inappropriately fearful, you might do things like make smaller grants to try and stretch the funds, give a one-year grant because you worry the money won't be well spent, or force grantees to jump through excessive and punitive hoops in the name of due diligence.

One global philanthropy expert, Charles Keidan, now editor of the global philanthropy magazine *Alliance*, recalled this happening to him during his first foundation job in the UK.

> When I directed a family foundation, I was tougher on grantees than I would be today. I was cognizant that in the early days, the family was making big gifts to organizations based on fundraising appeals at a gala, more on the basis of relationships than evidence. I felt we had to use the money well, to be catalytic and strategic. So, I asked grantees questions they weren't ready to answer. My motivation was good, but my execution was impatient and unsympathetic.[3]

One Eastern European donor wanted to position his foundation as more innovative and strategic by offering general operating funding and making it easier for nongovernmental organizations (NGOs) to apply. Although it was a family foundation, he relied heavily on the advice and guidance of lawyers, accountants, and auditors from his business. Once they got involved, the simple process designed to give NGOs a lot of freedom in how they used their funding spiraled out of control.

His business advisors didn't trust the NGOs and began changing the rules. They asked fear-based questions such as, "How do we know these organizations won't steal the funds if we provide general operating support?" and "How do we know if they manage their books properly?"

They turned what was supposed to be an easy application process into a full-blown audit. They insisted on looking into the NGOs' bank accounts and accounting documents. They created a massive application process. They even asked the charities to create a separate bank account to receive the funds so they could track how the money was spent.

This scarcity mentality held the charities hostage. Instead of quickly receiving flexible funding, they had to wait nine months for a grant to fund a specific program. They had to invest a lot of their time managing and reporting on the grant. The donor allowed his fearful advisors to have this influence and inflict a scarcity mentality on his foundation. In doing so, he got in his own way.

Fear of Disappointing Others

Philanthropists don't like to disappoint people. I sure don't, and I bet you don't either. Unfortunately, philanthropy provides ample opportunities to disappoint. Sometimes it feels like the number one thing we do! Disappointing others most commonly happens by politely saying, "No." "No" to applicants that don't fit our funding guidelines. "No" to friends who ask us to contribute to their favorite charity. "No" to nonprofit leaders who want us to serve on their board.

One ultra-high-net-worth donor served on an NGO board that caused her stress. She didn't think they were making smart decisions or fulfilling their potential. Her efforts to help them were ignored. She really wanted off the board, but she had made a commitment and feared disappointing them. Even though the board had become a waste of her time and drained her energy, she feared saying, "No."

The fear of disappointing others also manifests itself when funders refuse to share what they've learned. For example, a corporate giving program conducted research on three different issues they're interested in funding. Findings and recommendations were summarized into a report. After reviewing the report, they selected one issue to support, but they were afraid to share the report publicly. They worried they would disappoint the people and organizations working on the two issues that weren't selected. Stuck in this scarcity mentality, they choose to hold back information that could prove helpful to other people working on that issue, out of fear of disappointing them.

Fear of Learning You Aren't Right

We all want to be right. After all, we're smart people. In fact, we're brilliant. We've bought and sold businesses, trained to become professional musicians, and led nonprofit organizations. We might draw upon a lifetime of challenging experiences that help us deeply understand the strengths and needs of others. We may have graduated from elite universities or the school of hard knocks. Whatever our backgrounds, we know a lot. And we want to be right!

But many funders fear learning they aren't right. They don't want to find out they aren't as smart as they think when it comes to solving the world's problems. So they stop asking questions. They stop learning. They stop looking for better approaches to reaching their goal. This is a scarcity mind-set in action. A funder prefers to stay in denial rather than risk learning they're wrong. If they could overcome this fear and recognize ways they need to change, they would increase their ability to make an impact. But fear overcomes their desire to make a difference.

This happens to many professional athletes who want to give back to their community after retirement. Most want to create their own foundation, without fully appreciating how hard it is to manage a nonprofit organization, create and run quality programs, and raise funds to sustain it. There are lots of other options. You can create a donor-advised fund instead of starting a foundation. That way someone else can manage the back-office operations, stay on top of taxes and reporting, and issue the checks. Or instead of creating new programs, you can invest your resources to expand and strengthen existing ones.

Charles Way agrees this would be a good idea, but it doesn't take into account the vision that most professional athletes have for themselves. Way is a former National Football League (NFL) player with the New York Giants. After his retirement from football, he spent 15 years with the Giants as their director of Player Development, then was recruited to the NFL to become director of Player Engagement. He's now a managing partner with Purple Bridge Management. With the Giants and the NFL, he helped players prepare for life and career after football, including philanthropy. Says Way:

> Sure, donor-advised funds would be a great solution. But not too many athletes know they exist and could be a better alternative to starting a foundation. It's also important to realize that, depending on the socioeconomic situation you come from, and the impact that situation had on you, oftentimes that determines how involved and passionate you are about that initiative. Which further fuels the desire to start a foundation—because from their experience, if they don't do something to make their community's situation better, then no one will.

In other words, they could benefit from learning that the approach they think they should take might not be best. There are alternative ways of giving back that might be better for you and more impactful for the communities you want to help. But it's hard to learn we might not be right.

It's easy to stay in our cocoons. We can hold tight to our beliefs and not fully understand the context of a problem or the scale of its solution. We often receive news via apps on our computers and smartphones, filtered to us via unknown algorithms that track what they think we want to know and feed us an increasingly narrow band of information. As a result, it's hard to learn from the opinions of people who have different cultural, political, or professional views.

Thankfully we aren't limited to what our devices tell us! We can learn from the people who are directly impacted by the issues we want to support. But too often we don't. For many, talking to "others" seems scary. So does hiring them or inviting them to join our boards. After all, we might learn we need to question our assumptions, or change the way we work. It's easier to base our philanthropic decisions on the decisions of other ultra-high-net-worth donors, academic research, and environmental scans. Rather than step foot in the blighted neighborhood we want to strengthen, we step into our offices and turn on our computers to learn.

Fear of Loss

In my experience, philanthropists fear two kinds of loss. Loss of the person you thought you were and loss of control.

Fear of losing the person you thought you were goes along with the previously mentioned fear, the fear of learning you aren't right. But it goes deeper.

You might participate in a workshop about undoing implicit bias and learn you have more racial bias than you realized. A *lot* more. Turns out, you aren't the "colorblind" person you thought you were. You conclude that all this "racial equity" stuff you've been hearing about might just be too much for you to deal with. After all, it will require you and your philanthropy to change significantly. You fear losing the person you thought you were, and you decide it's easier to stay in denial, thank you very much.

I feared losing the person I thought I was during college. I decided to study abroad in Ecuador. I had always envisioned myself as someone who could join the Peace Corps, live in the global South (we called it the Third World back then), and help people in developing countries. After all, I had a double major in anthropology and political science and a double minor in Latin American studies and Spanish. What more could I need?

But there I was in rural Ecuador. I had gotten scabies after living with my gracious indigenous host family, sleeping on a woven mat on the dirt floor of their hut. I was slumped over a toilet throwing up uncontrollably, while simultaneously trying to down a bottle of Pepto Bismol. I couldn't stop itching. I was exhausted, homesick, and desperately missed American pizza.

In retrospect, my predicament makes me laugh. At the time, however, I deeply questioned myself. I wondered if I was really the person

I thought I was. And I realized the answer was, "Not exactly." The reality of living in a poor community in Ecuador was a heck of a lot different than imagining it from Bloomington, Indiana! I experienced a loss of the person I thought I was, and it was hard.

Philanthropists also fear the loss of power and control. There is a lot of power in philanthropy. There is the power to ignite social change by strategically using your philanthropic capital to advance your goals. And there is a lot of power simply being the person with access to wealth. This creates a power dynamic: The giver gives and the recipient receives. Guess who holds the power? With power comes control. Donors get to choose which causes they support, whom they fund, and what they expect will happen with those funds.

Here are some of the ways that funders, out of fear, try to hold on to power and control:

Not offering general operating support. General operating (also known as core support) is a grant in support of a nonprofit organization's mission rather than specific projects or programs. It provides the working capital nonprofits need to sustain their day-to-day operations, address changing needs, and take advantage of unforeseen opportunities. It's the type of funding most nonprofit leaders want, yet too few funders provide. David Callahan, founder and editor of Inside Philanthropy and author of *The Givers*, argues that many funders don't want to provide general operating support because they fear they will lose control when they let the nonprofit figure out the best way to use the grant. They would rather have control over the money by giving nonprofits clear objectives and goals and tracking their progress to make sure they are meeting their objectives.[4]

Not retaining outside expertise. Many wealth advisors and family offices could provide substantially more services to help their clients reach their philanthropic goals. And given the anticipated $68 trillion intergenerational transfer of wealth over the next several decades, providing philanthropy services is a great way to engage the next generation and retain clients across generations. If they don't have the expertise in-house (which most don't), they could retain or refer outside philanthropy experts to help them. But they have a misguided fear that if they involve others, they might lose the client or damage the client relationship. They fear losing control. Instead of helping their clients transform their giving (and increase the likelihood that they keep the next generation as clients), they continue providing minimal, subpar, and transactional philanthropy guidance.

Losing control of donor legacy. Loss of legacy is another fear, especially in family foundations or family businesses. When I worked at the David and Lucile Packard Foundation, new-employee orientation included watching a video about the foundation's history. We learned how Dave and his friend Bill Hewlett started Hewlett-Packard out of a garage, the reasons he and his wife Lucile began their foundation, and the values of their family. It was a terrific way to help preserve the legacy of the family and foundation among the hundreds of employees who would play important roles in the foundation over decades.

Another donor, however, embraced a scarcity mentality when designing the legacy of his family foundation. A successful business leader, he was generous when it came to giving back to his community. In designing his board members' succession plan, however, he didn't just outline the role of family and nonfamily members on the board. He named specific people who would be asked to join the board if there was a vacancy, and in what order. And he put it in the foundation's bylaws.

Fast-forward to today: The donor has passed away. Among the individuals he named, most have little awareness about or interest in the foundation, and many are retiring. I can appreciate that he wanted to ensure that his foundation would be stewarded by people he trusted. But his fear of losing control of donor legacy is preventing the current foundation leadership from developing the board they need to guide the foundation into the future.

Fear Masked as Guilt

You feel guilty because you have access to wealth others don't have. You feel, therefore, that you shouldn't invest in yourself. You say to yourself, "How can I justify hiring an executive coach, investing in a communications plan, or getting help to implement our strategy when people are starving, girls are being kidnapped and sex trafficked, and we have an epidemic of drug addiction?" What you're doing, though, is letting your guilt get in the way of logic.

When you ask yourself, "How can I justify these expenses?" the right answer is, "How can I not?" After all, your role is that of champion. Your job is to help your cause by any means necessary, and that includes the "unconventional" approach of strengthening your organization's knowledge or infrastructure.

Sometimes the Fear Is Justified

It's also important to recognize there are fears in our world of philanthropy born from the very real dangers we sometimes face.

In 2018, Open Society Foundations had to move 100 employees out of their office in Budapest to Berlin, because of the repressive and hostile environment created by the Hungarian government's arbitrary interference.[5] Richard and Rhoda Goldman created the Goldman Environmental Prize to honor the achievements and leadership of grassroots environmental activists from around the world. Many of the prize winners faced harassment, physical abuse, intimidation, false criminalization, unjust arrests, and jail sentences (two were murdered after receiving the prize).[6] Activist donors who accompanied human rights leaders during El Salvador's civil war in the 1980s were often at physical risk for their safety.

Similarly, several globally recognized philanthropy leaders were happy to be interviewed for this book but were unwilling to be acknowledged or quoted, out of fear. Some work in countries with shrinking space for civil society and feared negative political and professional repercussions for sharing certain opinions.

The danger that some funders face can become tremendous obstacles to doing good in the world.

But these situations are by far the exception and not the rule.

Don't Hold Yourself Hostage to Your Fears

Make no mistake about it: We all feel fear from time to time. Sometimes this fear is rooted in reality, and sometimes it's not. Regardless of its source, we're the ones who choose whether we'll allow fear to become an obstacle that gets in the way of achieving our goals. We have the power to overcome our fears and bring about transformation. As Jean Case, philanthropist and CEO of the Case Foundation, shares in her book *Be Fearless,* "I am always inspired by people who challenge themselves and those around them by asking the question: What would you do if you weren't afraid?"[7]

We need talented philanthropists like you to step up, take risks, and make a difference. We need you to banish your scarcity mind-set and embrace a mind-set of abundance. We need you to put your own oxygen mask on first, so that you can help others and change the world. We're counting on you. Your community is counting on you. The world is counting on you.

Notes

1. http://www.msnbc.com/the-last-word/odonnell-it-time-question-tom-sellec.
2. Author interview with Meredith Shields, August 29, 2019.
3. Interview with Charles Keidan, August 12, 2019.
4. https://www.insidephilanthropy.com/home/2014/11/20/control-why-so-many-funders-fear-general-support-and-cant-st.html.
5. https://www.opensocietyfoundations.org/newsroom/open-society-foundations-close-international-operations-budapest.
6. https://www.goldmanprize.org/blog/fighting-for-their-lives-goldman-prize-winners-under-threat/; https://af.reuters.com/article/drcNews/idAFL8N1HR5DK.
7. J. Case, *Be Fearless: 5 Principles for a Life of Breakthroughs and Purpose* (New York: Simon & Schuster, 2019).

3 | You Respond Too Slowly

If you've seen the movie *Zootopia*, you might recall the scene in which the two main characters, a fox and a rabbit, head to the Department of Mammal Vehicles to learn about a missing otter. Rushing in, they are horrified to discover the DMV is staffed by sloths! What follows is a painfully funny exchange with the slow-moving sloth employee. A transaction that should take three minutes instead takes the entire day. Day turns into night before they get the information they need.

Philanthropists are just like those sloths. They respond too slowly. And it's just as painful to watch.

In philanthropy, slowness is a problem because people's lives are at stake. The environment is at stake. A community in crisis is at stake. If philanthropists genuinely believe they can help change the world—as you do—they should hurry up and get on with it!

Instead, here's what typically happens. A town floods, but a local foundation can't make an emergency grant to the Red Cross without full board approval, and the board doesn't meet again for four months.

An entrepreneur creates a donor-advised fund following the sale of her business (and collects a tax deduction in the process) but is too busy to make donations from it. A corporate foundation proudly puts its new strategic plan on its website, but 18 months later has not begun implementing it.

Why are philanthropists so slow? By far the biggest reason is lack of external accountability. One form of external accountability is federal regulation of charitable giving, which varies by country and by philanthropic vehicle (e.g., private foundation, public charity, donor-advised fund, checks written by individuals, etc.).

In the United States, foundations are required to give away about 5% of their assets annually. Charitable lead trusts (CLTs) provide charities with cash flow for a specified time period. Aside from that, there is almost no pressure to give quickly, or even give at all. Holders of donor-advised funds (DAFs) have zero requirements for when they must contribute to charities (although some leading DAF sponsors, such as Fidelity Charitable, have commendably taken initiative to require their DAFs to make grants within a few years). And there is no expectation for how quickly individuals contribute directly to charities with cash, checks, or credit card payments.

Theoretically, nonprofits seeking funds could hold philanthropists accountable for being too slow. They certainly are the ones who bear the brunt of philanthropic dillydallying. Unfortunately, there is a strong power dynamic preventing such accountability. Nonprofits don't want to bite the hand that feeds them.

What's most interesting to me is that while working within this almost accountability-free zone, donors and foundations self-impose restrictions that no government would ever bother to require. They create and then hold themselves hostage to cumbersome policies and processes that are not required by law but which do slow them down. Instead of figuring out the most expeditious way to get from Point A to Point B, philanthropists put hurdles in their own way. These hurdles look helpful—conducting an environmental scan, attending a conference, cleaning out the office—but actually become barriers to speed.

Here are a few examples I've experienced with my clients. Do any of these feel familiar to you? A family foundation confines itself to lengthy strategic planning processes that convene board members dozens of times before their strategy is finalized. A donor collects endless data to learn about a social problem and then is so overwhelmed by the data that she doesn't know what to do with the information. A community foundation can't make decisions until after the grants committee meets in person, and that only happens twice a year.

Why do philanthropists hamstring themselves and reduce their speed to impact? No one does this intentionally. No funder wakes up in the morning saying, "Let me postpone my impact for one more day." Most funders have no idea they are slowing themselves down. They don't notice their sloth-like behavior, much less how it gets in their way.

They are delusional philanthropists.

Are you one of them? My guess is yes, at least some of the time. We all are.

Philanthropists respond too slowly for three main reasons: They toss junk in their way, they make the simple complex, and they become bloated with bureaucracy.

As you read about each of these, think about whether and how often this happens to you. Better yet, jot down a few examples of how you slow yourself down. You can do this on a Post-it note, in your journal, or in some white space in this book. That will help you identify ways you can speed things up later.

Clogging the System with Unnecessary Junk

Funders set their goals, and then they actually create a bunch of junk that gets in their way. They use this junk as an excuse for moving so slowly.

When I speak with philanthropists, I hear about this junk all the time. One woman genuinely wanted to start a foundation, but she tossed a wedding in her way: She decided she needed to help plan her daughter's wedding—a year away—and couldn't even think about the foundation until after. A private foundation was ready to refresh its strategy but tossed a U.S. president in its way: President Donald Trump was unexpectedly elected, so the foundation board decided to postpone strategic planning for four months to "see what happens." A donor said his astrological chart told him to wait a month before deciding whether to convert his foundation to a donor-advised fund!

We all do this. We all set our sights on what we want to accomplish, and then we create things that get in our way and slow us down.

When I set out to write this book, I immediately—without realizing it—tossed in a bunch of junk. What I needed to do was start writing. Instead, I decided that first I needed to take a week off work and completely unclutter my house. And get to inbox zero. And finish planning our family vacation. And schedule the kids' summer camps (five months before summer). "How could I possibly focus on a book if I'm worried about laundry, a playroom, emails, and how my twins will be spending summer vacation?" I concluded.

The same thing happens in all industries. My friend, Andy Bass, a renowned business consultant in England, pointed this out to me. He explained that people spend excessive time just preparing to make a change. He calls it "planning to start to prepare to get ready for change." He says, "In organizations, this might mean everybody has to participate in endless data gathering, go to mandatory workshops, get certified as a Black Belt, and so on. Trainers call it 'sheep dipping.'"[1] Andy is exactly right. The good news is that since we created all this junk, we can just as easily eliminate it.

Complexifying the Simple Instead of Simplifying the Complex

Instead of determining the easiest and most streamlined solution, philanthropists often create a convoluted one. Occam's Razor is a principle created by William of Ockham seven centuries ago, which states that given two options or two competing theories that lead to the same result, the simpler one is preferred.[2] Funders should follow Occam's Razor more often!

If you want to implement your strategy, it's as simple as identifying your top implementation priorities, assigning people to be accountable to them, asking them to come up with a list of the 5–10 things they need to do next, and then holding their feet to the fire by asking for progress updates every few weeks. It's really that easy. What most funders do instead is turn a simple solution into a complex one. They spend months creating detailed implementation plans replete with Gantt charts, work plans, tactics, and timelines. Or they claim they're too busy to start implementing because their calendar is chock-full of meetings, events, and conferences for the next few months (none of which have anything to do with their new strategic direction).

I was once asked to coach a foundation leader who had received numerous complaints for running lengthy and unproductive meetings. Two-hour meetings regularly ran over to three or four hours. Rarely did he bring an agenda, participants felt little was accomplished, and meetings ended with everyone exhausted. I suggested shorter meeting formats with tighter, goal-oriented agendas.

Want to know his solution?

He convened this group three times over two months to discuss how to shorten the meeting. He totally missed the point. You don't need to more meetings to determine how to shorten a meeting. You need to streamline the meetings without increasing them. He complexified the simple and slowed things down.

Developing Bureaucratic Bloat

Bureaucracy allows unnecessary procedures and systems to rule the roost. These procedures made sense when you first started, but they no longer serve you. Or they never made sense, and you just lassoed them into your orbit because you weren't thinking critically.

Let me give you a few examples. Bureaucracy is active when you require four different people to approve a $500 grant. Bureaucracy is at work when takes an average of nine months for your organization to make a grant. And it's alive and well when you invest the time to develop a written policy on how staff should clean the foundation's kitchen, but you won't invest in systems to streamline grantmaking.

Now, before you declare, "That doesn't apply to me," I'm here to tell you it does. I don't care if you are a single person writing charitable checks from your kitchen table or the head of the largest foundation on the planet. Bureaucratic practices start small. In fact, initially they are undetectable. Like black mold, they start in the far corners of our altruistic intentions and accumulate, undetected, until it's too late. Then you're getting sick and you don't know why.

I once talked with a philanthropic family that wanted me to help them create a giving plan. They estimated the project would take 24 months. I explained it could be done in 24 days if they were motivated— maybe a few months at most. "Why wait?" I asked. "Because our family meets twice a year, once by phone and once in person," my contact explained. "We think these important discussions should happen in person. We need one in-person meeting to hire the consultant, and two more to discuss and agree upon the plan." While I don't disagree with the value of face-to-face communication, this family was allowing unnecessary procedures (e.g., voting must happen in person, we only meet every six months, etc.) to dictate the speed at which they could attain clarity and alignment in their family philanthropy. The bureaucratic tail was wagging the charitable dog, and it was slowing things down.

Why does bad bureaucracy happen to good philanthropists? Again, no one wakes up thinking, "Let me make life harder for myself and others!" It's all done in the name of altruism.

You think you are being good stewards of your resources by requiring four signatures on every grant approval. You think you are engaging your family in your charitable giving by insisting on in-person decision making. But really you are becoming bureaucratic and slowing things down. You are delusional in your altruism.

You aren't applying common sense to your giving. You aren't looking under your own hood to identify blockages and eliminate them.

Committing to Speeding Things Up

Most philanthropists respond too slowly by tossing in junk that impedes their progress, creating unnecessary complexity and allowing bureaucracy to grow and subsume their charitable goals.

But that's not the kind of philanthropist you want to be.

I know you don't want to be a sloth. You don't want litter your philanthropic orbit with cosmic debris. You don't want to add unnecessary complexity to what should be straightforward solutions. And you certainly don't want to create a bureaucracy! You know the world is changing rapidly, and you want to be part of it. New problems are emerging, and you want to help solve them. Many of the world's problems already have solutions—you want more people to learn about those solutions and implement them.

I know this because you bought this book. No one buys a book titled *Delusional Altruism* unless they recognize they might be making some mistakes and genuinely want to fix them. That's great! Because the world needs philanthropists who can speed things up. The world needs philanthropists with impact velocity. The world needs you. Let's go!

Notes

1. Author interview with Andy Bass.
2. https://www.britannica.com/topic/Occams-razor.

4 | You Have Too Many Steps

Guess what? In philanthropy, it turns out *we* are the bottleneck. We clog our systems. We prevent funding from flowing to those who need it most.

Why does this happen? We have too many steps.

Yes, we—including you. You who proclaim to be "streamlined." You who fund evidence-based solutions and arm yourself with logic models. You who are on the frontlines of whatever issue or cause you care about.

You have too many steps for every aspect of your giving. Too many steps for deciding what issue to focus on, and too many steps to make a grant. Too many steps in setting strategy, and too many steps in implementing it. Too many steps in hiring staff, retaining consultants, managing your finances, preparing for board meetings, and making decisions.

I hope you catch my drift. You have too many steps!

We all have too many steps—myself included. As a result, we slow down our speed to impact.

Let me tell you a story about being a bottleneck.

I've been the bottleneck to my nine-year-old daughter's ability to see at night in her bedroom. For months—OK, honestly, for about a year—she has been complaining that her ceiling light was burned out and asking if I could please replace the bulb. Every time she complained, I would think about the steps I'd need to take to meet her request.

1. Research all those newfangled light bulbs before I buy more (do I want LED or incandescent or halogen? And what is a "lumen" anyway?).
2. Install the new overhead light fixture we bought for her two years ago. Might as well do that too when I install the bulb, right?
3. Buy new light bulbs.
4. Find the stepladder stored behind the Christmas tree in the garage and bring it to her room.

And on it went.

Last night, I did something different. I looked up at her lightless fixture, ran downstairs, took a bulb out of a lamp we never use, ran back upstairs, climbed on her bed, and installed the light bulb. It took a total of two minutes. She turned on the light and danced around her room—literally—singing, "Thank you, Mom, for giving me light!" I felt like an idiot. What a bottleneck I had been! I had too many steps, and the only step I needed was the one she had asked for.

I don't want to be that bottleneck, and neither do you.

What "Too Many Steps" Means

What do I mean by "too many steps" in philanthropy? Sometimes we call it bureaucracy, as in Chapter 3: "You Respond Too Slowly." Some people call it red tape. Sometimes there are simply too many steps, tasks, and activities that a funder inadvertently puts in the path toward reaching a goal. I'm talking about a rigid conformity to rules that hinders decision making. Unnecessary duplication. Practices that are unnecessary, inefficient, convoluted, and inflexible.

Here are a few examples of needless steps that I've encountered among philanthropists. Not just your average philanthropists, mind you, but fabulous, skillful, and super-smart people. Leaders who are committed to social change, justice, and equity. People who have dedicated their lives to helping others. People just like you. Because needless steps don't just happen to bad people. They crop up among the best of us. You are one of those brilliant and dedicated philanthropists the world needs, and they happen to you, too.

I bet these stories will sound familiar. As you read them, jot down any examples you can think of—either those your organization is guilty of or those you've experienced elsewhere. Count how many pointless steps are involved.

Sometimes funders create too many steps by trying to be transparent. Here's an example: A foundation wanted to be "transparent" when it hired evaluators, so no one could accuse it of favoritism. Its solution was to require proposals from three different evaluators every time it needed to retain one. It didn't matter the size of the project, the demonstrated quality of an evaluator's work, or the urgency of need. A request for proposals (RFP) had to be issued and three proposals had to be received for any engagement. If only two evaluators submitted proposals, staff had to go out and dredge up more evaluators and encourage them to apply until that third proposal came in. As a result, staff spent months creating RFPs, finding evaluators, and reviewing proposals that were ultimately unnecessary and added nothing to the foundation's transparency—simply stating clearly who they retained and why would have sufficed. Chances are, they knew who they wanted to hire in the first place.

Often funders create too many steps for their grantees. One couple allocates $50,000 each year out of their donor-advised fund. They do this by giving out 10 grants of $5,000 each. To select the recipients, they require nonprofits to fill out lengthy application forms, submit three years of audited financial statements, obtain letters of recommendation from community leaders, explain how the project will be evaluated, and host the couple on a half-day site visit to showcase the organization.

It likely costs the nonprofits about $1,500 in staff time to obtain a $5,000 grant.

It doesn't have to be this way. Philanthropists can easily eliminate steps and cut the red tape if they choose. After all, they are the ones who created all those steps in the first place. The Headwaters Foundation in Montana has eliminated lengthy board dockets entirely. The foundation's board approves the overall strategic framework and initiatives (including the purpose, grant range, and timeline), and trusts the staff to make funding decisions and approve grant requests. This frees up tremendous amounts of staff time, and they use it to help their grantees.[1]

The Vadon Foundation in Seattle has done a great job eliminating steps. It has the most straightforward and respectful application process I've ever seen: "To reduce the administrative burden on potential partners, we ask that interested grantees initially send us an introductory email or call our offices to discuss your program. If there seems to be potential for collaboration, we can mutually determine what materials or information would be useful for further discussion."[2] And guess what appears immediately to the right of this statement on their website? The foundation executive director's full contact information.

Too Many Steps Cause Too Many Problems

These excessive steps cause four types of problems and prevent you from making your mark on the world. They reduce speed, reduce quality, cost money, and make you miserable. And I know you don't want to be slow, inferior, expensive, or cranky!

Let's examine each problem.

Too Many Steps Slow Things Down

Too many steps will decelerate decision making, delay funding allocations, and grind implementation to a halt. While you wait six months to approve a grant request, your grantee could lose top talent to other organizations, because they don't know whether they'll have the funds to make job offers. Your grantee will have to spend too long continuing to search for talent.

Too Many Steps Reduce Quality

A consultant colleague once received an RFP from two partnering foundations who sought a nationally recognized consultant with experience developing and managing early childhood initiatives. The RFP was full of unnecessary expectations and legalese, taking 19 pages to explain how to submit a 10-page proposal and outlining all the activities the consultant should undertake and in what order. They'd had months to write the RFP but allowed the consultant only weeks to apply. They refused to allow the consultant to talk to the decision makers so she could fully understand their objectives, and she was required to be available on a specific day to fly in for an interview in the event she was selected as a finalist. This was a sneak peek at a funder collaboration that would be unnecessarily complex, and she wanted no part of it. She was uniquely qualified to deliver stellar results for these funders, but because of their rigid conformity to their needless steps and pointless practices, she didn't apply—and they lost out on a quality consultant. I am sure there were other top consultants who also took a polite pass.

Too Many Steps Cost You Money

Funders often think their systems, processes, and tactics are necessary for due diligence and effective stewardship of philanthropic assets. It turns out the opposite can be true. To check this, I advise my clients to use a simple technique: Calculate the cost of people's time and use that data to inform their decisions.

You can quickly calculate an hourly wage by adding the annual salary plus benefits and dividing it by 2,080 working hours per year. According to the *2018 Grantmaker Salary and Benefits Report* of the Council on

Foundations, the average program officer salary in the United States was $95,341.[3] Add 25% in benefits (the median average for all U.S. foundation employees) and the average hourly rate for a program officer is $57 per hour.

Now tally everyone's time spent on the activity you are tracking—spending three weeks preparing for board meetings, for example, or finding numerous consultants to decide among. You can immediately calculate the cost of all those needless steps, and I bet you will be shocked at the amount!

I worked with one funder to do this after they cast a wide net to solicit consultant proposals for a project in order to demonstrate transparency and equity in consultant selection. We estimated that foundation staff spent 108 hours over two months reviewing 45 consultant proposals and making a final selection, for a total cost of $6,600 in staff time. This was for a $30,000 consulting contract! In other words, the funder spent more than one-fifth the cost of the consultant just on finding one.

Too Many Steps Make You Miserable

You hate these steps. They make you grumpy. Consider these examples:

You, the foundation CEO, loathe the end-of-year ritual known as the performance review. You dread it because it always takes a month of your time even though you only have 10 employees. You dread the perfunctory back-and-forth exchange with each employee and the frustration of reviewing performance against last year's goals, which are no longer relevant because your strategy has since changed. You dread this because your performance review process has too many steps, most of which don't help you achieve your goal of incentivizing and rewarding excellent performance.

You, the celebrity activist, hate that every charitable decision you make is vetted by your stable of "handlers." You feel like a Ping-Pong ball as your desire to help homeless pets is bounced around from agent to publicist to assistant to nonprofit and back again. The worthiness of the cause is vetted against its media value. There are too many steps, and all you want to do is support an organization that's doing a great job.

You, as an individual, are increasingly frustrated that it takes you so long to determine your giving strategy. You look around and see your well-heeled friends attending events, joining donor circles, and taking global glamping volunteer trips to the Andes before they decide which causes to support. You figure you need to do that, too, so you jump right in. But just before you hit the "purchase" button on your volunteer vacation, you stop yourself. "This is ridiculous," you think. "I don't need a guide carrying me up the Inca Trail to understand what low-income Peruvians want and how I can best help them."

Why Do We Have Too Many Steps?

We have too many steps because we are delusional. We have too many steps because—although we are paying attention to *what* we give—we aren't paying attention to *how* we give. Either we are oblivious to the red tape we've wrapped ourselves up in or we are aware of this problem but aren't doing anything about it. We are stuck in our ways. "That's the way it's always been," we lament. And then we keep doing the same thing.

Often all these steps made sense at an early phase of our philanthropic journey, but they no longer serve us today. In fact, "red tape" was originally used by King Charles V of Spain in the early 16th century to *increase* governmental efficiency! Important dossiers requiring urgent discussion were literally bound in red ribbon or string. This distinguished them from less important documents bound in ordinary string. But a concept for efficiency became "too many steps" by the age of computers and information technology.[4]

These steps exist in every nook and cranny of philanthropy, no matter what kind of funder you are. I don't care if you are issuing checks from your donor-advised fund or running the Bill and Melinda Gates

Foundation. You have too many steps. And the noble work you do as a philanthropist is too important to cause you to be inferior, slow, costly, and cranky!

Notes

1. Author interview with Brenda Solorzano, CEO of Headwaters Foundation, May 13, 2019.
2. http://vadonfoundation.org/how-to-apply.php.
3. https://www.cof.org/content/2018-grantmaker-salary-and-benefits-report.
4. https://en.wikipedia.org/wiki/Red_tape.

5 | You Are Too Overwhelmed to Take Your Next Step

A serious, but largely overlooked, problem in philanthropy is feeling overwhelmed. You know what I'm talking about. You might have woken up this morning feeling overwhelmed by the day ahead of you. You could feel overwhelmed right now. It might be because the ideas you're reading about in this book are triggering changes you want to make, but you aren't yet sure how to make them. Or you might be overwhelmed because you haven't gotten around to scheduling the dental appointment, dermatology check-up, and half dozen other health appointments you should probably make.

What is overwhelm? According to wellness writer Michelle Rees, "Overwhelm happens when the sheer volume of thoughts feelings, tasks, and stimuli in our daily environment shifts our brain and nervous system into a reactive, stressed state."[1] The result? Easy things become hard and hard things become impossible.

I felt that way recently while trying to finish up work, pack for a long weekend, take my daughter back-to-school shopping, and register my kids for dance class—all before noon!

In addition to zapping our creativity and problem-solving skills, overwhelm creates a relentless cycle of inactivity. We stop in our tracks. We don't know the right path forward, which step to take, or even what direction to choose. Overwhelm costs money, drains time, and suffocates talent.

Think feeling overwhelmed is not a big deal for philanthropists? Think again.

Think of the woman who is so overwhelmed with managing her family foundation after the death of her husband that she cannot even consider potential solutions, such as transitioning the foundation into an easier-to-manage donor-advised fund, or retaining a consultant to help her run it. The foundation falls into disarray, fails to make its 5% payout, and triggers tax penalties.

Think of the CEO of a philanthropy-serving organization who feels overwhelmed by the prospect of firing her communications director, because she's worried that she won't have any communications support during a major change in the organization's strategy. She tolerates the communication director's poor performance and bullying behavior, which results in a toxic work environment, low staff morale, low productivity, and poor communications. As a result, two top performers leave in frustration.

Six Ways Philanthropists Are Overwhelmed

In my experience, philanthropists experience six distinct types of overwhelm. As you read the list, jot down how many of these you've experienced in the past year.

1. **Are you overwhelmed by the world's problems?** The world holds more than 7.5 billion of us. Sometimes it feels as though we face unlimited challenges. Climate change, income inequality,

influenza pandemics, food insecurity, war . . . just to name a few! Many funders feel overwhelmed by the sheer size and depth of such problems.

2. **Are you overwhelmed finding a cause to support?** Some people come to this work with a clear passion and focus. Their child had brain cancer and they want to prevent the disease from striking other families. For the rest of us, however, it can be overwhelming to determine which issue to tackle. We care about so many needs: domestic violence or mental health? Climate change or inequality? Is it better to double down on one issue or spread our contributions across a wide range of causes? There are no right or wrong answers, but the choices can daunt us. Toss in trying to involve the wildly different interests of your adult children or the predilections of your company's CEO, and you start to feel like a deer in the headlights.

3. **Are you overwhelmed by choices?** Once you know which causes you want to support, you still need to decide *how* to support them. There are an estimated 10 million nongovernmental organizations (NGOs) worldwide.[2] That's a lot of potential grantees to choose among! And your choices are not only numerous but often they are big: Determining whether to let go of employees who don't fit your new strategy. Identifying the most effective approach to increasing access to drinking water without inadvertently harming people. It's common to feel overwhelmed by guilt or anxiety (or both) in the face of such decisions.

4. **Are you overwhelmed by taking action?** You've set goals and developed a plan. It's smooth sailing from here to make it all happen, right? Wrong. At this stage, many funders are sitting on a plan with five goals, ten objectives, and four cross-cutting themes. Strategies are getting mixed up with tactics, everything feels like a priority, and no one knows what they are supposed to do next. They are overwhelmed. Their response? To "busy" themselves in meetings, calls, and emails that accomplish little.

5. **Are you overwhelmed by change?** We all think change is great . . . until it happens to us. You might be managing wealth you've recently inherited, recovering from the surprise outcome of an election, or taking on your first CEO role. When we change, we are forced to let go of habits we are comfortable with. We step

into the unknown, and often into areas we've tried to avoid. It's easy to feel overwhelmed and disoriented by change, and unsure how to respond.

6. **Are you overwhelmed by lack of time?** This one's a doozy. Most people think they don't have time. You are probably saying to yourself, "OK, Kris, I get all this, but I have no time to deal with it. Just look at my calendar—I'm booked solid for the next three months. My inbox is overflowing. And I have that big event coming up!" I understand. When I started writing this book, I wondered how I would fit "write two hours a day" into my calendar. But the belief that we have no time is the easiest culprit to resolve. You have more control over your time than you realize, especially if you stop mindlessly giving it away to people and issues that are not your top priorities. Meetings don't need to last an hour, strategic planning need not take a year, and you don't need to embark on a multistate learning tour. Compare your calendar against your top priorities. You'll be stunned to realize how little of your time is allocated to what's most important. Read Chapter 10, "You Are Fast," to learn how to increase efficiency in your life and in your giving.

Feeling overwhelmed is delusional because you don't recognize the damage it's causing you and your philanthropy. You don't know how much control you have to reduce overwhelm. And you aren't doing anything about it. Overwhelm is holding you back from changing the world, and you're allowing it to do so.

Let's look at what's contributing the feeling of overwhelm. As you read, make a note of when you take one of these actions. Also, pay attention to how much is within your control.

Eight Ways You Contribute to Feeling Overwhelmed

As odd as it seems, overwhelm often comes more from our minds than from the physical world. That is, we may indeed have a boatload of tasks to take care of, but how we view our situation has a lot to do with whether we feel helplessly overwhelmed or appropriately busy. Our thoughts tip the boat in one direction or the other.

Here are eight ways you unintentionally contribute to a feeling of overwhelm:

1. **You wear it like a badge of honor.** When asked how you are, how often do you respond, "I'm busy"? I'm guessing fairly often. I'm guilty of this, too. In fact, you might even boast about how busy you are. It might be your nonstop travel schedule, your upcoming board meeting, the gala you are planning, or juggling work and kids during the summer.

   But being busy and feeling overwhelmed is not a badge of honor. Your booked schedule is not proof of your importance. It's probably proof of your exhaustion! In fact, keeping busy might be a form of procrastination. Instead of stuffing our calendars, we need to create more unstructured time to relax, think, and do nothing. In fact, studies show that periods of being idle makes us more creative and better at problem solving.[3]

   The "busy brag" is also contagious and can negatively impact organizational cultures. Netflix and Virgin Group have begun combating this by offering employees unlimited vacation time. Not only does this help them attract top talent, it neutralizes a culture of "busy bragging" even as employees are still held accountable for results.[4] Carl Richards, author of *The Behavior Gap*, offers this practical advice: "Take the 'busy' badge, throw it in the trash, and replace it with one that says, 'rested.'"[5]

2. **You set unrealistic expectations.** One way we do this is to set up a series of tight deadlines with no real plan for meeting them. Another example is scheduling relentless back-to-back meetings, with no time to think or follow up on what we agreed to do. A colleague told me his foundation has a culture of double-booking meetings: For example, you might schedule an hour-long meeting with a colleague to discuss an important matter, only to discover that you actually have just 10 minutes because she booked another meeting at the same time. Think of how much overwhelm that practice is causing!

3. **You don't have a strategy, much less a plan.** It's easy to feel overwhelmed when you don't know what you are trying to do and you don't have a plan. You end up engaging in lots of disconnected activities. You get pulled in different directions and jump on too

many charitable bandwagons. As a result, you feel overwhelmed by a growing list of obligations, and you get frustrated that you aren't making headway on any of them. You need a strategy to help you prioritize which tasks to do when—and which to ignore, at least temporarily.

4. **You don't have systems in place.** Perhaps you don't use basic systems and processes to help you conduct your work. As a result, you're frequently late and overwhelmed while completing routine activities. The systems you need might be simple, such as clearing your email inbox each day, or complex, such as installing a new grants management system.

   One family foundation trustee described the chaos her family experienced without a grantmaking process. The board had no process or schedule for reviewing proposals or approving grants. This was intentional, because they thought the lack of a grantmaking system would allow them to be nimble and make quick decisions. In fact, the opposite was true. "We were all over the place. . . . As proposals rolled in, we had to drop what we were doing and respond. We felt like we were being really responsive. But really, we were just disorganized. On one hand we'd say we needed to hurry, but then we'd reschedule board meetings, and funding decisions got postponed for six months."[6]

5. **You don't invest in technology that could help you.** There are myriad ways that investments in technology make us faster, more effective, and less exhausted grantmakers. This might include online grant applications, employee volunteer systems, and giving platforms. Technology investments can also help our grantees to scale up their solutions.

   For example, Business of Good Foundation (Ohio) supports mentoring to help first-generation, low-income college students persist to college graduation. It does this by supporting America Mentors, which uses MentorcliQ technology on a smartphone or tablet to match students with mentors and enable guided interactions between these pairs, fostering strong relationships through timely and relevant conversations. All for free. The outcome? More than 3,000 students have been mentored and graduation rates increased from 8% in 2011 to 80% in 2017. The foundation hopes there will be a time when all first-generation college students have mentors.[7]

6. **You don't invest in people who can help you.** You don't need to go it alone. There are plenty of people with expertise who can help you—you just need to engage them. Who am I talking about? Virtual administrative assistants, speech writers, communications experts, family offices, strategic advisors, and event planners. Employees who could handle work you don't have the time or expertise to do. I'm also talking about people who can handle non-work-related tasks for you, such as mowing your lawn, cleaning your apartment, and preparing your taxes.

   Why invest in outside help? I can think of at least three reasons:

   First, you will free up your time and brainpower to do what you are best at. If you're best at engaging employees in meaningful volunteer opportunities, why would you spend your time on data entry?

   Second, you can always improve. Why be good when you can be great? Why be great when you can be fabulous? A trusted advisor can help you prioritize your goals and hold you accountable for meeting them.

   Third, when you invest in people who are smarter and better at an activity than you are, you might find that the quality of your organization's work improves dramatically. After all, if you have an entire group of people attacking projects from their own individual strengths, things start getting done quickly.

7. **You don't take care of yourself.** It's easy to feel overwhelmed when you run yourself ragged. We often forget how much our physical, mental, and spiritual health contributes to our success. Does any of this sound familiar? Lack of sleep, lack of exercise, unhealthy eating, and not enough time spent with the ones you care most about—family, friends, pets, and yourself. Not to mention that this can contribute to serious problems such as diabetes and depression. The conventional wisdom is true: You can't take care of others until you take care of yourself.

8. **You believe feeling overwhelmed is normal.** You've felt so harried for so long that you've come to expect it. You've forgotten what it's like to feel calm and on top of things. In fact, you wonder

whether you ever felt this way. If you've gotten to this point, you need an intervention—and quickly! This is especially challenging and insidious when those around you are suffering the same problem. When your colleagues, family members, and friends constantly describe being behind, busy, and stressed, you feel pressured to feel the same way.

What amazes me about the list above is that everything on it is usually within our power to change—or at least influence. In many ways, we enable and facilitate our own feelings of overwhelm.

Of course, overwhelm is also triggered and exacerbated by experiences and traumas beyond our control. You might live in a community experiencing a natural disaster or violence, experience racism or homophobia, have a serious health problem, or have lost a loved one. There are a lot of real-world factors that can overwhelm us, whether they come from our workplace, community, national politics, or personal identity and experience.

When oppression, physical health problems, mental health concerns, and similar major life issues are involved, it is important to take action. Counseling, support groups, religion, peer groups, and family can be powerful sources of strength. So too can volunteering, community organizing, and participating in social change activities to eradicate the situations that cause these types of traumas.

Sometimes the contributors to overwhelm are powerful and constant. Other times they are more subtle. Regardless, they all have an effect. Although we might not be able to remove some of these at their source, we can at least try to mitigate them. This can partially be accomplished by some of the techniques discussed in this book.

Notes

1. https://www.wholelifechallenge.com/how-to-reduce-overwhelm-and-get-your-life-back/.
2. https://en.m.wikipedia.org/wiki/Non-governmental_organization.

3. https://www.nytimes.com/2019/04/29/smarter-living/the-case-for-doing-nothing.html?inf_contact_key=a23388258010909ab2f895e76bec07b8680f8914173f9191b1c0223e68310bb1&login=email&auth=login-email.
4. https://www.huffpost.com/entry/being-busy-is-nothing-to-brag-about_b_5a4b9a6de4b0d86c803c7971.
5. https://www.nytimes.com/2019/02/19/your-money/sketch-guy-knowledge-workers-need-rest.html.
6. Confidential interview with family foundation trustee.
7. Email correspondence from Tim McCarthy, Business of Good Foundation, September 22, 2019.

6 | You Are Fooled by Your Own Efforts

Over the past 20 years, I've spoken with thousands of philanthropists and haven't found a single slacker. Just the opposite. They put in lots of effort. But many confuse effort with impact.

Many well-intentioned philanthropists are fooled by their own efforts. They grit their teeth and take action, but it doesn't result in much. That's because that grit and action aren't aligned toward a common goal. Donors are under the delusion that their vast efforts will change the world simply because they're busy.

Just peek into the calendars and to-do lists of any philanthropist. Board meetings, staff meetings, and meetings to plan meetings. Business travel, webinars, and back-to-back calls. Conferences to plan. New initiatives to launch. Grants management software to install. Reports to write. Fundraising events to attend. Proposals to review. Emails to catch up on.

Those can seem like important things. After all, you need to convene your board members and respond to email. All that effort on such important stuff must result in something, right?

Not really.

I recently spoke to a foundation CEO who lamented that she and her team would be devoting the next six weeks to preparing for a board meeting. They would have to drop everything they were working on to get ready. The board meeting amounted to a dog and pony show. The board expected them to find and prepare outside experts to speak at the meeting, organize fancy dinners, and graphically design presentation materials. Each program team was to give multi-hour updates on progress since the last time the board met six months ago.

The trouble is, none of it mattered. All this effort was actually preventing them from doing their important work.

In the six months since the last board meeting, the foundation's previous CEO had resigned, the board undertook a national executive search, and the foundation's strategic planning efforts were put on hold. The new CEO began just two weeks before our conversation.

The important work of the foundation was to allow the new CEO time and space to develop her vision for the foundation, finalize the strategic plan, and lead her team to implement the strategy. Instead, she was leading her team to create PowerPoint presentations. But the board liked seeing all these signs of a busy organization.

Why do we confuse busyness with productivity and results? Philanthropists find themselves busy working on the wrong stuff for three main reasons: They don't have a clear strategy. They aren't implementing that strategy. And, as a result, they get distracted by the latest trends and go off course.

You Don't Know Where You Want to Go

As obvious as it may seem, first you need to know what you are trying to accomplish. If you don't know what you want to do, it's unlikely you will do it. American baseball legend Yogi Berra summed it up best: "If you don't know where you are going, you'll end up someplace else."

The best way to know what you want to accomplish is to formulate a clear strategy. Let's define what we mean.

Strategy is a framework within which decisions are made that influence the nature and direction of the enterprise.[1] In this case, the "enterprise" is you. You as an individual or you as an organization (e.g., family office, donor-advised fund, giving circle, Fortune 100 company, or philanthropy association). Strategy is a tool for making decisions and choices that are congruent with where you want your philanthropy to go.

One thing I learned from consulting expert Alan Weiss is that when we think about strategy, it's helpful to divide it into two components: strategy formulation and strategy implementation. Formulating your strategy means identifying your desired future state. What is the change you want to see in the world or in your community? What charitable impact do you want your company to be known for? What kind of philanthropist do you want to become?

Implementing your strategy means moving from your current state (where you are today) to your desired future state, ideally as quickly as possible. We'll learn more about strategy implementation later in this chapter. For now, let's focus on strategy formulation. Or, more typically, the reluctance of philanthropists to formulate their strategy.

Too often, philanthropists don't have a strategy. They haven't identified their desired future state, so it's hard for them to find the best path to where they want to go. In fact, it's darned near impossible.

If they don't have a strategy and don't know where they're going, what are philanthropists doing? Sitting still? Meditating? Napping?

Nope. They are very, very busy. Doing lots and lots of stuff.

They are attending conferences, reviewing proposals, designing new community initiatives, going to meetings, speaking with legislators, filling vacant positions, conducting site visits, hiring consultants, scanning the field, and preparing their taxes.

They are doing lots and lots of stuff. None of it is "bad" stuff. I'm sure it's interesting stuff. And the grants they make along the way are likely helping people. But they're focused on the *wrong* stuff. They are busy with a lot of activity, but the activity is not aligned toward a single goal. They have no strategy. They lack a framework within which to make decisions that affect the nature and direction of their philanthropy—decisions like "What's the most important use of my time?" and "Which nonprofits are best equipped to accomplish our goals?" Without this decision-making framework called a strategy, many funders are flailing in the wind.

But they sure are keeping themselves busy.

You Don't Know How to Get There

Once philanthropists have formulated their strategy and understand their desired future state, it should be easy to achieve it, right? Wrong.

As hard as it might have been to develop a strategy, the harder part is implementing it! Strategy most often fails in its implementation, not its formulation.

Why? Because instead of implementing the strategy, everyone starts doing stuff. But not the right stuff. They start working on the same old stuff they were working on before their strategy changed. They continue working on the old strategy, not the new one! There are four mistakes funders make that lead to this implementation implosion.

The first mistake is that the leader—the donor, CEO, or board chair—assumes that everyone knows how to implement the new strategy. "Everyone" might mean you and your spouse, your board, your corporate giving department, or your staff of 300 employees. They were all involved in the planning process, so they should know their next steps, right? Wrong. They don't. I know this because every time I advise philanthropists on strategy implementation, I interview everyone involved. I ask them, "What are the top three priorities for implementing your new strategic plan?" Without failure they identify several dozen "top" priorities!

This leads us to our second mistake. Those involved don't know their next step because they have not determined the top implementation priorities. In the decades I've spent advising funders to formulate and implement their strategies, the biggest problem with implementation (and the easiest one to fix) is they have not determined the three or four most important things that need to happen next to implement the strategy. If they don't know top priorities, it's impossible to know who is accountable for them, and what their own role is in addressing them.

I'm talking about the top priorities for your entire operation, whether you are a single-family office, a foundation, a donor-advised fund, or a corporate giving program. Everyone needs to know what these are, who is accountable for them, and what their own role is in addressing that priority.

Your top priorities might be as simple as: Learn more about the problem of homelessness in our community, learn from other funders about what's working to end homelessness, and identify homeless-serving organizations we might want to support. Or they could be more complex if your new strategy requires a big shift in approach: Develop a communications plan, launch a new signature initiative, and hire a chief operating officer.

The third mistake is not reallocating your time to align with your implementation priorities. If your top priorities are to identify best practices in ending homelessness and find potential nonprofits to support, then guess what? You should be spending your time identifying best practices and finding grantees! Makes complete sense, right? But many philanthropists forget to apply common sense. They literally don't look ahead in their calendars and reallocate how they spend their time. Instead, they make a fourth mistake.

The fourth mistake is they keep on doing all stuff they were doing before they set their strategy. They literally walk out of the strategic planning retreat, go back to their offices, open their busy calendars, look at all the stuff that's already scheduled, and continue doing it. For example, let's say you previously made a lot of small grants out of your donor-advised fund to support a wide range of causes in your community, from the arts to mental health, education, and homelessness. Your calendar was probably filled with activities such as notifying potential nonprofits about funding opportunities, reviewing proposals, attending events, participating in a local initiative to improve access to the arts, and leading an education funders network.

But now you've decided you want to pick one issue and really make a difference. You are doubling down on ending homelessness (your new strategy). You'll notice that none of the activities I just mentioned will help you with your top priorities to learn about best practices in ending homelessness or find potential grantees. Yet most funders ignore this reality. All that old stuff is scheduled out on their calendars, perhaps for a year, and so they keep doing it. Perhaps out of obligation. Perhaps out of guilt. But usually it's because they made the first three mistakes: They assumed everyone knew how to implement the strategy, they never identified their priorities, and they never reallocated their time to align with their priorities. No wonder they keep doing the same old stuff!

They might do this for weeks, months, or a year. One foundation leader told me she anticipated it would take their staff an entire year before they could stop doing all the old stuff and shift to the actions required to implement their new strategic plan. She justified this by calling it the Strategy Transition Year!

Let me make this clear: You don't need a year to change gears. You need to stop doing the things that no longer help you achieve your goals and start doing the things that do.

You Suffer from Donor Distraction Disorder

Why is it a problem that funders don't have clear strategies and a plan to implement them? Not only do they end up busying themselves by working on the wrong stuff but sometimes they head off course in the entirely wrong direction.

Ideally, strategy is a funder's North Star. It should be the tool they use to determine their top priorities and their path forward. As new opportunities appear on their doorstep, they can compare them against their strategy to determine whether the opportunity will help them achieve their goals or take them off course.

Without a strategy and a plan to achieve it, two bad things can happen to good philanthropists: They inadvertently pursue new directions based on whatever threats or opportunities present themselves, and their organizations can get pulled apart by diverse internal activities. Let's examine these further.

1. Chasing shiny philanthropic squirrels. Without thinking, and absent a strategy, you inadvertently set a reactive direction—reacting to other people's ideas, to trends, or to threats in the environment. Sometimes this is as simple as "going along to get along." You conform to what's expected of you in order to maintain acceptance and security. Everyone else seems to be doing it, and you don't want to be criticized for not participating.

You know what I'm talking about because this has happened to you. It happens to all of us.

A surprise candidate is elected prime minister. You decide this changes everything you've worked on in the past few years, and instead you should invest all your time and resources into "movement building." A new initiative is being developed by other funders in your community and you want to be part of the excitement, even though it's an issue you've never funded. You just returned from a global conference where the buzz was about the United Nation's Sustainable Development Goals (SDGs) and you decide you should reorganize your philanthropy around these goals.

Now, chances are there is nothing wrong with the new approach itself. Movements need building, that new initiative is probably meeting an important community need, and who can argue with global goals such as "gender equality" and "clean water and sanitation"? The problem occurs when you don't already know what *you* want to accomplish with *your* philanthropy, and you don't have a plan to get there. When you lack clarity, it's easy to get pulled into the latest compelling idea or trend.

2. Getting pulled apart from within. In addition to being distracted by external changes and opportunities, your strategic vacuum results in your philanthropy being pulled apart internally. Why? Because you have talented people on your team. And in this vacuum, they take initiative to propose and try new endeavors. While their initiative is commendable (you didn't hire slackers!), their disparate activities have the potential to derail the direction of your philanthropy. For example, while on vacation your trustee learns about an innovative approach to youth development and he urges you to explore it (even though you don't fund youth development). Your vice president of programs decides policy advocacy is important and begins requiring all program officers to ask applicants to incorporate policy advocacy into grant requests. Your IT department purchases new employee engagement and workplace-giving software without consulting the director of corporate charitable giving.

Fooled or Fools?

Many of you picked up this book, with its title *Delusional Altruism*, because you were looking for scandals. Juicy, outrageous, and unseemly stories about bad philanthropists. Look, I love a gossipy tidbit just like everyone else, but that's not what this book is about. Because on the whole, I don't think that's what philanthropy is about.

Sure, there are examples of bad behavior in philanthropy. Let's take a look at a few of them. As you read through these, count how many of these examples you've encountered:

- **The time wasters:** The funder that forces nonprofits to waste time. One program officer at a large U.S. foundation privately admits that the foundation reviews less than 20% of grantee reports. One non-profit grant recipient told me he spends about 40 hours preparing grant reports for this foundation.

- **The mean:** The foundation trustee who refused to allow the foundation to invest in software so that nonprofits should apply for funding online. Why? Because he thought nonprofits should "work hard for their money."
- **The renegade:** The successful business leader who decided, on his own and almost without consulting anyone, to build a new medical clinic for Hispanic-American residents of his community. The clinic was built, opened, struggled, and closed in less than two years. Why? There was already a clinic with a solid reputation serving the same community. He didn't consult the Hispanic community or learn about assets and needs. He just acted alone.
- **The ego-driven:** The nonprofit board member who reneged on a $50,000 pledge because another board member pledged a larger amount. She didn't want to be shown up.
- **The criminal:** The donor who sexually harassed the nonprofit development director.
- **The toxic:** The foundation executive who tolerates bullying behavior, creating an oppressive work environment.
- **The corporate socially irresponsible:** The Fortune 500 company that uses philanthropy as a cover for bad business practices.
- **The spotlight seeker:** The celebrity who donated and helped raise more than $10 million for earthquake relief efforts. Yet investigations found he spent millions of those dollars on his operation (lavish offices, salaries, consultants' fees, travel, and mounting legal fees) and left little lasting community impact.
- **The bully:** The donor who publicly insults grantees and partners, without concern for negative repercussions, because he knows he's one of the few sources of philanthropic support in his town and grant recipients will be afraid to confront his behavior.
- **The shape-shifter:** The funder who forces grant seekers through rewrite after rewrite of proposals because their own project goals and priorities are continuously changing.
- **The dagger-through-the-heart funder:** The foundation that withheld grant funding during a significant nonprofit leadership transition to "see what happens." Instead of supporting the nonprofit to make the transition successful, they watched the nonprofit flounder and then close its doors.

- **The tax-benefit grabber:** The donor who gains a significant tax benefit by opening a donor-advised fund but years later has not bothered to make any grants from it.
- **The power tripper:** The business leader who encouraged his colleagues to become philanthropic. He described the joy of choosing which cause and nonprofit to support as being "like a kid in candy store." As if choosing between helping find a cure for AIDS or ending homelessness was like choosing between Swedish fish and saltwater taffy.

Sadly, these stories are real. And they create real problems. These philanthropists are seriously fooled by their own efforts! For the most part, they want to make a difference. But they most certainly get in their own way on the road to useful—not to mention impactful—giving.

But that's not the majority of philanthropists, and it's certainly not you. Emma Turner, director of Philanthropy Service at Barclays Private Bank in London, shares her experience:

> The donors we work with have a very strong social conscience. They genuinely want to make a difference. When I ask them, 'Why philanthropy, why now?' they almost always tell me that they never expected to have this much money in their lifetime. They feel lucky, they have more than they need, and they want to give back and make the world a better place. In 12 years of philanthropy advising, I've only met one person who wanted to be knighted for their charitable giving![2]

The vast majority of philanthropists are genuine in their altruism, just like you. You want to leave this world better than you entered it. You recognize that you bring a lot of strengths *and* that you have a lot to learn. You want to continuously strengthen your philanthropic muscles.

Notes

1. Author's conversation with Alan Weiss, February 15, 2017. See also, B. Tregoe and J. Zimmerman, *Top Management Strategy* (New York: Simon and Schuster, 1980).
2. Author interview with Emma Turner, August 13, 2019.

7 | You Ask the Wrong Questions

Whether we realize it or not, our lives are ruled by questions. Asking ourselves a productive question sends us down a path of impact and joy. Asking ourselves a misguided question sends us down a bumpy road, limiting possibilities for us and for our organizations.

Philanthropists ask themselves the wrong questions all the time. Their questions restrict their thinking, tangle them in tactics, force them to make impossible choices, and increase their risk.

Before you can ask the right questions, however, you need to recognize the wrong ones so they can be avoided.

I primarily hear funders asking themselves three kinds of wrong-headed questions. As you read on, jot down any examples of times you fell into one of these traps. Doing so will help you identify simple changes you can make to ask the right questions and transform your giving.

Wrong Question #1: "*How* Do We Do It?"

In the introduction to this book, I told you that *how* you give is as important as how much you give or to which causes you give. Your "how,"
then, is of paramount import.

Yet here I am telling you that the wrongest of wrong questions is the
"how" question. What gives? Can understanding "how" be both critical
and derailing?

The thing that makes this question dangerous is its timing. Used at
the right time, it will transform your giving like nothing you've ever
seen. Used at the wrong time, it will sink you.

Philanthropists ask "How?" too quickly. In particular, they ask
"How?" before asking "What?" They'll ask, "How will we accomplish
this?" and they'll generate a bunch of answers. Next, they'll rush
into action, implementing those answers. They think they're being
productive, but asking "How?" too soon actually sends them down the
wrong path. It leaves them further behind than when they started.

What funders need to determine first is *what* they want to do. Have
you ever been in a planning session in which the discussion went around
in circles without resolution? I bet it was because people jumped to
asking "How?" before asking "What?"

The problem this creates is that you can't know the best approach if
you don't know what you are trying to do. You force yourself to choose
among options before you've identified your objective or established criteria for decision making. As a result, funders either choose the wrong
"how" or become paralyzed and do nothing.

For example, let's say you recognize that your school system does
a poor job providing students an arts education. You might ask, "How
should we improve the arts instruction in our school district? Should we
retrain our existing teachers, hire better teachers, or bring in local artists
to teach in classrooms?"

If you don't know what you are trying to accomplish overall, though,
it's impossible to know whether improving arts instruction is the right
thing do to, much less which of those options will obtain the best result.

Only after asking questions such as, "What's our goal for arts education?" or "What should a comprehensive arts education plan include?" can you begin to think about the best way to address the issue.

Another way to distinguish the "what" from the "how" is to separate strategy from tactics.

Strategy is the "what," as in "What change do we want to create?" and "What type of philanthropist do I want to become?" *Strategic questions* help you form your strategy. They push you into articulating answers to the question "What are we trying to accomplish?"

Tactics are the "how." They're the activities that must be undertaken to achieve your strategy. *Tactical questions* help you figure out how to implement your strategy once it's been formulated. They get you to answer the question "How will we accomplish it?"

Now, don't get me wrong. The tactical "how" questions aren't evil. In fact, they're super-important questions that need to be asked. But funders shouldn't rush to ask them first. They should only be asked *after* you've answered your strategic questions. Only by answering your strategic "what" questions can you possibly know the right tactical "how" questions to ask.

For example, when a philanthropic family is developing its giving plan, they should ask strategic "what" questions such as: "What change do we want to see in our community?" "What difference do we want to make?" "What are the goals for our family?" Answering these questions will give them clarity on their purpose, the type of impact they're striving for, and the type of philanthropic family they want to become.

If what I'm saying sounds obvious, it's anything but. For example, I've seen countless families embark on creating a giving plan by asking all kinds of tactical "how" questions: "How often should our board meet?" "How big should our grants be?" "How do we involve the kids?"

Why do we gravitate toward tactical questions? They seem easier to answer and implement, so we feel like we're making progress. We can check these tactical items off our to-do lists. They don't require deep exploration. Andy Carroll, senior program director of Exponent Philanthropy, has been observing this for more than 30 years:

It's so easy for donors to focus on tactics because figuring out what you want to accomplish requires knowing yourself, knowing your field or community, and focusing. To become clearer about your values and goals, it really helps to have a trusted partner willing to engage you. Many donors don't have someone who is good at listening and asking questions. Some funders worry they will appear ignorant, many underestimate the knowledge and relationships required to make impact, and others think they know it all already—so they jump into tactics.

For example, it's simpler to answer the question "How do we reach millennials on social media?" than it is to answer "What are our communication goals?" The tactical social media question can be answered with a social media campaign. You know, you can start tweeting and snapchatting. Strategic questions, however, make you think more deeply about what you're trying to accomplish through communications.

The danger of rushing into "how" before asking "what" is that you easily get carried down the wrong path. Or lots of wrong paths. Chasing millennials on social media might be the wrong "how" if what you want to accomplish turns out to be improving federal policies for youth in foster care. When your philanthropy heads down the wrong path, you don't accomplish your goals. And you waste a lot of time and money along the way.

Smart philanthropists like you make this mistake all the time. We all do.

Now that you understand the problem of asking "How?" before asking "What?," let's tackle Wrong Question #2.

Wrong Question #2: What's the *Best* Way to Do This?

Let's say you took my advice and asked yourself, "What do we want to accomplish?" before asking, "How should we do it?" (Good for you!)

Unfortunately, you're now poised to fall into the trap of asking Wrong Question #2: "What's the *best* way to do this?" It seems like a good question, right? After all, you want the best. In fact, you deserve the best, and so do the communities you serve.

The problem with asking, "What's the *best* way" to do something is that it stops most people in their tracks. They begin to wonder, "What *is* the best?" "Am I smart enough to come up with the *best* way?" "What does *best* even mean?" This question evokes fear. People are afraid to toss around ideas, because they might not be good enough. This means, ironically, while you will identify some ways to accomplish your goals, they likely won't be the best way.

The question philanthropists should ask instead is "What are *all* the possible ways we could do this?" Allow yourself or your team to brainstorm every possible approach, tactic, and crazy idea. Let the ideas flow. You need to identify as many possible ways to do something as you can think of before you can determine the best way.

My friend Mark Levy tipped me off to this idea. He is the author of *Accidental Genius: Revolutionize Your Thinking Through Private Writing*, and he knows a thing or two about coming up with good ideas. He used to lead brainstorming sessions with advertising executives on Madison Avenue. He instinctively knew that asking, "What's the best ad campaign you can create?" would stifle creativity. Instead, one of the techniques he used was to have them brainstorm *all* the ways they could meet or exceed their client's goals. Opening themselves up to every bizarre and crazy idea they could they come up with helped them find the best one.

This applies to philanthropists just as much as to Mad Men.

Take the case of Ellen, a high-net-worth donor. Ellen proudly told me the goal of her charitable giving was to reduce youth violence in her community. She did this by giving annual grants of $5,000–$10,000 to 10 different nonprofits. But she wasn't getting the results she wanted.

She asked my advice on the best way to improve her approach and shared three options she thought were best: Providing grants to more organizations, increasing the grant amount to $20,000, or offering college scholarships to youths participating in the programs.

When I asked what her objective was, she was clear. She wanted to reduce rates of youth violence among middle school students by 30% in five years.

If that was indeed her primary objective, none of her options for achieving it was good.

Giving small grants to more organizations would not accomplish much, because the organizations were not working together. Doubling the amount of funds wouldn't make much impact, because the amount would still be small compared to the scale of the problem. The incentive of a college scholarship four or more years from now won't be very influential to middle schoolers.

She had limited her options by trying to figure out the "best," and none of them were great.

I advised her to ask her team, "What are *all* the ways we can reduce youth violence?" Together they brainstormed a long list. They eventually landed on a coordinated strategy to partner with local government, law enforcement, juvenile courts, schools, and other youth-serving organizations to address the root causes of youth violence and track progress.

Only when you've identified all possible options can you choose the best among them.

Wrong Question #3: "Can We Start Right Away?"

You've established your strategy and you understand your objectives. You've identified all the ways to achieve your strategy and chosen the best ones. Congratulations! Now you're ready to roll up your sleeves and get to work, right? Wrong.

The third wrong question commonly asked by funders is, "Can we start right away?"

What's wrong with that? You know I'm all for increasing speed in philanthropy—I devoted a whole chapter of this book to it! And I know you're anxious to start implementing your great new idea. After all, people's lives are at stake. But the problem with asking, "Can we start right away?" is that you haven't yet assessed the risk.

Risk is inherent in just about everything we do.

There's risk in riding a bike in traffic and there's risk in hiring your next employee. There's risk in investing in a new nonprofit, and there's risk in launching your signature funding initiative.

As a philanthropist, you are well positioned to take risks. You have access to wealth, you aren't mired in government regulation, and unless you work in corporate philanthropy, you don't report to shareholders. That creates a fertile environment to try new things. In fact, a great use of philanthropic dollars is the riskier "first money in" to support initial research or the testing phase of a project to determine whether further investment is warranted.

But not every risk is worth taking. Many philanthropic decisions turn out to be flops. You might hire the wrong person, fund an ineffective organization, or fail to achieve results. Ignoring risk can cost money, delay progress, damage your reputation, and even harm the people you want to help.

Unfortunately, many philanthropists make decisions without asking questions to assess risk. They learn about a new program at a conference and immediately begin replicating it. They are asked to join a funding collaborative spearheaded by a well-known donor and they instantly agree. They've created a new innovation and jump to implement it.

"Assessing risk sounds complicated," you might be thinking. I know you want to make a decision now and get started right away. But relax. Assessing risk is actually quite simple. It's a matter of taking your bright, shiny new idea and assessing it against four criteria: cost, benefit, strategic fit, and difficulty of implementation. This allows you to determine whether it's a prudent risk worth taking.[1] I will tell you how to do this in Chapter 12, "You Are Unstoppable."

Why Does Asking the Wrong Questions Cause Problems?

Asking the wrong questions, such "How do we do it?" "What's the best way to do this?" and "Can we start right away?" is a common mistake we all make. Think back to the last time you asked one of these questions. I bet it wasn't that long ago. Unfortunately, these questions can invite costly mistakes. At best, they take you off course. At worst, you have unflattering coverage on the front page of the *New York Times* because your approach is hurting the people you want to help. Your funding initiative was a bust, and now everyone knows! You don't want that. When you say, "I want to use our philanthropy to improve our community," you truly mean it. And the best way to do that is to start with the right questions.

Luckily, that's the topic of the next chapter! In fact, Part II of this book is devoted to eliminating delusional altruism and transforming how you give. Because how you give matters.

Ready to be transformational? Read on!

Note

1. Michael Robert and Alan Weiss, *The Innovation Formula* (New York: Harper & Row, 1988).

PART II

Transformational Giving

8

You Start with the Right Questions

Questions are surprisingly powerful. The right questions spur learning, fuel innovation, create clarity, build trust, mitigate risk, and save money. To have a transformational impact as a philanthropist, you need to start with the right questions.

In fact, research shows that starting with the right question is the genesis of innovation and value creation. According to David Stuart, author of the *New York Times* best-selling book *Great Work: How to Make a Difference People Love,* "The effect of asking the right questions is statistically profound. In our research we saw that asking the right question increased the odds of someone's work having a positive effect on others by 4.1 times. It made the outcome 3.1 times more likely to be deemed important, 2.8 times more likely to create passion in the doer, and . . . 2.7 times more likely to make a positive impact on the organization's bottom line."[1]

This chapter examines the 12 most important questions high-performing philanthropists should ask regularly. Don't be fooled into

81

thinking that any one or two of them are more important than the others. At times, you'll want to ask them all. Asking (and answering) them will transform your giving and accelerate your speed to impact.

Question 1: Why?

Ask "why?" to understand your purpose. Ask "why?" to question assumptions. Both answers are critical to transform your giving. If you ask "why?" with these two reasons in mind, you will attain clarity, inspire others to join you, and turbocharge your impact velocity.

First, let's look at asking "why?" to understand your purpose.

In his best-selling book *Start with Why*, author Simon Sinek implores readers to determine their "why" to identify their purpose, cause, or belief. People need to understand *why* they do what they do, not just *what* they do or *how* they do it. Businesses should know their raison d'être. He explains that people do business with those whose purpose aligns with their own beliefs. People don't buy *what* you do, they buy *why* you do it.

The Elton John AIDS Foundation believes AIDS can be beaten. It knows its purpose. It asked and answered, "Why do we exist?" As a result of this clarity, the U.S.- and U.K.-based foundation has successfully raised more than $450 million over the past 25 years to challenge discrimination against people with HIV/AIDS, prevent infections, provide treatment and services, and motivate governments to end AIDS around the world.

Why is knowing your "why" important in philanthropy? I believe it's because clarity trumps strategy. You need clarity on your charitable purpose (your "why") before you can accomplish much with your charitable giving. Simon Sinek notes that Martin Luther King, Jr., " . . . gave the 'I Have a Dream' speech, not the 'I Have a Plan' speech."[2] You need to know your purpose before you develop your plan. Others will join with your purpose because it aligns with theirs.

The Lippman Kanfer Family Foundation in Akron, Ohio, knows their purpose. They understand the "why" of their family philanthropy. In fact, they used their "why" to develop a unique approach to organizing how they give. While the foundation's mandate is "to repair and enrich the world through thriving communities," the answer to *why* that foundation exists is slightly different: to "build and sustain a multigenerational family culture of *tzedakah*," which means "philanthropy" in Hebrew. That's right. Joe Kanfer, chair of GOJO Industries (the inventors of Purell), along with other family members, determined that the purpose of the Lippman Kanfer Family Foundation is to encourage their multigenerational family to be philanthropic while facilitating thoughtful giving. It's especially important to them to come together to do this work as the family grows and spreads out around the world. As a result, they organize their grantmaking into themed three-year cycles. Every three years the family chooses a societal issue, learns about it together, and makes grants based on what they learn.

Second, ask "why?" to question assumptions.

In philanthropy, there is no shortage of causes to support. There is no dearth of social or environmental problems to tackle. Likewise, there is no shortage of good-sounding solutions. In fact, there are all kinds of important "shiny objects" you hear about at philanthropy conferences or read about online. Things like trauma-informed care, emotional intelligence, crowdfunding, and collective impact. If you don't ask "why?" you might begin funding one of these solutions without knowing if it's right for you.

Let's say your foundation's executive director announces, "I recommend we fund a new citywide campaign to increase public transportation." That sounds like a great idea, right? Who could be against more public transportation? It helps people get to school and work, while saving the environment.

But the question you need to ask at this stage is, "Why?" In this case you might ask, "Why should our foundation support public transportation instead of other citywide goals?" or "Why does transportation advance our strategy?" or "Why should we be involved in policy advocacy?"

Asking "why?" does not imply that an idea is bad. Public transportation, trauma-informed care, and crowdfunding are all hugely important.

When you ask "why?" to question assumptions, you get to the substance of why *your* philanthropy should be involved in this work. Asking "why?" helps you revisit the overall purpose of your funding and keeps you focused on the long game.

I'm not advocating that you channel your inner two year old. Don't ask "why?" to be obnoxious or incessantly contrarian. Ask "why?" to make sure whatever you are doing is the right thing for you to do at that time. It couldn't be easier. It goes like this:

- "We should diversify our board of directors." Why? Diversity might be critically important, but is our board ready to be inclusive of diverse perspectives? Are there other things we might do as a board first, such as understand our own implicit biases or learn about the history and context that created our wealth, so that we are well prepared to diversify the board?
- "We should create a Giving Tuesday campaign." Why? Have we thought about what we want to accomplish? Is this the best way to encourage others to give, or are there other options?
- "We should start a foundation." Why? Why a foundation and not a donor-advised fund? Are we ready for the responsibility of managing a nonprofit organization?

Asking "why" is not to be confused with bogging down your process. You can ask "why?" and consider the possibilities with integrity, then move on quickly.

When you ask "why?" to understand your philanthropic purpose and question assumptions, you are well on your road to philanthropic impact. You are also ready to ask your next question.

Question 2: What?

Philanthropists should ask, "What?" In particular, they should ask "what?" before they ask "how?" By asking "what?" first, you gain clarity on the goal you want to accomplish. (In Chapter 7: "You Ask the

Wrong Questions," I described the particular peril of asking "how?" before asking "what?")

For example, you might learn that a staggering 81.7 million children in Asia suffer from stunting as a result of malnutrition, that undernutrition is the underlying cause of 45% of all child deaths globally,[3] and that the global cost of malnutrition is $3.5 trillion per year (not including the cost in suffering).[4] You want to do something about it.

Ask yourself: "*What* impact do we want to have on child malnutrition in Asia?" By asking "what?" first, you can attain clarity on what you want to accomplish. More importantly, it allows everyone on your team to come to agreement. *What* you want to do might be to increase government investment in malnourished communities. Or it might be to empower mothers to prevent and detect malnutrition in their children. Those are two different objectives, requiring different courses of action.

If *what* you want to do is increase government investment in malnourished communities, you could then ask "how" questions such as "How do we determine which branches of government to work with?" or "How can we become a trusted source of information and expertise to governmental leaders?" If what you *want* to do is empower mothers to prevent and detect malnutrition in their children, you might ask, "How can we promote breastfeeding?" or "How can we train mothers to monitor their child's nutritional status?"

Another reason to ask "what?" before "how?" is that it prevents your ideas from getting shot down. In groups, whether it's your family, staff, or community stakeholders, when you start discussing "how" to do something before you agree on "what" you want to do, it's easy to start shooting everyone's ideas down.

It goes like this: "I think we should buy vans to transport kids to after-school programs." "No, that's too expensive." "We should give kids bus passes and they can take public transportation." "Bad idea—it's not safe and we can't control the routes." "We need a searchable, online directory of after-school programs." "That's too hard to maintain."

And on it goes: One person lobs a "how?" and someone else shoots it to the ground. Meetings end without conclusion and everyone feels frustrated.

When you start by asking "what?" you might conclude that you want high-quality after-school programs within a mile of every school. Armed with agreement on your objective, you can now turn your attention to alternative ways of achieving it (e.g., map existing after-school programs to identify locations and gaps, identify transportation assets, assess transportation options, offer training to improve program quality).

Question 3: What Do I Know Already?

I have great news for you! You already know 80% of the answer to any question you have about philanthropy.

Now for the bad news: Most of us don't take the time to think about what we already know. This is a problem, because when we don't start by asking what we already know, we don't allow our best ideas to germinate and flourish. We also waste time and money getting other people to answer our questions.

Don't worry, I have an easy solution to this common problem: Start by asking yourself, "What do I already know?" If you do this, you will answer your question faster and at less cost.

Whenever you have a question in philanthropy, you should first spend some time—even an hour—to brainstorm everything you already know about the topic and write it down. I mean literally, pull out your notepad, laptop, or easel paper. Do this by yourself or in a group. Ask yourself, "What do I (we) already know?"

It doesn't matter if your question is "How can we provide better philanthropic services to the clients of our multi-family office?" "Should we start a corporate foundation?" or "How can we help more low-income students attend university?" I guarantee you will identify 80% of what you need to know.

For example, let's say you want to know this: "How can we use our philanthropic dollars to prevent drug abuse?" You're not a drug abuse expert, but you might have learned a lot by funding a related issue, mental health. You might recognize that both issues are stigmatized, people who suffer from them are often too embarrassed to seek treatment, there aren't enough treatment options, and health insurance companies do not sufficiently cover either type of problem. All this knowledge and insight can help you answer your question, "How can we use our philanthropic dollars to prevent drug abuse?"

Or your question might be "What's involved in starting a corporate foundation?" Even though you've never started a foundation, you might have started several businesses. You know what it takes: file articles of incorporation, hire and manage employees, set up an office, develop operating procedures, and manage assets. You've probably served on several nonprofit boards, so you understand nonprofit governance and budgeting. You can apply all that experience and more to help answer your question "What's involved in starting a corporate foundation?" I bet you'll be 80% there.

Instead, what funders typically do is immediately look to other people for the answers. They don't even stop to reflect upon what they already know. They dive right in, finding other "experts" to help them answer 100% of their questions. They do this by looking online, reading articles and reports, commissioning research, and hiring consultants.

Let me tell you about Marcie. A talented woman with decades of philanthropic experience, Marcie left her leadership role at a philanthropy organization to become the CEO of a community foundation. She wanted to increase the foundation's assets through a planned giving campaign. She told me she didn't know anything about planned giving and asked if I could recommend a consultant she could hire. I told her that was the last thing she needed to do.

I reminded Marcie that even if she had zero planned-giving experience, she knew a lot about things closely related to planned giving. Planned giving is a type of fund development, and she had plenty of fund development and donor relations experience, having raised money from members of the philanthropy organization for over a decade. She had designed and launched other kinds of campaigns, so she had expertise in setting campaign goals, developing implementation plans, and project management. She had become an expert in communications, including developing communications plans, messages, and collateral materials.

Fund development, donor relations, campaign management, and communications are all critical components of a successful planned giving campaign. I advised Marcie to sit down for an hour to reflect on everything she knew about these topics and write them down (the 80%). Only then should she think about the aspects of planned giving she didn't know anything about (the 20%).

Question 4: What Don't I Know?

You know a lot. And yes, there's a lot you don't know.

Many philanthropists generate their wealth through enormous success in business. Others are hired to work at foundations for their content expertise. But it's delusional to think that just because you are a successful hedge fund manager, celebrity, civil rights attorney, or climate change expert, you are therefore an expert in everything. And it certainly doesn't make you an expert in philanthropic giving or social change.

After you ask, "What do I already know?" you should ask, "What don't I know?"

Let's go back to Marcie.

After Marcie wrote down everything she knew related to planned giving (the 80%), she thought specifically about what she didn't know (the remaining 20%). There was a lot, such as:

What are best practices in planned giving?
What are common planned giving mistakes to avoid?
What's the difference between a charitable remainder trust and a bequest?
How do you have conversations with people about money and death?
How do people from different cultural and religious backgrounds think differently about planned giving?

And don't forget, there's all the stuff you don't know that you don't know. She realized there was a great deal she needed to learn, but she didn't even know what it was!

Now that Marcie had a pretty good handle on what she didn't know about planned giving, she could quickly fill those knowledge gaps by obtaining specific information. Rather than feeling overwhelmed by an entire dimension of fund development about which she first thought she knew nothing, she could reach out to financial advisors to understand the range of philanthropic vehicles used in planned giving. She could learn from knowledgeable colleagues who advise donors about whether her planned giving approaches and message needed to be tailored to different cultural groups.

And if she still wanted to hire a planned giving consultant, she could talk with the consultant about her specific needs to determine whether the consultant was the best fit. That would allow her to focus only on what she truly needed and hire the experts. She might need someone to help her handle delicate conversations about legacy giving, identify planned giving prospects, and develop relationships with estate planning attorneys, but not how to design the campaign or develop a marketing and communications plan.

By identifying everything she already knew (the 80%) and getting help with just the 20% she didn't know, she saved time, saved money, and began securing planned gifts sooner.

This leads us to our next question.

Question 5: Who Else Needs to Be Involved?

No matter what you want to do with your philanthropy, you can't do it alone. You need to regularly ask yourself, "Who else needs to be involved?" And then you need to meaningfully involve them.

Why? First, as we've discussed, no matter how brilliant and fabulous you are, you don't have all the personal or professional insight and experiences you need to do whatever you are trying to do. Second, our solutions—and our philanthropy—need to be as interconnected as our problems are.

Let's take a look.

No one could possibly possess all the experiences and information needed to inform your philanthropy or create the change you seek. You might be a donor who wants to help people whose lives are quite different from yours. Or you could be a celebrity who wants to support kids who are living through the same things you did growing up. You might have extensive professional knowledge about the issue you care about, or none. It doesn't matter where you fall on the spectrum. Regardless of how much or how little insight you bring to the table, your philanthropy should involve others. Especially those you seek to help.

Imagine a smartphone app to help busy moms that was created by men with no children, who didn't talk to busy moms when they developed it. It makes no sense. Imagine designing a grantmaking strategy to help migrant workers, without learning from migrant workers to understand their strengths and challenges or involving them to create solutions and opportunities. That doesn't make sense either. Unfortunately, that happens often in philanthropy.

But you don't want to be that kind of philanthropist! You want your philanthropy to be best positioned to create change. That's why you ask, "Who else needs to be involved?"

Mark Smucker, CEO of the J.M. Smucker Company, recognized a need to refresh the company's purpose due to changing consumer and societal dynamics. He realized he couldn't do it alone, although he certainly could have tried. After all, he was the fifth-generation leader of his family's business, which had started in 1897 as a small custom cider mill in Orrville, Ohio, and had grown into a Fortune 500 company. But as a purpose-driven leader, he knew the purpose of his family's company had always been more than profit. And he realized that to fully live its purpose, Smucker's entire operation and all 7,000 employees needed to be aligned to it. So he involved a cross section of employees that included individuals from all aspects of the organization and all levels of seniority. Working together, 40 employees, Mark, and a consulting firm spent an afternoon brainstorming, vetting, and voting on a refreshed direction for the company's purpose. Ultimately, they landed on: Feeding connections that help us thrive—life tastes better together.[5]

The second reason why you need to ask, "Who else needs to be involved?" is because the challenges we face don't exist in a vacuum. Our problems exist in an interconnected universe of systems, governments, organizations, financing, environments, and stakeholders. Our solutions—and our philanthropy—need to be interconnected as well.

Pick any issue you care about: elder abuse, rising populism, poor sanitation. Regardless of the issue, there are groups of people, organizations, systems, financing, and regulations intertwined with it. Spend 15 minutes brainstorming about them and I bet you will come up with a bunch.

Let's say you want to improve education in your hometown. Your list of people and things connected to education could include teachers, principals, unions, parents, students; the school district; teacher training programs; textbook publishers; and city, county, state, and federal government regulations, funding, and systems. Speaking of systems, it's not just the education system that's involved with education. The child welfare, juvenile justice, transportation, zoning, and health care systems might have roles to play in improving education, too. Your list goes on and on.

In order to tackle the problem, you need to involve these systems, organizations, and stakeholders to fully understand the problem, determine the best solution, and implement that solution.

Let me give you an example. When the David and Lucile Packard Foundation wanted to tackle the problem of summer learning loss in California, staff realized they couldn't do it alone. They asked, "Who else needs to be involved?" They immediately engaged three key summer learning organizations, the Partnership for Children and Youth, ASAPconnect, and the National Summer Learning Association, to form a consortium and help them design Summer Matters, a seven-year initiative to ensure that California's education leaders embrace high-quality after-school and summer enrichment as essential to the overall success of children who need it most. This expanded to a larger steering committee that included county offices of education from across the state, other funders, and a children's advocacy organization. Quickly, they involved teachers, libraries, parks, universities, school board members, after-school programs, technical assistance providers, evaluators, and the California State Department of Education. Eventually the list of partners and grantees grew exponentially into a statewide network with more than 85 member organizations.

A few years into the initiative, the Packard Foundation wasn't seeing the results they expected. They convened their network to brainstorm solutions. They asked themselves again, "Who else needs to be involved?" and realized they had not sufficiently involved school superintendents. They recalibrated their approach and engaged 73 superintendents as champions for change. These superintendents played a critical role advocating for expanded, high-quality summer learning opportunities and increased funding in their districts. Results quickly improved.[6]

That's why you need to ask, "Who else needs to be involved?" when you are developing, launching, and implementing your philanthropy.

How do you determine whom else to involve? It depends on what you are trying to accomplish. A good place to start is with the people and communities most impacted by whatever you want to do. Keep in mind, there can be a lot of diversity within that group! For example, if you want to increase kindergarten readiness by encouraging moms to read to their children, you must recognize there are many kinds of moms: teen moms, older moms, single moms, and lesbian moms. Moms of various ethnic and cultural backgrounds. Moms who have a hard time reading (e.g., due to dyslexia, poor vision, or illiteracy). Moms who speak a language different from yours. Think about the variety of perspectives you should include.

You can then ask yourself questions such as:

- Who else is connected to them (e.g., caregivers, teachers)?
- What other organizations are involved?

- Who are their partners? Their detractors?
- Who influences them?
- What systems are they part of?
- What laws and regulations govern them?
- How are they financed?
- Who stands out as making a difference on this issue?
- Are there models or best practices we should look at?
- Who are the leaders and experts?

You can brainstorm answers to questions like these and a picture will emerge of others you might involve. From there, you can begin to prioritize whom to involve first.

Now, let's talk briefly about when and how to involve them.

When should you involve others in your philanthropy? Early and often. Think about your work in stages. There are opportunities to involve other people at every stage: idea generating, testing, planning, implementing, evaluating, and refining. Keep in mind that the people you involve might change over time. The folks who advise you on developing your plan might be different from those who help you implement it. You might rely heavily on your attorneys and accountants when you first create your foundation, then later work with a philanthropy advisor to determine funding areas and a governance structure. As you clarify the focus of your giving, you might involve community members, content experts, and other funders.

How do you involve them? There is no limit to the ways you can involve other people in your philanthropy. Get creative! I find involvement falls into three categories: informing, decision making, and doing.

Informing means that you are learning from others and using that information to determine your best course of action. For example, a corporate funder might talk to philanthropy leaders at other companies about their employee volunteerism programs in order to determine their approach to employee volunteerism. You can inform yourself through many means, ranging from reading articles, picking up the phone and calling colleagues, watching webinars and attending conferences, conducting listening tours and town hall meetings, engaging others in your planning sessions, convening an advisory group, and commissioning research (e.g., interviews, focus groups, and surveys). When I advised the Charles and Helen Schwab Foundation as it developed grantmaking programs to prevent poverty and reduce homelessness, then–National Program Director Rick Williams and I flew across the country to meet with national experts and foundation leaders to understand best practices and promising approaches. What we learned informed the Schwab Foundation's grantmaking and identified potential partners.

Decision making means just that. Think of all the different types of decisions you make as a philanthropist: determining your funding priorities, deciding whether to create a private foundation or limited liability corporation (LLC), selecting an organization to host your donor-advised fund, setting strategy, making funding decisions, and so on. Involving others in decision making means they get to decide. They don't just share their opinion; they get a vote. You might do this by hiring people into decision-making roles in your organization, inviting them to join your board, involving them in the leadership council of your community initiative, or creating a community grants committee that makes funding decisions.

Rawa, a fund in Palestine, engages community members to set funding priorities, prospect ideas and projects, make funding decisions, and allocate resources for innovative community development. With funding from the Rockefeller Brothers Fund, Global Fund for Community Foundations, Al-Maamal Foundation, and others, Rawa's collaborative process seeks to "foster communication, learning, networking, solidarity, and exchange between fractured and separated Palestinian communities."[7]

Doing involves the diverse people and organizations you involve when it's time to roll up your sleeves and do the work. These "doers" can include employees, board members, grantees, partners, consultants, researchers, virtual assistants, volunteers, grant writers—basically anyone who can help with the "stuff" involved in implementing your philanthropic goals.

For example, the Con Alma Health Foundation in New Mexico heavily relies upon its 15-member board of trustees and 15-member Community Advisory Committee to build authentic connections with grantees, partners, and communities throughout the state. Both groups reflect the diversity of ethnicities and geographies of New Mexico, including members of the Navajo Nation, the Pueblo Tribal Groups, and the Apache Nation. These individuals don't just govern and advise, they roll up their sleeves and help. They make connections with and between nonprofits and host foundation gatherings in their own communities. They travel to remote parts of the state and help people understand how to apply for grants. They are empowered to engage with others as representatives of the foundation. This shared leadership model ensures that grantmaking decisions are informed by diverse perspectives and experiences.[8]

Question 6: What Are Our Best Practices Internally?

We often look to *external* sources for best practices, hoping that others have figured out the ideal way to accomplish something and that we can simply duplicate it. But chances are, you have a lot of *internal* best practices you can build upon. The problem is you aren't fully aware of your own best practices! And if you aren't aware of them, you aren't taking full advantage of them.

Looking to *external* sources for best practices means you are asking everyone else but yourself what the best way to do something is. We do this through Google searches, conducting needs assessments, commissioning environmental scans, and posting queries on list serves. These aren't bad activities, but they are problematic. They are problematic because they can take an immense amount of time, divert your attention, and cost money.

A better approach is to start with your *internal* best practices. These are practices that you already employ and handle exceptionally well. Perhaps you do them sometimes, but not all the time. Or maybe some members of your team do them, but not everyone. An internal best practice could be anything, such as:

- Hiring the most experienced people to work at a celebrity's foundation, rather than the celebrity's friends and family
- Supporting a program team that reads a new article each month and discusses its implications for the team's grantmaking strategies
- Involving an evaluation expert in the development of new funding initiatives, rather than waiting to assess progress years down the road

But when is the last time you searched inside yourself or your organization for these internal best practices? If you are like most philanthropists, the answer is rarely or never. With a little time and intention, you can identify your best practices, expand them, and make dramatic improvements in your philanthropy.

Let's take an easy example: time management. If you want to learn how to better manage your time, you could seek external best practices by searching "time management" online and getting more than 72 million results. You'll find all kinds of advice—from organizing your day between "maker" and "manager" time to categorizing your activities based on urgency and importance. All good tips. But you don't have time to read and prioritize 72 million of them!

What if instead you started with your own best practices for time management? What has worked well for you when managing your own time? If you've never paused to think about it, try it right now. Spend 15 minutes jotting down or thinking about your best practices over the next few days. I bet you will come up with an insightful list. For example, here are a few of your colleagues' best time management practices:

- "Never scheduling back-to-back meetings. I need time in between to follow through on my 'next steps' and prepare for my next meeting."
- "I block out an entire day to focus on a big project rather than spending one hour on it every day."
- "Answering email three times per day, rather than all day long."

Similarly, there are hidden best practices that exist among funders. Even if your staff is tiny, there's likely to be someone who's developed a practice that everyone can learn from. If you are a donor with no employees, you probably have created exceptional practices with some grantees that could be extended to all.

You can find your own best practices by looking for distinctions and patterns. Start with where you have multiple experiences doing the same thing: launching an event (employee volunteer days, for example), managing similar employees (program officers), or funding multiple locations (you support medical services at 10 different Chinese orphanages). What's working exceptionally well with some people or at some locations that is not working as well at others? Those are the distinctions you should examine. Are there patterns of success among them? Identify those. For example, they could be patterns of leadership, management, technology, communications, and so forth.

Perhaps you've participated in seven different collaborative funding efforts, but only three of them achieved measurable results. What distinguished those three? Was it having the right partners at the table? Having an evaluation plan at the onset? Dedicated personnel to keep everyone on task? Look for patterns and you will find your best practices. Now, write them down and be sure to implement and build upon them when you embark on your next funding collaborative.

Make it an internal best practice to regularly search for internal best practices! Seriously, you can easily incorporate this into your existing work at events such as staff meetings, quarterly meetings among your collaborative partners, or annual family retreats.

Question 7: What Are All the Ways We Can Do This?

As we learned in Chapter 7, if you first ask, "What are *all* the ways we can do this?" instead of asking "What's the *best* way to do it?" you will accomplish your goals faster and more effectively.

So start instead by asking, "What are *all* the ways?" Allow your team to brainstorm every imaginable possibility.

If you want to increase your grantees' impact by helping them learn from each other along the way, you might first think of the grantees convening. But if you give your team permission to think creatively, you might also come up with: pay for grantees to visit each other, create an online community where grantees can ask and answer questions, strengthen personal relationships between grantees so that they will naturally turn to each other for help, and ensure grantees are not penalized for sharing mistakes.

Involve people outside your team to help generate ideas—namely, the people you are trying to help. I bet your grantees can think of a lot of ways they'd love to learn from each other!

And once you've identified a plethora of options, you can prioritize two or three among them.

Question 8: If You Could Do It All Over Again, What Would You Do Differently?

There is one question that is guaranteed to save time and money and help achieve dramatic results. It's a simple question, but the answers you receive could change your outcomes and the way you think about your philanthropy.

That question is this: "If you could do it all over again, what would you do differently?"

Yes, it's really that simple.

If you ask others that question while or after they attempt the same thing you're trying to do, I promise you will reap benefits. Listen to what they have to say, implement their suggestions, and you will save time, financial resources, and headaches. You will also have a much more successful grantmaking program, and it will happen faster than if you hadn't asked this question. Why make the same mistakes someone else already made, when we can learn from each other and collectively bring greater impact to the communities that we serve?

Let me give you an example. I was helping a community foundation design and launch a youth development initiative, so we visited other communities across the country that were doing the same thing. We asked each of them, "If you could develop your initiative all over again, what would you do differently?"

Each one of them said, "If I could do it all over again, I would develop a communications plan from the very beginning." Bingo!

The organizations all agreed that without such a plan, they were hindered throughout their entire initiative by poor communication and coordination and lack of awareness among key stakeholders. This is exactly the type of practical information we need to navigate our philanthropic journeys.

This crucial question was asked by another foundation, and one organization responded that they should have gotten out of the office and into the community they served before developing their strategy. In this case, they were addressing issues facing the elderly. They had reams of data about illness, clinical services, nutrition, and mobility. But they didn't go talk to those who serve the elderly, or to the elderly themselves. They missed the important moments of deep understanding that can come when one sees how local, state, or national policies play out on the ground. Their impact was not what it could have been.

The conclusion is simple, right? Ask the question, listen to the answers, implement the suggestion, save yourself time and resources, get faster results, and have greater impact. Don't be afraid to reach out for advice to a fellow donor, consultant, or foundation that has worked on similar issues. I guarantee it works!

Question 9: How Can We Speed This Up?

If you want to increase your speed to impact, regularly ask yourself, "How can we speed this up?" Brainstorm possible solutions and try out the best ones. People, this is not complicated. We just forget to do it!

In Chapter 10, "You Are Fast," I share all kinds of tips to speed things up and I encourage you to read that chapter. In the meantime, ask yourself how you can speed up just about anything you are doing with your philanthropy. No matter what you are working on, I guarantee it can be accomplished with greater velocity.

Ariane Brunet, Margaret Schink, and Julie Shaw asked themselves how they could speed up grantmaking to enable women activists to respond quickly in unanticipated situations, especially in areas of escalating violence. Time is of the essence to allow activists to seize small windows of unforeseen opportunities to create change or to protect themselves from immediate danger. To determine the best way to speed up their giving, they involved 80 activists and donors from around the world to collectively design their rapid-response grantmaking model and launch the Urgent Action Fund for Women's Human Rights. The Fund uses online, text, and mobile funding applications to respond to requests within 72 hours and allocate funds days later. Together with their sister funds, they support women in Asia, the Middle East, Eastern and Western Europe, Latin America, Africa, Canada, Russia, Turkey, and the United States. Since its founding in 1997, its annual budget has grown to $1.5 million USD and they've allocated more than 1,000 grants in 97 countries.[9]

But you don't need to design a new funding model to be speedy. Whether you are dispersing funds, deciding how to expand your investment portfolio to include impact investments, or creating a scholarship program, you can probably shave off half the time you normally spend. To do this, you might need to change your practice or invest in yourself. For example, instead of filing your own tax documents, you can hire an accountant to file them. Instead of reading 20 articles and attending a workshop about impact investing, you could retain an expert to advise you and make recommendations. Or you could make no financial investment at all. Cut the length of your weekly staff meetings in half by emailing out updates in advance, starting on time, and adhering to outcome-oriented agendas.

Question 10: If This Was to Become Best-in-Class, What Would It Look Like?

Set yourself up for the greatest possible success by asking, "If this was to become best in class, what would it look like?" Asking this question reframes your thinking. You aren't simply collaborating with other funders; you are creating a best-in-class funding collaborative. You aren't just improving sanitation in rural India; you are designing an award-winning approach that could become a global model for other countries.

Asking this question forces you to strive for the best. You realize that it matters *how* you do what you do. The pieces you put into place. The talent you hire. The partners you engage.

Focus group expert Naomi Henderson recommends the use of "best-in-class" questions to elicit feedback from focus group participants. Some examples:

- "What would it take for this (product) to get a gold star?"
- "What would it take for this to get an A?"[10]

You can channel your inner focus group moderator and ask similar questions:

- "If this (initiative) were recognized as a national best practice, what would it look like?"
- "If, five years from now, funders from around the world came to us to learn how we (solved this problem), what will we tell them?"
- "If this (donor-advised fund) were to win an award, what would it be for?"
- "If this (corporate giving program) were 'best in class,' what would that look like?"

Now, hold on a second. I know what you're thinking. You're thinking you are too small to become a national model. You don't have enough funding to demonstrate how your approach works. You'd just like to make a difference in your hometown, thank you very much. You don't need to be a global best practice.

Don't let small thinking hold you back. You don't need to be a billionaire to get a gold star. (And good for you for caring about your hometown.) But "If this were to become 'best in class,' what would it look like?" is a question we all should ask. It forces us to think differently. And it requires us to put in place the talent, systems, and structures we need to build something award worthy.

You surely don't have all the resources you need to tackle the opioid crisis, but you can ask yourselves questions like "Who are the best partners we can bring to the table?" and "What other financial resources can we leverage?" and "If 10 years from now there were zero deaths from opioid overdoses in our hometown, what will have needed to change, and what can we start doing now to change it?"

And guess what? You don't need to ever become that national model, win an award, or get that gold star. The point is that you reframed your thinking. You tried. And in trying, you are setting yourself up for greater success.

Question 11: What's the Risk?

Not every idea is a good one. Not all innovations should be pursued. Before jumping onto the next philanthropic trend or funding an untested idea, simply ask yourself, "What's the risk?"

Everything has some risk. Risk of failure, damaged reputation, financial loss, or strained relationships. But how do you identify potential risks? And how do you determine whether a risk is worth taking?

I have two techniques that I use with my clients to identify and assess risk. What I love about them both is they cost nothing and you can start doing them today!

The first is the Risk List. Together with your colleagues (your team, partners, stakeholders), brainstorm all the potential risks associated with what you are about to do. Write them on easel paper and discuss them. Ask yourself three questions:

1. What is the likelihood of this happening?
2. What is the severity, if it did happen?
3. What can we do to lessen or prevent this risk?

Let's say you are deciding whether to partner with a national non-profit organization to raise awareness about an issue and expand their services. Potential risks might be:

- Damage to your reputation, if there are any significant problems or scandals with that nonprofit
- Failure, if evaluation results are poor
- Financial risks, if the costs of service expansion are more than anticipated
- Your funding tied up with one organization, limiting your ability to support other projects
- A CEO who resigns unexpectedly, causing the project to falter

You might conclude that if a scandal broke out, the risk could be severe. However, it is highly unlikely because the organization is well run and you have a long-term relationship with the CEO. You could also mitigate this risk by conducting some additional due diligence. You could talk with staff at varying levels of the organization, learn from the nonprofit's other funders and partners about their experience working with them, and search online for any potential concerns.

By answering these three questions, you might eliminate some risks and identify concrete steps you can take to prevent others from happening. But don't leave that initial list on a shelf! Instead, bring your "risk list" to every team meeting involving your investment and briefly discuss what you've done, or can do, to continue to keep risk at a minimum. Cross off old risks once you've handled them. Add new risks as they emerge and use this process to quickly address them.

The second technique is to determine *prudent* risk. In other words, is it a crazy, off-the-wall idea that hasn't been thought through? Or is it a risk worth pursuing? Start by assessing the idea or opportunity against four criteria: cost, benefit, strategic fit, and ease of implementation. Assess your opportunities against these four criteria to reveal whether the opportunity has high potential. If it does, you can begin developing it. When you intentionally develop it, you might surface additional challenges (possibly eliminating it from further consideration). This involves assessing pros and cons, creating best- and worst-case scenarios and the critical factors that lead to each, and identifying risks and rewards. Only if this development process indicates that a risky idea is worth pursuing should you move to implementation.[11] I describe this process in greater detail in Chapter 12, "You Are Unstoppable."

Question 12: Does This Bring Me Joy?

Philanthropists should gain more than they give. Yes, you read that correctly.

I'm not talking about self-dealing. I don't mean they should financially gain more than they give. And I'm certainly not suggesting that gains in publicity or celebrity status should surpass charitable contributions.

I'm talking about joy.

Giving should bring you joy. The joy of knowing you helped improve someone's life. The joy of realizing that with your philanthropic contribution, a village will have clean drinking water, fewer people will die in car accidents, or an emerging leader has the resources to put her dream for gender empowerment into action.

The work we do as philanthropists should also bring us joy, regardless of whether it's speaking, planning, meeting with grantees, traveling the globe, managing people, or reviewing proposals. There's a lot involved in being an effective funder. How we spend our time each day should bring us joy, too.

That doesn't mean philanthropy isn't hard. Being philanthropic can test our endurance and try our spirits. As philanthropists, we feel embarrassed when we recognize our own unconscious discrimination against people with disabilities. It's disappointing when your new innovation is a flop. It's painful to support people who have just experienced trauma, such as the loss of a child or a natural disaster. It's hard to tell a nonprofit leader you aren't giving him a grant.

Sometimes the joy gets squeezed right out of us with overflowing inboxes, people we don't like to spend time with, and frantic year-end deadlines.

But on balance, you should feel dramatically more joy than frustration when it comes to your giving. When you reflect on your philanthropic efforts, whether it involves making public appearances, wrangling family members to agree on funding priorities, or the physical labor of building a school, delight should outweigh disappointment. You should feel overjoyed and not overwhelmed.

If your philanthropy is not bringing you joy, something's wrong.

Here's how to find out: Ask yourself regularly, "Does this bring me joy?" If the answer isn't a resounding "Yes!" it's time to make some changes.

Here's a fun exercise: First, create a list of everything you do in your philanthropy—and I mean everything, from strategic planning to meeting with your financial advisors to answering email. Feel free to group your activities into categories if that helps you.

Second, make three columns and label them:

1. Brings me joy (it gives me energy and I love it)
2. I can delegate (even though I can do it and I might even like doing it)
3. I hate doing (it sucks the life out of me)

Third, for each activity, check the appropriate column. Be honest.

Fourth, circle all the activities that bring you joy. These are the activities on which you should spend 80%–100% of your time. Period.

Everything in the "delegate" category can be assigned elsewhere: to an employee, an intern, new software, or maybe even someone outside of your organization. Get an assistant. Reorganize your team. Promote someone who would find joy doing this activity.

Items in the "hate" category should be stopped, changed, delegated, or at least reevaluated.

I do this exercise every year. Recently, I realized that there were many communications activities I liked doing and could do—such as posting on social media—but that were taking too much time away from things that I enjoyed even more. I found I could easily delegate these tasks to someone who is better and faster at it than me. I created an entire job description out of the communications-related activities that I could delegate and/or disliked doing. Then I hired a marketing and communications firm to do them.

Now I spend more time doing things that bring me joy, like writing this book. I spend more time helping philanthropists increase their impact and less time posting about it on Hootsuite.

By being intentional about what gives us joy (rather than on what just responds to our sense of obligation), we stay engaged in the activities that matter the most. We are less distracted from our missions. We can think more creatively about how to change seemingly intractable social problems. We become our best and most productive selves. And we are able to share that joy with others.

Notes

1. https://www.forbes.com/sites/davidsturt/2013/10/18/are-you-asking-the-right-question/#5b7f9c476c5d.
2. https://www.ted.com/talks/simon_sinek_how_great_leaders_inspire_action?language=en.
3. https://www.powerofnutrition.org/.
4. https://www.alliancemagazine.org/conf-report/energy-curiosity-and-urgent-questions-on-the-avpn-agenda/.
5. Author email correspondence with Jill Penrose and Tamara Fynan of JM Smucker Company, September 19, 2019.
6. https://putnam-consulting.com/wp-content/uploads/Packard_SummerLearningReport_WEB_2017-03-23.pdf.

7. http://rawafund.org/our-model.
8. https://assets.campbell.edu/wp-content/uploads/2019/05/RPA-New-Mexico_LR.pdf.
9. https://urgentactionfund.org/.
10. https://books.google.com/books?id=qE9g_gYZhz8C&pg=PA7&lpg =PA7&dq=%E2%80%9CWhat+would+it+take+for+this+product+ to+get+a+gold+star?%E2%80%9D+focus+group+questions&source =bl&ots=f_ZFtR9izA&sig=ACfU3U3ijDkQ6z2mGVSHb6q2T7rQk LByrQ&hl=en&sa=X&ved=2ahUKEwjoxo6ojLfjAhWQbc0KHUgr Ck8Q6AEwAHoECAYQAQ#v=onepage&q=%E2%80%9CWhat %20would%20it%20take%20for%20this%20product%20to%20get %20a%20gold%20star%3F%E2%80%9D%20focus%20group %20questions&f=false.
11. Michael Robert and Alan Weiss, *The Innovation Formula* (New York: Harper & Row, 1988).

9 | You See and Act Abundantly

There's an old saying that goes "You have to spend money to make money." This is true in philanthropy as well as in business. But here's the trick: Money isn't our only tool. We have plenty of other assets at our disposal, such as time, knowledge, relationships, and creativity. Which leads me to my favorite paraphrase of that old saw: You have to act with abundance to create abundance.

You might wonder what I'm talking about, as you seek to find the essential funds and resources required to make life more abundant for the individuals, communities, and institutions you want so much to support. So let's explore how investing in yourself and your organization—and adjusting your mind-set to believe that you are worth this abundance—can in turn lead to abundance for your cause.

I learned this lesson years ago when I worked for a small nonprofit in San Francisco. In those days, the fancy new technology was fax machines! We used fax machines the way many of us use email and social media today—to get out the word quickly to legislators, the media, and our supporters. Sometimes we would send out several fax alerts a day, trying to mobilize people to do the things we supported and believed in.

Although our finances were tight, our leadership decided we needed to send every dollar possible to our program recipients in Central America. Meanwhile, we ourselves existed in a mind-set of extreme austerity—scarcity, in fact. So, purchasing a fax machine for $900 was out of the question. Instead, we were instructed to borrow a fax machine that was located 10 blocks away—half a mile—whenever we needed to send out our alerts. At minimum, this process would take about an hour from beginning to end, but it often took much, much longer.

I was oblivious to our scarcity mind-set for quite some time, until a team of us made a trip to Central America to visit with an organization that was a recipient of our funds. When we walked through the door, the first thing I noticed was a fax machine—a huge one that probably cost around $3,000. I was shocked that this organization—which was relying upon international donations—could afford a fax machine at all, much less one that was so expensive, when we—the people bringing the donations—were spending at least an hour each day borrowing someone else's.

So, I asked the director of the organization, "How can you afford this?"

He looked at me like I had just asked how he could afford to breathe. "Well, of course we need a fax machine," he told me. "Sending faxes is vital to our work."

I realized then that our scarcity mentality had held us back. We didn't think we deserved to invest in ourselves. And we weren't paying attention to how much staff time this caused us to waste each day. What could we have accomplished if we spent an hour each day calling potential donors instead of walking 10 blocks to send a fax? I bet we could have raised a lot more money to send to Central America!

As you consider your own situation, think about how your scarcity mind-set hinders talent, stalls creativity, and hijacks opportunity for systemic change. The good news is that there's a sure way to overcome a scarcity mind-set: by doing exactly the opposite and adopting an abundance mind-set.

The Abundance Mind-Set

An *abundance mind-set* is a belief that investment in yourself is important, and the more you put into your operation—and yourself—the greater the return. I firmly believe that adopting an abundance mind-set, which is the antithesis of the scarcity mind-set I discussed in Chapter 1, leads to better outcomes and greater change in the world. The greater your abundance mind-set, the greater your impact velocity.

Many people naturally assume that wealthy people, foundation leaders, and celebrities feel abundance. And we assume their mind-set reflects this abundance. After all, they have big money, big ideas, and often big passion. While it's true that they do have an abundance of resources and desire to do good, that doesn't mean that they themselves have a corresponding abundance mind-set. Instead, they often feel guilty about investing in themselves, their organizations, and their philanthropy. They think all their money should go directly to grantees, and not be frittered away on overhead. Their mind-set is one of scarcity, not abundance.

Of course, adopting an abundance mind-set doesn't mean leasing a floor of luxury office suites or flying foundation trustees to exotic resorts. What it means is believing that you not only deserve to strengthen, grow, and improve so that you are best positioned to help others, but that you must. That you can continuously improve, despite adversity. It means investing in the people, technology, operations, and expertise that help you and your team deliver value on your mission—and therefore to the grantees and communities that you serve. You think big.

What does it look like when you have embraced an abundance mind-set? Here are eight sure indicators:

1. **You are proactively generous.** You take initiative to share your time, experience, expertise, reputation, and resources. You regularly ask yourself, "What do we have in abundance that could add value

to this situation?" I'm not talking here about monetary generosity. Sure, you can give a grant. That is generous and important. But you can also open doors for emerging leaders, offer honest advice to a nonprofit struggling through a transition, and take a leadership role in tackling a controversial issue.

For example, philanthropists often conduct research (needs assessments, environmental scans) to determine whether or how to fund a particular issue. Based on the findings, the funder might decide *not* to fund the issue at this time. Philanthropists with a *scarcity* mind-set will keep the research findings to themselves. Often they are fearful of negative repercussions of sharing the information. After all, community members and those interviewed for the research might get mad that the funder decided not to support their worthy cause. Philanthropists with an *abundance* mind-set will be happy to disseminate the findings widely with the field. They have confidence they made the best decision for themselves, *and* they recognize that others can learn from their research.

2. **You have courage to continuously grow and develop yourself.** This can include intellectual, emotional, spiritual, and skills development. You might assume this means investing financial resources to support your development, but it doesn't have to. Even if you can't afford to retain an advisor or attend a workshop, there is an abundance of high-quality and free resources that can help you— podcasts, webinars, articles, white papers, and peer networks. Need proof? Just visit my website putnam-consulting.com or the website of any philanthropy-serving organization.

Your abundant growth and development often requires courage. Courage to believe you deserve to grow and improve. Courage to carve out time in your day for your growth. Courage to listen to the opinions of people whose perspectives are radically different from yours (this can be as simple as watching a different cable news channel), because you feel confident in your beliefs *and* realize you can learn from others. Courage to change your beliefs or your philanthropy based on what you learn.

3. **You are resilient.** We know that that society's problems were not created overnight and nor will they be solved overnight. Tackling these issues likely means testing unproven ideas, taking risks, and

making "big bets." When you do that, you are likely to fail along the way. Heck, even when we make "safe bets" we might flounder! Abundant philanthropists recognize that the road to social change is full of potholes, unexpected detours, and blown-up bridges. They have a Plan B and probably a Plan C. They can rebound and recover from a loss or failure and learn from the experience. My friend and consultant Richard Citrin, coauthor of the book *The Resilience Advantage: Stop Managing Stress and Find Your Resilience*, explains that resilience is more than bouncing *back* to your previous state: "Resilience is our ability to address our adversities in an effective manner and to learn from them so that we bounce forward and improve on how we handle situations in the future."[1]

4. **You embrace inclusion.** It's no secret that our world is becoming more polarized and increasingly intolerant with each passing day. You understand that solving entrenched social problems requires that we come together to identify common goals. To develop these goals, we must include voices and solutions across a broad spectrum. This requires an abundance of empathy, trust, and tolerance.

   Carly Hare recognizes the need to embrace an abundance of vulnerability and grace in philanthropy. Hare is the executive director of CHANGE Philanthropy, a coalition of philanthropic networks whose vision is to transform and challenge philanthropic culture to advance equity, benefit all communities, and ignite positive social change. "We need to remember that we are all entering conversations about inequities from different places on our life journeys. We need to allow people the grace to be themselves, be vulnerable, feel discomfort, and heal so that together we can have courageous conversations. If we don't do that, we stay in a delusional state. We stay ignorant," explains Hare.[2]

5. **You believe you deserve the best.** I'm not talking about the best luxury yacht or Hermès Birkin bag. I'm talking about believing that you and your philanthropy deserve the best information, ideas, technology, and talent. That that problem you want to tackle deserves the smartest minds and best-equipped organizations to help solve it. That your relationship with your board chair is so important, you both deserve investing your time and effort to strengthen it. That it's worth spending $250 extra on that nonstop flight (avoiding

the time-wasting ritual of reviewing dozens of cheaper but longer options), because you know you will accomplish more for your philanthropy if you arrive rested and not exhausted.

You believe you deserve the best because you want to give your best.

I cannot emphasize enough that believing you deserve the best does not *necessarily* mean that you spend money. It could mean that you make sure you get enough sleep each night. It could also mean you want your philanthropic practices to be informed by the best ideas. As part of her effort to better understand food systems and identify opportunities where her foundation could play a role, Mary Anthony, executive director of the 1772 Foundation, contacted a best-selling author and award-winning expert on local food and nutrition to see if he might be willing to answer some questions and share his experience. The author was perfectly willing and ended up spending an hour talking with Mary. The conversation cost her nothing, and her philanthropy was informed by a nationally renowned expert.

6. **You think big.** Think for a moment about what you would like to accomplish through your philanthropy. Now, imagine yourself five years from now. Will you have achieved your goals if you focus on the limitations of your current grant budget? If you busy yourself in never-ending data gathering or copy editing your board meeting materials? If that's all you do, you will not. You realize that if you want to reach your goals over the long run, then you've got to start thinking big right now. This also means thinking about what you can accomplish beyond the confines of your grant budget.

Mitzi Perdue thought big, and well beyond her grant budget. In 2019 she heard Paul Hutchison, founder of the Child Liberation Foundation, talk about how to rescue and rehabilitate survivors of child trafficking. The talk changed her life. She wanted to support his work. But as she sat in the audience, she calculated that by donating to his organization she would need to cut back on her donations to other organizations.

Then she thought beyond her foundation's grants budget.

She thought of a prized possession: a seventeenth-century de Medici Cardinal's desk given to her by her late parents (her father had founded the Sheraton Hotel chain). She realized she could auction the desk and donate the proceeds. She then wondered if others might have items they would be willing to donate to raise funds for anti-trafficking organizations. Within months, Perdue created the Global Anti-Trafficking Auction. Operating with a mind-set of abundance, she leveraged her contacts to find other wealthy individuals and celebrities willing to contribute. A New York auction house agreed to manage the auction and forgo their commission. That meant people could use the anti-trafficking auction to convert their tangible items to cash for donation without having to pay the usual 20%–25% commission. Perdue secured PBS for production of a 30-minute television show about the event. She arranged for a major hotel chain to display images of auction items and promote the auction at their properties. As of the time of this writing, auction items pledged for donation include a yacht, a building, a sapphire and diamond necklace worn by actress Marlene Dietrich, a 69.7 carat ruby from the early Qing Dynasty, and 12 Imperial banquet plates that belonged to Tsar Alexander II. All because Perdue was willing to think big and beyond her grant budget.

7. **You take prudent risks.** We all know the old saying "Nothing ventured, nothing gained." Getting a return on your investment requires accepting some amount of risk, and you embrace it. When you make an investment in your grantees, this requires trusting that people will do the right thing with the resources you're giving them. Instead of obsessing about their overhead or trying to micromanage them, you say, "Here's money for your planning, or your board development, or whatever you need to do to strengthen your organization. I trust you." With an abundance mind-set, are you looking at the world through rose-colored glasses? I don't think so. The more you put into something, the more you get out of it. There are solutions to every problem, but they often require taking chances.

8. **You invest in your capacity and talent, and that of your grantees.** So far, I've tried to emphasize that abundance is a belief, a mind-set. Being abundant does not *require* spending money. Now I want to tell you that philanthropists also need to invest financially in themselves to increase their effectiveness and impact velocity. That means you. You also need to invest more in the nonprofits you support—the ones helping you accomplish your mission. Let's take a look.

Investing in Yourself

Embracing abundance includes investing resources in yourself, your philanthropy, and your organization. You want to power your philanthropy with innovative ideas and top talent. You want expert guidance to navigate your philanthropic decisions. You want your foundation built upon well-oiled systems, useful technology, and agile leadership.

To do that, you need to invest in yourself.

Here are a handful of places where investing in yourself—and your philanthropy—will reap rewards:

1. **Organizational capacity.** When you have limited capacity, it can be hard to think with an abundance mentality. But making a big impact doesn't mean you have to be the biggest funder. Sometimes it means identifying your gaps in operations or knowledge and finding the most efficient way to fill them.

   The Heising-Simons Foundation in Silicon Valley was preparing for significant growth over a three-year period due to an influx of assets. This included tripling its staff, tripling its grantmaking budget, and building out new offices to accommodate its growth. CEO Deanna Gomby knew the foundation would need a strong communications function, but at the time the foundation lacked a communication plan and had limited capacity. She enlisted the help of consultants to develop an initial plan, identify options for staffing-up a communications department, develop a communications budget, and provide interim communications support until communications staff could be hired.

2. **Talent.** Think about the talent you need to launch, manage, and grow your philanthropy. This could include in-house staff (a CEO, program officer, or assistant), outside advisors (your philanthropy advisor, impact investment advisors), an organization that provides back-office management (donor-advised fund sponsor or family office), or your trustees. It also includes you.

   Now, think about how to obtain top talent, and what investments you might need to make in their success. From your board chair to the administrative assistant, your team could have greater impact if they had the support, training, and leadership opportunities. This could involve retaining a trusted advisor, increasing program staff's grantmaking authority, eliminating bureaucratic hurdles within your operation, training assistants in customer service and allowing them to resolve problems, developing a pipeline of leadership, or bringing all your outside advisors together to coordinate their approaches to helping you.

You can also pay ongoing attention to diversity, inclusion, and equity within your philanthropy. In their report "The Exit Interview," the Association of Black Foundation Executives identified that many black professionals were leaving jobs in philanthropy because they felt isolated; had limited opportunities for professional-track training, networks, or support systems; and sometimes felt their expertise was not valued by colleagues. They recommended opportunities to "improve career pathways for Black philanthropic professionals in grantmaking institutions and ensure their perspectives are brought to grantmaking decisions."[3]

3. **Technology.** Remember that fax machine story? The right technology can help your organization communicate more quickly and effectively and reach decisions faster. While it's true that you don't need every shiny new gadget that comes on the market, you and your team do need ready access to technology such as upgraded computers and software; online grant application, grants management, and constituent relationship management (CRM) systems; cybersecurity; and tools for sharing and collaborating. These are not luxury toys but necessary tools to help you create impact. Some innovative foundations are elevating the role of technology in their strategy and grantmaking by embedding technologists into their program teams.

4. **Learning.** Creating a culture of learning in your organization requires a focus on *intentional* learning. That includes sharing knowledge even when there may not be a direct benefit to your organization.

One community foundation gives an annual award to a non-profit that best exemplifies excellence in management. The rigorous application reviews nonprofit staffing, planning, technology, community engagement, and more. One year, the foundation decided to turn the process inward. They filled out that application themselves and committed to publishing it as an annual report. That meant publicly admitting areas of weakness. But it also showed their donors, nonprofits, and community leaders they were serious about running a strong organization and were willing to learn and improve.

Investing in Your Partners

Ultimately, every investment you make in yourself is going to benefit your nonprofit partners—and help you implement your strategy and achieve your goals. However, there are a few things you can do to invest in them directly:

1. **Take time to build a trusting relationship with grantees.** You want your grantee partners to come to you when a problem is emerging or when new opportunities arise. One nonprofit arts organization was using four different Excel spreadsheets to manage donors, attendees, ticket sales, and more—but was too afraid to ask their funders for a grant to create a single database. They worried their funders would think they were poorly managed and stop funding them. So, they hobbled along, wasting time and losing money. They had lots of funders, but none with whom they had a trusting relationship to discuss their true problems and ask for the help they really needed.

2. **Stick with grantees through challenging times.** Changing the world isn't going to happen overnight, and your grantees need your sustained support over a prolonged period of time to create lasting change. Life is probably nerve-racking enough for your grantees without them constantly worrying whether or not you'll still be providing support to them a year—or a month—from now. This is especially the case in challenging times. When Advocates for Children and Youth (ACY) in Baltimore, a longtime nonprofit partner of the Annie E. Casey Foundation, struggled with the departure of its CEO and lost a massive portion of its funding, the foundation decided to stick with them.

   The foundation could have held back funding to wait to see what happened during the executive transition. Instead, it intentionally invested in ACY to make the transition a success.

Explained Rafael Lopez, who was at the time an associate director at Annie E. Casey Foundation, "The composition of talent in our field is changing daily. We need to be supporters of organizations that do the hardest work on the ground, and we must recognize infrastructure changes as critical. Our field historically sees professional development as a luxury, but you can't address the toughest challenges without leaders to drive change."[4]

3. **Make sufficient investments in your grantees' infrastructure, organizational capacity, and long-term planning.** This might include providing multiyear funding, paying for the true costs of running programs, and offering core operating support. You can learn more about these approaches and others in Chapter 11, "You Transform Lives." It does no one any good if your grantees don't have enough funds to operate efficiently and to effectively pursue their mission and goals.

4. **Support the competition.** There's generally not a lot of "competition" in philanthropy, but there is in business. Corporate funders express an abundance mind-set when they invest in projects regardless of whether that investment also helps their competition. For example, when Blue Shield of California ended the year with a surplus, it created a $20 million grantmaking program to support accountable care organizations at 18 California hospitals, health systems, clinics, and physician organizations. They celebrated the fact that it would benefit even their competitor insurance companies. They had their eyes on the prize of serving underserved populations, reducing health care costs, and enhancing the quality of care.[5]

Investing in Philanthropy's Infrastructure

You might also consider opportunities to strengthen the infrastructure and ecosystem of philanthropy. By this I mean supporting organizations that "provide a necessary support system for amplifying philanthropy's effectiveness."[6] This includes philanthropy-serving membership organizations, professional support organizations, and peer networks. It can also include research and advocacy organizations.

Why is this important? A strong philanthropic infrastructure helps us all to learn and improve, strengthen our capacity, and leverage the experience and funding of other philanthropists. Worldwide Initiatives for Grantmaker Support (WINGS) believes "As philanthropy grows in importance, and extends into new areas of the globe, it is important to ensure that there is an adequate support system to enable philanthropists to take advantage of opportunities and to protect against threats."[7] This is especially important in regions of the world where philanthropic infrastructure is still emerging and where there is less political space for civil society.

The Narada Foundation has been a leader in growing philanthropy's infrastructure in China. They provided a three-year grant to launch the Non-Profit Incubator in 2007, the first incubator of nonprofit organizations in China. Within five years, a substantial number of new grassroots NGOs had emerged and taken root. Narada also co-initiated and funded the China Foundation Forum, where private foundations network and learn from each other. The Forum quickly evolved into a highly influential organization, attracting nearly 1,000 foundation and nonprofit participants at its 2017 annual conference.

"The effects for the sector of supporting infrastructure are multiplied," explains Yanni Peng, CEO of Narada Foundation. "It encourages new organizations to be set up, builds NPO's capacity, enhances the sectoral information and data flow, establishes sectoral ethics and standards, strengthens networks at various levels, and is an advocate for a better legal and regulatory framework."[8]

How Will You Know If You Are Embracing an Abundance Mind-Set?

As you adopt these practices, how will you know when you and your organization are successfully making the transition from a scarcity mind-set to an abundance mind-set? When you or the people in your organization have an abundance mind-set, you'll routinely hear questions and statements like this:

- Who are the top experts in the country (or world) who can advise us?
- How much more impact can we have if we add additional capacity to our funding initiative?
- Who are the best people we can get and what is the most strategic use of their time?
- If our program was to become a national model, what would that look like? What can we put in place now to accomplish that?
- If we really want to make a difference on this issue, we need to make a multiyear commitment (because we understand that change takes time).
- What tools, resources, or technology will help our grantees become more effective?
- Let's magnify our impact by leveraging relationships and partners.
- It's OK if our corporate funding initiative also benefits our competitors. It will improve outcomes for everyone, and we will learn a lot.
- Let's survey our grantees to better understand their experience with us so that we can improve.

Once you start hearing comments like these, and seeing the improved outcomes they lead to, you'll wonder how you ever managed in the "bad old days" of a scarcity mentality. And as your abundance mind-set becomes strong, you'll know the value of the standard airline advice to "Put your own oxygen mask on first." You can't help others unless you help yourself.

Notes

1. Richard S. Citrin and Alan Weiss, *The Resilience Advantage: Stop Managing Stress and Find Your Resilience* Business (New York: Expert Press, 2016).

2. Interview with Carly Hare, August 1, 2019.

3. https://www.abfe.org/wp-content/uploads/2014/05/ABFE-The-Exit-Interview.pdf.

4. https://putnam-consulting.com/wp-content/uploads/GenChange_TRANSITION.pdf.

5. https://www.blueshieldca.com/bsca/about-blue-shield/media-center/aco-development-grants.sp.

6. https://wings.issuelab.org/resource/what-makes-a-strong-ecosystem-of-support-to-philanthropy.html.

7. Ibid.

8. https://www.alliancemagazine.org/feature/infrastructure-strategic-priority/.

10

You Are Fast

Do you believe your work matters? I do.

You're giving people in rural communities greater access to metal health services. You're strengthening economic expansion in Africa.

Your philanthropy matters. If you believe that too, you should make dramatic improvements as *quickly* as you can. Why? Because every delay prevents your ability to make a difference. When we're talking about preventing drug overdoses or reforming immigration policies, we're talking about changing people's lives for the better.

To increase your impact, increase your speed.

9 Ways to Get Time Back in Your Day

First, let's spend some time talking about you.

If we want to increase your speed to philanthropic impact, we need to look at how you spend your time. We need to get rid of all that stuff

123

that distracts you from your priorities, prevents productivity, and gets in your way. The world needs you, and it needs you to take control of your time.

Protecting your time is critical to your success. It might sound counterintuitive but taking control of your time allows you to *give* more of it on what matters most. Management guru Peter Drucker was legendary for being generous with his time. A corporate CEO recalls hoping to get an hour of his time, and instead got four. A business student hoped for a phone interview for his school newspaper and received lengthy insights. How could Drucker give his time so freely? He zealously protected it. "Your accomplishments and your effectiveness," Drucker wrote, "are set, or limited, by the way you manage your time, your scarcest resource."[1]

Everyone can improve their time habits, even if the changes are simply tactical.

Here are nine practical ways I've helped my clients free up their time so they can focus on their most important work. I bet they will help you as well.

1. Start Your Day Attending to Your Priorities, Not Someone Else's

What was the first thing you did this morning when you woke up? If you're like most people, you checked your smartphone. In fact, over half (58%) of American adult smartphone users check their smartphones within the first 10 minutes of waking. Nearly one in four (24%) check it within the first *minute* of their day![2] This habit is hard to break. You're worried you might miss something important, so you start your day by grabbing your phone and clicking through endless emails, scrolling the news, or replying to WhatsApp chats.

Do you want to know what you are doing when you check your phone or email first thing in the morning? You are *giving away* control of your time and energy to someone else. Instead of waking up and focusing on what *you* want to accomplish, you allow other people's agendas to supersede yours. Who are those other people? Whoever happened to email you last night. The editors at BBC World News who determine news story placement. When you wake up in the morning and immediately turn your attention to other people's requests or the stresses of the world, you give up control. You need to stop!

2. Spend the First Hour of Your Workday Doing Something Creative

Whenever you first sit down to work—whether it's on the couch before your kids wake up or at the office—do something that generates ideas, tackles a project, and gives you energy. It might be taking the time to brainstorm your next funding initiative, thinking about how to reorganize your team, or writing.

3. Allocate Your Time According to Your Priorities

Too often we know what we want to accomplish, but we never seem to get it done. Instead, determine your top priorities and then *actually block out time in your calendar to accomplish them.*

Do this exercise: First, write down the top one to three most important things you want to accomplish this quarter or this year. It could include hiring your foundation's first executive director or finally making that baby album for your kid before he heads off to college. Second, print out your calendar for the next three months. Then take a highlighter and mark all the time you *currently* have scheduled to work on your top priorities. It's stunning, right? Because you probably have little or zero time allocated. No wonder you never get it done! Now, go into your calendar and start blocking out time to work on your priorities. Even if you can only squeeze in 20–30 minutes per day to start, it's amazing what you can accomplish. In 20 minutes, you could brainstorm your top qualities for an executive director, contact a foundation association to ask for sample job descriptions, or ask colleagues to recommend search firms.

Trust me, this works. About two years ago I wanted to publish this book. I went so far as to write "publish book by year's end" on a yellow Post-it and stuck it next to my computer so that I'd see it every day. And then I let a bunch of other stuff get in the way. Client deadlines, speaking engagements, scheduling activities for my kids. I hadn't made the book a priority, so nothing happened.

A year later, I changed. I made the book one of my top three priorities. Then I made a list of the most important things I needed to do to publish it. I blocked out time in my calendar to work on the book every day, even if all I did was something minimal. The result? I had a signed contract with one of the world's most prominent business book publishers five weeks later.

4. Ask Yourself, "How Can I Do This in Half the Time?"

No matter what you are doing, you can probably do it faster (or eliminate it entirely). Habitually ask yourself how you can accomplish anything in half of the time you typically take. This might be preparing a speech, reviewing grant proposals, or conducting your weekly staff meeting. Force yourself to come up with a solution that requires half the time. Chances are that this will involve some other changes as well, such as more efficient meeting preparation or streamlined grant applications— and that's a good thing! You can also think about what you can eliminate.

Remember that calendar you printed out when we talked about allocating your priorities earlier in this chapter? Pull it out again. Now take a pen and look at every item. Cross out activities that aren't necessary or could be accomplished in half the time. In-person meetings could be accomplished by video call. Calls can be accomplished by email. Your two-day planning retreat could, with ample prep work, be reduced to one day. That 20-page report you're writing could be summarized in three pages instead—and trust me, everyone will appreciate it.

5. Say No

How many times a week do you get requests to "pick your brain" or "grab a quick cup of coffee"? It's not always necessary to meet someone in person to give career advice or consult about a project. You have to start saying no to all those requests for your time that are not advancing your own personal or philanthropic goals. Of course, it's important to be open, especially to grantees and the community, but there are ways you can be helpful without draining your time.

For example, one of my clients, Nonet Sykes, was the director of race equity and inclusion at the Annie E. Casey Foundation. Casey has made tremendous strides operationalizing equity across the foundation and has been a pioneer in this work. As a result, Sykes was flooded with requests from other funders to learn from her experience. Many offered to fly her out to meet with their staff and present to their board. She wanted to help other funders become more equitable and inclusive, but she also needed to make sure that didn't take away from her own role in the foundation. She often had to say, "No."

As a result, she decided to document how the foundation operationalized equity in its work and share it with the field. In fact, this became part of Casey's race equity and inclusion strategy—not a separate distraction. Casey commissioned several case studies and reports, including "Operationalizing Equity: Putting the Annie E. Casey Foundation's Racial and Ethnic Equity and Inclusion Framework into Action,"[3] "Deploying Casey's REI Framework,"[4] and a collection of other race equity resources for funders.[5] These resources are now hugely helpful not only to other philanthropists but to Casey's own staff and board. This approach saved Sykes tremendous amounts of time previously spent in meetings and trainings.

6. If You Are 80% There, Move

If you've accomplished 80% of what you are trying to do, it's time to move on. Stop laboring over the final details of a project. Success is not about perfection. As consulting expert Alan Weiss has shared with me, too often we find ourselves spending an inordinate amount of time on that last 20% of anything we do, but those details tend to be far less important. It's better to get it nearly done and start moving on it with the confidence that you will figure out the rest along the way. For example, if you're writing an article or a speech and you've covered all your main topics, don't spend excessive time debating whether you should make five points or seven points, or in what order. Give the speech. If you're launching a new funding initiative and you've done enough evidence-based research to develop 80% of your strategy, don't spend more time endlessly gathering data. Start implementing.

7. Prevent Interruptions

Distractions and interruptions are no joke. They interrupt our flow, take us off course, and drain our bottom line. According to a study from the University of California, Irvine, an average worker gets only 11 minutes between each interruption, and it takes an average of 25 minutes to get back to the original task.[6] If that weren't bad enough, those interruptions cause us to make 20% more mistakes on our original task.[7] Other research found that "when employees are asked to formally calculate the time they lose to interruptions, they routinely come up with 40%–60% of their most productive time; that's about 3–5 hours every day." Interruptions cost the U.S. economy $588 billion a year.[8]

Fortunately, there are some easy solutions to decrease disruptions. Go through your computer, tablet, and smartphone (you know, the one you no longer check first thing in the morning) and remove all the notifications. You don't need beeps informing you of new emails or banners announcing breaking news stories. Visually inform others you are unavailable by posting a sign or wearing headphones. Use technology to your advantage by blocking time on your calendar as "busy," changing your Out of Office reply to indicate you'll respond tomorrow, and using the Do Not Disturb button on your phone. As a last resort, change locations. Find another office or café where you can work. Your colleagues and your children can't interrupt you if they can't find you!

8. Identify Your "Productivity Propensity"

What are the conditions under which you are most productive? My husband works best while listening to music, but I need complete silence. Are you better focusing on one project for four hours, or would you get more done spending 60 minutes each day on the project? Get clear on *your* ideal conditions for productivity and rework your schedule or arrange your office so you can be your most productive.

9. Assign It to Someone Else

As a general rule, if someone else can do the work, hand it off. Assign certain tasks to a staff person, board member, consultant, or intern so you can focus on what only you can tackle. For managers, that might mean having staff summarize their performance discussions with you and then emailing you those write-ups. If their summary is accurate, great—file it. If it's not, reply with corrections and then file. You've dispersed the work of writing up the performance summary, and you've helped that person understand and internalize the conversation.

Remember your printed calendar? Go through it one more time. This time, read through your scheduled activities with an eye toward what you could delegate. Can someone else attend the funder collaborative meeting or write the blog post? Right down the actual names of people ("Mariano"), or at least the type of person you need ("writing consultant"). Now go find and delegate it to them.

For example, one donor was starting a new foundation, and she was frustrated that it was taking so long to get things moving. She began tracking her time and realized that there were plenty of activities that she could easily delegate to an assistant. She had spent so much time working hard and feeling overwhelmed that she hadn't thought about the best use of her time. After she took a step back and analyzed her time, she decided to hire a part-time assistant to handle scheduling, review proposals, do basic research, and look at office space. This freed her up to focus on big-picture issues: clarifying the foundation's mission, building partnerships, and getting the work underway. Yes, this up-front work may actually take time in the beginning, but the reward is that you can zero in on the approaches that hold you back over the long term. In other words, go slow for a moment of internal reflection so you can go fast in the long run.

Three Ways to Speed Up Your Teams and Organizations

Once you've tackled the challenge of your own personal time and work habits, you can turn your attention to speeding up your teams and organizations. Whether it's just you and an assistant or a staff of hundreds, you are likely working with other people to achieve your philanthropic results. Below are three practical ways you can quicken the pace of your work together.

1. Think Like a Mechanic

Mechanics lift the hood to determine why a car has stalled. They change air filters because they know a dirty air filter can reduce air flow to your engine. They check tire pressure to ensure optimal fuel economy and the lowest rolling resistance. They check fluids because lubricated car parts operate better and last longer when fluids stay clean. And they do this on a maintenance schedule, because regularly making minor improvements keeps your car running smoothly.

You need to think like a mechanic. You need to regularly lift up the hood of your philanthropy to notice what's slowing you down. Where are you wasteful, duplicative, or redundant? What are your barriers and blockages? Identify those, then systematically eliminate them. For example:

- Are you asking grantees questions you already know the answer to? Stop asking that question or create an online application that pre-populates last year's data.
- Does your policy require five employees to sign off on all grants, regardless of whether you are awarding $500 or $50,000? Change the policy to allow one person to approve grants under $15,000.
- Do you insist that grantees submit final reports but then learn that your team never reads them because the information is rarely useful? Eliminate the report, change the questions, or change how you learn from grantees. The Robert Sterling Clark Foundation, a private foundation committed to helping create a vibrant New York City, realized their grantees' reports didn't help them understand what grantees had learned during the grant period. So they switched to an oral reporting process. "We interview grantees at the end of the funding period, and then we do whatever writing needs to be done coming out of that conversation," explains Lisa Pilar Cowan, vice president.[9]

You can help your team make some quick and easy improvements—and feel good about it—by simply asking everyone on your team to identify one aspect of their work that seems exceptionally slow, cumbersome, or unnecessary. It might be the length of time to make a grant, the number of meetings they are expected to attend, or a policy that no longer meets its intended purpose. Ask them to come up with potential solutions to speed things up. Then implement the best ideas.

Another approach: Each week or month, as a team, identify one part of your work—financial management, family meetings, site visits—and collectively identify ways you are bogged down. Are you forever having the same discussion with no resolution? Have funding decisions already been made prior to site visits, rendering them unnecessary? Brainstorm possible solutions together, and prioritize immediate next steps, including who is accountable for what and by when.

These might seem like minor improvements. But together they can add up to significant change that optimizes your speed to impact. Of course, not everyone embraces change. Some people might feel defensive. The point is not to cast blame but to continuously improve. Often improvements don't happen because you haven't had time to focus on them. People say, "That's just the way things are done around here," or your organizational environment doesn't encourage change and continuous improvement. What made sense for your philanthropy when it first started, or even five years ago, might not make sense in today's environment—and may even be holding you back.

Give yourself some quick wins by keeping the following in mind: Keep it simple, focus on the low-hanging fruit, make it fun, and reward people when they speed something up. Don't try to change everything at once. And make sure whoever is in charge (donor, CEO, board chair) makes improvements too. Be a champion of change from within!

2. Assess the Cost of Your Time

Philanthropists don't often think about the cost of their time or compare that cost against the value gained. But you can quickly tabulate the costs of your time, identify waste, and speed things up.

For example, one public charity foundation board was debating whether to continue an annual grants program that allocated $100,000 by giving $5,000 each to 20 nonprofits. The goal of the program was to meet basic needs in their community, and they wanted to be open and responsive to emerging issues. Their process required identifying and notifying potential grantees, reviewing 60 proposals and budgets, selecting 30 finalists, conducting site visits with those finalists, summarizing site visit findings, making funding decisions to select 20 grantees, processing 20 grants, and reviewing 20 annual reports. Whew, that's a lot of work to make $5,000 grants! I suggested they calculate the cost of the staff time to manage this grant program and use that data to inform their decision. (See Chapter 4, "You Have Too Many Steps," to review an easy way to calculate staff costs.)

In this example, I'd guess each site visit would take an average of eight hours, including scheduling, preparing for, traveling to and from, conducting, and summarizing. Assuming a U.S. program officer makes an average hourly rate of $57, that amounts to $456 per site visit. Multiply that times 30 visits, and you've spent $13,680 just on the site visits "needed" to give away $100,000! If you calculate the entire cost of the program officer's time, you approach a figure of one-quarter to one-third of the grant budget taken up just by implementing the darn thing.

Another good example is the cost of holding board meetings. I have consulted with numerous foundations on projects that absolutely stalled because of an upcoming board meeting. Staff members will say they're not available for three weeks because they're preparing—vetting projects with colleagues, summarizing grants, editing the summaries, rehearsing presentations, collating materials, etc. If your board meetings are held four times a year, you're wasting a total of 12 weeks simply preparing for board meetings. That's three months each year! And that doesn't include the post–board meeting recovery period when staff are exhausted and unproductive, trying to get through a backlog of 300 emails.

You can easily calculate the cost, in time and in dollars, of anything you do. Next, think about the value you gain with that investment of time and money. Are you finding that the total cost and amount of time spent is too high for the value gained? Did you learn your people aren't spending time on their most important work? Terrific news! You've just identified an opportunity to speed things up (and save money too).

Ask yourselves what changes you could make to more effectively use staff and board time for decision making. Perhaps you can give staff the authority to approve grants up to a specific dollar amount. That's what the Headwaters Foundation did. They ask their board to preapprove an overall grants budget tied to a specific grant program and trust their staff to make the best funding decisions. Or you might recognize that the time spent writing and editing one-page summaries, paragraph summaries, and one-sentence summaries of every grant is a mind-numbing waste of brainpower. That's what the Blue Shield of California Foundation decided. They streamlined how they made funding decisions and reduced the size of their quarterly board materials from 300 pages to 30 pages.

3. Build for Speed

Whenever you create something new or revamp an existing effort, ask yourself, "What is the fastest way we can do this?" Then build that. You want to make dramatic improvement quickly, not get mired in sluggish, incremental change. There are a few ways to do this.

First, anticipate the 80/20 rule. The 80/20 rule, also known as the Pareto Principle, states that 80% of the results will be generated by 20% of the input. In other words, there are all kinds of ways to achieve your goals, but 20% of them will generate 80% of your outcome. (The term was coined by management consultant Joseph Juran and named after Italian economist Vilfredo Pareto, who recognized that 80% of Italian land was owned by 20% of the population.)[10] Knowing this, you can try to proactively identify that 20% during your planning stage, and focus your time and resources on those efforts.

For example, if you want to maintain and grow family wealth across multiple generations, having a family governance structure in place that provides a clear mission, education, and communication might be the 20% of effort that will drive 80% of your results (more than tax or wealth planning).[11]

Second, start with the end in mind. Define success and work backward to achieve it. Remember the funder above who wanted to meet basic needs by allocating $100,000 to 20 different organizations via a labor-intensive funding process? If success is defined as more people in your community having their basic needs met for food, shelter, or health care, you can work backward to determine the fastest way to accomplish that with your $100,000 investment. You might identify a few options: Advocate for policy changes to increase public funding for basic needs. Make a $100,000 grant to expand your local foodbank. Invest in a local collaborative to decrease chronic homelessness. When you approach your work with a lens of speed ("What's the fastest way we can help people put food on their table?"), I'm guessing "Spend lots of time giving small grants to a wide range of organizations" would not rise to the top!

Third, ask, "If we were to build this today from the ground up, what would it look like?" If you are trying to increase the speed to impact of an existing program, it's easy to get stuck making incremental improvements. A fix here, a tweak there. But if you reenvision it entirely, you free yourself to design it for optimal results. Give yourself permission to start from scratch.

The Commonwealth Fund in New York City did this when it considered renewing funding for its signature program, the Commonwealth Fund Fellowship in Minority Health Policy at Harvard University. The fellowship prepares physicians of color to lead health systems and advocate for policy change to improve health care delivery and health outcomes for vulnerable populations. The program had begun 20 years prior and much had changed since then, including health care reform, best practices in adult learning, and the use of technology to convene, educate, and position leaders. There was still a need for this fellowship, given that much had *not* changed in the diversity of health care leadership. The Fund's leadership rightly asked, "If we were to build this fellowship program from the ground up today, what would we create?"

The leadership learned that it would create a program that contained many elements of the current fellowship, such as enabling the fellows to obtain a master's degree focused on health management or health policy focus and using a cohort model so fellows could learn from and support one other. It also identified new elements and improvements it would want to make: creating a strong and active alumni network connected to the Fund; developing fellows' skills in health care finance, managing complex organizations, and coalition building; and greater senior job placement assistance.

The Fund opened up the placement of the fellowship to other universities through a competitive RFP process and received multiple proposals. In the end, it decided to continue supporting the existing fellowship at Harvard University, with improvements made. It also started a new fellowship program at Yale University's School of Management, to test a different program model and allow clinicians across disciplines to receive a master's for executives in business administration.

Create Aerodynamic Funding

When it comes to receiving funding, it would be difficult to find a nonprofit leader who is worried about things moving too quickly. Yet the hoops philanthropists often ask grant seekers to jump through are so labor intensive that we end up decreasing the number of applicants, overburdening the organizations we seek to help, and delaying progress. I was once asked to determine why a foundation received so few proposals from certain parts of the state it served. The reason was that nonprofits in those areas were so frustrated by the foundation's lengthy approval process, constantly shifting priorities, and lack of communication that they stopped applying for grants!

If we declutter the grant process, we strengthen our philanthropy and speed up our transformation.

The William and Flora Hewlett Foundation in California has made significant changes to some of their grantmaking practices, while increasing their impact. First, they make grants up to $1M on a rolling basis, requiring only president approval (the board has reviewed and approved grant strategies, and does not need to approve each grant). This practice allows Hewlett to be both responsive and timely in meeting needs. Second, when it comes to general operating support grants, Hewlett regularly accepts documents already written for other purposes—e.g., annual reports or applications written for other funders—rather than requiring a custom proposal. Each of these process modifications helps Hewlett be nimble and places the grantee's experience at the center of their efforts.

The Hewlett Foundation is not the only one that allows nonprofits to submit proposals written for other funders. The much smaller Robert Sterling Clark Foundation in New York does this, too. "We find that the proposals they have written for other funders work just fine for us. They give us the info we need to get started, and then we can Google their 990s, talk to colleagues in the field, and, most importantly, meet with them and observe their programs," says Lisa Pilar Cowan, the foundation's vice president. "It is a better (and more fun) use of their time and ours to talk, rather than for them to sit in their offices writing to our specifications, only for us to sit in our offices, reading."[12]

The R.J. McElroy Trust in Waterloo, Iowa, decided to become the "easiest place to seek funding for good ideas" while allocating up to $2M annually to inspire and transform young people. They made dramatic changes to their application and review process, including reducing the application from four to six pages down to a one-page letter and not requiring any additional attachments (if the foundation wants to learn about the nonprofit's board, annual budget, or tax status, they look it up online themselves).

As a result, applicants now spend an average of three hours to request funds (down from 10 hours), and the foundation understands the requests better. Staff spend less time summarizing proposals and more time offering friendly advice to grant seekers. "I estimate that changes we have made in recent years to streamline our grant application and reporting process save our grantseekers (in total) about 840 hours each year," according to Stacey Van Gorp, former executive director.[13]

How the Robert Wood Johnson Foundation Did It

In August 2013, the Robert Wood Johnson Foundation made its first round of grants to nine organizations in its Forward Promise initiative—designed to improve health and life outcomes for young men and boys of color. They initially received 1,226 proposals—the most they had ever received for one initiative in the foundation's 40-year history. They needed to screen those 1,226 proposals down to 373 that qualified for deeper review, then to 20 finalists that would receive site visits, and finally to the nine that would be recommended for funding. Quite an endeavor!

Surprisingly, one of the fastest parts of the whole process was whittling down the 1,226 proposals to 373—normally a time-consuming task even with far fewer to consider. Why did it work? The foundation had previously invested time and resources in a robust and sophisticated online application and review system. All of the applications were submitted online, and teams of reviewers from around the country were electronically assigned specific proposals to read. The criteria were entered online so reviewers could score proposals online, and scores could quickly be tabulated. Winnowing the huge batch of proposals went shockingly quickly, because the foundation had taken the time and invested the resources up front to think through and design an ideal process, supported by the necessary technology.

With those examples in mind, consider these possible simplifications for your own organization:

Take the time to think about what information you really need from a grantee in order to make an investment decision. Are there portions of the application you just skim over before getting to the full intention of the work? Some foundations have stopped requiring all grantees to submit a full application and instead asked for a simpler letter of intent. What information could a letter of intent provide that would help you decide whether you need to review a fully fleshed-out proposal? Eliminating the workload for your grantees also means eliminating the time you spend reviewing needless information.

When to Go Slow to Go Fast

While I'm encouraging you to speed things up, the fast approach is not always your best approach. Here are three times when it almost always makes more sense to slow down to achieve the results you want.

1. **Your instinct says no.** Philanthropy can be a lot like dating. Sometimes your date looks good on paper (good income, nice family) but your gut tells you something isn't right. When that happens, you should take the time to look more closely. It's the same with philanthropy. One donor was looking for an intermediary organization to lead a new initiative, and one seemed to be the right fit on paper (it had content expertise, brought the right relationships, and had served as an intermediary in other initiatives). Even so, the donor didn't feel right about the organization's CEO. But he felt pressed for time. Instead of trusting his instinct, he funded the organization. It turned out to be a bad investment. The nonprofit CEO publicly embarrassed the donor in a meeting and couldn't achieve initiative goals. By not trusting his instinct, the donor ultimately reduced his speed to impact.

2. **You're building relationships.** You can't rush a relationship, especially when you're entering a new field, working with new communities, or approaching your work in different ways. Strong, trusting relationships will advance your philanthropy in the long run and help you weather storms. It's worth the investment of time and resources to develop trust and maintain those relationships.

3. **You're hiring new staff.** The average hiring mistake costs 15 times a person's base salary.[14] This doesn't even include the costs of your lost time, lower employee morale, and reputational damage. It's more important to find the right fit than to simply fill the spot. One funder was in such a rush to hire a new leader that they conducted phone interviews only, without ever meeting their new hire in person. This turned out to be a disastrous decision that ultimately cost the trustees significant time and legal fees.

Luckily, these are specific scenarios that you can watch out for and easily identify. In almost every other situation, examine your processes and decision making with an eye to efficiency and prompt action, and you may well be surprised by the increased impact—and smoother relationships—you are able to achieve.

Notes

1. https://www.drucker.institute/thedx/guarding-time/.
2. http://assets.ctfassets.net/ob7bbcsqy5m2/
   31vsdady7mrKfa19B9cOnR/8eec316e95a91797fa1e4702cb366869/
   2018_RootMetrics_Lifestyles_of_Mobile_Consumers_Survey_
   Insights.pdf.
3. http://www.aecf.org/m/resourcedoc/aecf-OperationalizingEquity-
   2017.pdf.
4. https://www.aecf.org/resources/deploying-caseys-rei-framework/.
5. https://www.aecf.org/work/equity-and-inclusion/.
6. https://www.nytimes.com/2013/05/05/opinion/sunday/a-focus-
   on-distraction.html?searchResultPosition=4.
7. Ibid.
8. https://www.fastcompany.com/3044667/the-hidden-costs-of-
   interruptions-at-work.
9. https://www.exponentphilanthropy.org/blog/accept-proposals-
   written-funders/.
10. https://en.wikipedia.org/wiki/Pareto_principle.
11. https://www.bloomberg.com/news/articles/2019-02-04/tax-screw-
    ups-and-people-problems-experts-reveal-biggest-blunders-of-rich-
    families.
12. https://www.exponentphilanthropy.org/blog/accept-proposals-
    written-funders/.
13. https://www.exponentphilanthropy.org/blog/reducing-the-burden-
    on-our-grantseekers-and-ourselves/.
14. https://www.eonetwork.org/octane-magazine/special-features/
    seventipstoavoidingcostlyhiringmistakes.

11

You Transform Lives

In order to have a transformational impact on whatever issue you're passionate about, you need to give in ways that create lasting and sustainable change. To do that, you also need to transform yourself and how you give. How you give matters.

Giving happens in many ways. When we see images of horrific damage brought on by hurricanes, earthquakes, and mass shootings, we are moved to send money in response. Through a simple financial transaction, we've helped address an immediate need. The same is true when we support a local food pantry to provide a meal for a hungry family and when we donate to a homeless shelter to keep a single mother and her children off the street.

This type of transactional philanthropy is important and necessary to help those in immediate crises meet very pressing needs. For many donors, that's enough. But I know it's not enough for you. You want to do more. You want to address immediate needs, but you also want to change the conditions that created the needs in the first place.

More importantly, you recognize that in order to create this type of transformational change, the way you give probably needs to change too.

I call this Transformational Giving™.

Transformational giving requires that funders think about inequitable systems, policies, and root causes that may create, exacerbate, or maintain the problem, and help design long-term solutions to change them. It means thinking ahead 5, 10, or 30 years and creating solutions that will last.

It also means rethinking how you deploy your philanthropic dollars. This might be by offering multiyear grants, strengthening leaders, building the organizational capacity of nonprofits, and leveraging all your assets for social good. It often means getting outside your comfort zone and giving up some control.

First, let's talk about what you fund.

There are lots of ways to create change. You can provide direct aid, as musician Lenny Kravitz did through his Let Love Rule Foundation. He quickly mounted a relief effort to help Bahamians whose homes and lives were devastated in the wake of Hurricane Dorian—delivering medicine, generators, water, food, and more.[1]

You can invest in companies that develop scalable, innovative, and disruptive solutions to the world's most pressing needs, as the Sorenson Impact Foundation does. One of its early-stage investments was to Kinara Capital, an Indian lending company that provides loans to micro, small, and medium-sized businesses. These loans support and strengthen the small business sector that employs a large portion of the economy. The company has since created more than 47,000 new jobs.[2] In addition, Kinara's loans support the companies and entrepreneurs with an average 20% revenue increase.[3]

You can change the trajectory of one person's life, and in turn she helps exponentially more people throughout her lifetime.

Oprah Winfrey understands this. When she created the Oprah Winfrey Leadership Academy for Girls in South Africa, she didn't just want to provide disadvantaged young women with an education. She wanted to equip them with the intellectual and social skills necessary to assume positions of leadership in South Africa and abroad.[4] She knew that by helping to transform their lives, they would help others.

She's allocated $140 million over the past 10 years to equip hundreds of young women with free education (boarding and tuition) and holistic support to meet the girls' significant needs (from braces to medical care to support in dealing with traumas such as sexual abuse). Oprah visits regularly and holds "fireside chats" with the girls. Once the girls leave school, they continue to get support through networks. This includes designated host families for those who attend college in the United States.

As Oprah explains, "What our school does is work at creating a foundation of worthiness."[5]

Having spoken with thousands of philanthropists over several decades, I truly believe that people should give in ways that are meaningful to them. In ways that best engage their talents and passions. This varies by person and organization. It also varies by culture and religious belief. There is no single "right" way to give or path to follow.

I also think it's important for philanthropists to create lasting change. Transformational change. This chapter shares suggestions for how to do that. Both *what* to fund and *how* to fund it.

If these ideas are all new to you, that's great! There's lots to learn and many tools to add to your philanthropic toolbox. For many of you, these ideas will be familiar. You might deploy some, but not all. Or you might not deploy them consistently.

These suggestions are not meant to be prescriptive. As you read on, jot down examples of ways you give that create lasting change, and how you can do more. And take note of new approaches you can employ.

I know you want to genuinely change lives, transform communities, and save the environment. You want the world to be safer, healthier, happier, empowered, and more peaceful. You want to create long-lasting improvements. Me too.

Read on!

Change Systems

"We can't just put a Band-Aid on this. We need to change the system!"
How many times have you heard that statement? Probably a lot. Because
it's true. Most of the problems we tackle as funders are best solved in part
by changing the systems that created the problems in the first place. But
how do funders play a role in that change?

First, let's define what we are talking about. What exactly is a system,
and how would you know it if you bumped into it?

It turns out that systems are all around us. A system is "any group
of interacting, interrelated, or interdependent parts that form a complex and unified whole that has a specific purpose," according to Daniel
H. Kim, leading systems thinker and cofounder of the MIT Center for
Organizational Learning.[6] What's important to remember is that all parts
are interrelated and interdependent on each other. Otherwise it's just a
collection of parts (the solar system vs. a bowl of fruit).

The term "system" might sound wonky, bureaucratic, or above your
pay grade. "I don't care about systems; I just want to help people," you
might be thinking.

But when we recognize that we all live and work within many systems, we begin to appreciate their significance in helping people or
hurting them. Every day we interact with dozens of systems. Our kids
go to schools in our education systems. Those education systems determine who has access to reading specialists, the arts, and free lunch. In our
businesses we design systems for communicating with customers, growing sales, or administering health care benefits. In fact, we ourselves are
complex biological systems!

Systems can propel us forward or hold us back. When we hop
on the subway to meet friends for dinner, we benefit from riding the
public transportation system. When a dad cannot take his daughter
to a high-quality preschool because he already must take three buses
just to get to work, he's being held back by the public transportation
system. If we forgo the bus and hop in our cars, we drive in a system.
A decade ago, a combination of manufacturing (systems) flaws resulted

in out-of-control gas pedals across Toyota's fleet of vehicles. Thirty people died. Nine million vehicles were recalled in the costliest recall ever recorded.[7] The systems we live in matter!

If that's a system, what does it mean to change systems? As with most complex concepts, there is no single agreed-upon definition of "systems change" in philanthropy. Here, however, here is one I find helpful:

Systems change is "an intentional process designed to alter the status quo by shifting the function or structure of an identified system with purposeful interventions. It is a journey which can require a radical change in people's attitudes as well as in the ways people work. Systems change aims to bring about lasting change by altering underlying structures and supporting mechanisms which make the system operate in a particular way. These can include policies, routines, relationships, resources, power structures, and values."[8]

Three common elements of systems change appear to be somewhat universal. Systems change:

- Addresses policies, procedures, practices, and cultures across all components of the system
- Elevates voices and participation from those served by the system in creating change
- Is meant to improve experiences and outcomes for all stakeholders

"OK, got it," you might be thinking. "Now what do I do?"

As a philanthropist, you can support systems change in lots of ways. In advising my clients, there are three I've found most helpful. You can view your philanthropy through a systems change *lens*, use a systems change *framework* to guide your giving, and support systems change *movements*. Let's talk about each of these.

Strap on Your Systems Change Goggles

You can begin to look at the world through a lens of systems change. When you strap on your "systems change goggles," you can see the systems that touch the issues and communities you are working in. Then you can notice how those systems contribute to the problem or could contribute to the solution. You can start by simply asking yourself, "What systems are involved?" when thinking about any issue or problem you want tackle.

If you want to help children who have no parents, or whose parents have lost custody of them, you quickly realize they are under the care of the child welfare system. But these kids also interact with many systems that can help or hinder their care. This includes the education system, juvenile justice system, and health care systems.

To determine the best solutions to problems, you can learn more about these systems and what can be done to improve them. Once you begin seeing the ways systems negatively impact people and communities, you can determine how transforming the system can transform lives. Using a strengths-based approach, you can also notice when the system is helping people and identify improvements so that the system helps more people in more ways.

The Central Square Foundation uses a systems change lens to improve the learning outcomes of all children in India. The foundation, led by the cofounder of one of India's leading private equity funds, Ashish Dhawan, has a mission to transform India's school education system. For example, the Indian state of Rajasthan experienced low levels of educational attainment. So the foundation partnered with the state government, along with private, public, and philanthropic sectors including the Michael & Susan Dell Foundation and UNICEF, to establish schools in each of the state's 9,895 village councils. Their efforts also include improving governance, reducing teacher and school leadership vacancies, and upgrading school infrastructure.[9]

Depending on the size and focus of the philanthropic investment, this exploration may result in funding systems change as part of a broader philanthropic strategy. Or it might mean a philanthropy-wide emphasis on systems change. Lankelly Chase, an independent foundation in the United Kingdom, seeks to change systems that perpetuate disadvantage. Their entire mission is "to get to a place where people want to, know how to, and are free to create systems that are effective in responding to the interlocking nature of severe disadvantages such as homelessness, drug misuse, violence and abuse and mental ill health."

Use a Framework to Guide Philanthropic Investment

Reforming an entire system is likely to be too large a task for any one funder to tackle. Why not partner with others using a shared framework to guide your philanthropic investments?

The David and Lucile Packard Foundation, Gordon and Betty Moore Foundation, and Walton Family Foundation did this. With other partners, they developed a common framework for systems change that guides their collective investments in sustainable fisheries. The framework accounted for their various philosophies, objectives, and priorities; painted a clear picture of market-based systems changes that were needed to sustain fisheries; identified opportunities for philanthropic investment; and identified common metrics for success. In developing this framework, the foundations could see the ways their own philanthropic investments could contribute. They also saw the roles others needed to play for systems change to occur.[10]

The health care company DentaQuest focuses squarely on systems change through its philanthropy. The DentaQuest Partnership for Oral Health Advancement's sole focus is to create an effective and equitable system that results in improved oral health and well-being for everyone.[11] Their work is guided by a systems change framework. To improve oral health, they seek to change the systems of policy, care, financing, and the community.[12]

Support Systems Change Movements

We've all heard of the civil rights movement in the United States, the anti-apartheid movement in South Africa, and the global #MeToo movement. Many movements are less well known but no less important to those who benefit from them. Have you heard of a movement led by indigenous Guatemalan women to hold the Guatemalan government responsible for preventing global fashion companies from stealing Mayan textile designs? Fueled in part through a sustained partnership with the funder Thousand Currents, these women, part of the Asociación Femenina para el Desarrollo de Sacatepéquez (AFEDES), ignited a nationwide movement. They are poised to set an international legal precedent for indigenous peoples' collective intellectual property.

Thousand Currents believes their role in supporting the movement building of AFEDES is to invest without restrictions in their vision and goals. This included sticking with them through multiple changes in strategy and leadership. "Long-term social transformation presents many obstacles to our grantees' work. Funders need not present more," notes Solomé Lemma, executive director of Thousand Currents and cofounder of Africans in the Diaspora. "When funders can assimilate and act upon [the] wisdom that the people closest to the problems have the most important insights about their solutions, systems change becomes clearer."

So, what exactly is a movement? And how do you fund it?

A movement is a "network of individuals and organizations using the power of collective action to create cultural, economic, and political change."[13] They can be challenging to fund for a variety of reasons. For starters, most philanthropists don't fully understand them. My mom used to tell me not to invest in anything I don't understand. Most philanthropists feel the same way about giving their money away. If they don't fully "get" it, they likely won't fund it.

But movements, by definition, are tricky to wrap our heads around. They are decentralized and driven by many emerging and nontraditional actors (no lead organization to "fund"). They deploy diverse, sometimes unconventional strategies and tactics (they often upend the status quo and challenge existing gaps in the distribution of wealth, privilege, rights, and power—you know, the things that philanthropists are accustomed to having). And success is difficult to articulate (making it challenging to fit into your logic models and dashboards).[14]

Solidaire is a membership community of people with wealth who are committed to supporting progressive social movements. Lucky for us, in addition to facilitating the funding of social movements, they also want to help philanthropists understand movements and how to support them. They identify a "movement ecosystem" that includes creative disruption, organized communities, and political power. Further, they identify specific ways philanthropists can support each part of the ecosystem.

Because movements don't just happen. They require infrastructure.

Supporting movement infrastructure includes funding such things as leadership development, base building and organizing, strategy and planning, civic engagement, imagination and inspiration, technology, media and communications, and network building.[15] Things you as a funder *can* begin to wrap your head around.

Change Yourself to Change Systems

Changing systems also means changing ourselves. Julian Corner, the CEO of the Lankelly Chase Foundation, argues that it's both false and ineffective to think that as funders we can change systems without thinking about how we are implicated in those systems. "At Lankelly Chase, we have come to realize that changing systems has to start with changing ourselves. We can't be one thing and do or say another, because in an interdependent world that position will unravel over time and we will fail."

Working with a host of experts, the Annie E. Casey Foundation drew on existing tools and knowledge to develop a formal framework for its approach to changing systems within its own operation to make them more racially equitable. Casey's Race Equity and Inclusion Action Guide is available to any organization and includes seven replicable steps to advance and embed race equity within an organization's operations and culture. Further, Casey's work in race, equity, and inclusion provides a number of tools to help implement its framework, such as race equity and inclusion assessment tools that help governments redesign their decision-making processes.

Advocate for Policy Change

Of course, one of the primary drivers of systems change is policy.

Like systems, policies are all around us. They impact how we live, work, and interact with others. Wherever in the world you are reading this book right now, stop for a second. Strap on your invisible "policy goggles" and notice all the policies that touch your life.

It might be the fire sprinkler installed in the ceiling above your head, the result of local building code policies. The medical treatments you either have or don't have access to are the result of insurance policies or federal health policies. The homeless person you passed on the street today might be there as a result of a lifetime of interactions with inadequate education, child welfare, juvenile justice, mental health, and substance abuse treatment policies.

It used to be that you could scour the world and be hard pressed to find a philanthropist working in the public policy arena. Fortunately, that's changing as more and more funders realize that the root causes of the issues they want to address are themselves rooted within the workings of policy.

Let's be clear: The vast majority of "policy" work done by philanthropists is public policy *advocacy*. In its guide, *Advocacy Funding: The Philanthropy of Changing Minds*, GrantCraft (a service of Candid) defines advocacy as "a category of activities—usually carried out by grantees, but sometimes undertaken directly by foundations—whose primary purpose is to influence people's opinions or actions on matters of public policy or concern."[16] The GrantCraft guide points out that foundations generally use public policy advocacy to advance an idea that may be little known among the public, argue a position to defend a good idea from critics, or enrich the debate when a solution to a social problem is not readily apparent.

Many philanthropists shy away from policy advocacy because of fear. They fear the perceived limits and restrictions on their ability to influence public policies. But, depending on the country in which you work, you might have more leeway than you think. In the United States, while private foundations are prohibited by law from lobbying, they can engage in a wide range of direct and indirect policy advocacy activities. Grant-making public charities can engage in several kinds of lobbying activities in addition to advocacy. No foundation can support or oppose an electoral candidate, but all may engage in nonpartisan electoral activities such as voter registration or candidate education.

Philanthropists of all types are now engaging in policy advocacy. You might not think of a bank foundation as influencing policy change, but that's exactly what Lloyds Bank Foundation of England and Wales is doing. In 2017 they invested £2.6 million to influence domestic and sexual abuse policy and improve the commissioning environment for smaller charities.[17] Looking ahead, they plan to launch new national efforts to improve the criminal justice and welfare systems and address underlying drivers of disadvantage.[18]

Actress Mariska Hargitay (best known for her role as Detective Olivia Benson in *Law and Order: Special Victims Unit*) is another prominent activist. Through her Joyful Heart Foundation, she launched a national campaign pushing for the introduction of rape-kit reform bills, which includes six pillars for reform, in all 50 states. So far, 41 states and Washington, D.C., have passed laws supporting some aspect of the six pillars.[19] "To me, the [rape kit] backlog is one of the clearest and most shocking demonstrations of how we regard these crimes in our society. Testing rape kits sends a fundamental and crucial message to victims of sexual violence: You matter. What happened to you matters. Your case matters. For that reason, the Joyful Heart Foundation, which I founded in 2004, has made ending the rape kit backlog our number-one advocacy priority," explains Hargitay.[20]

Are you missing a key chance to change policy? Here are six ways philanthropists can support policy advocacy:

1. **Establish a vision.** Philanthropists can use their convening power to bring together all stakeholders and leading experts around a specific issue to spark discussion and identify potential policy solutions.

2. **Conduct research.** Donors can fund objective research to inform any policy debate. Research also can show the effectiveness or unintended consequences of a policy after it is enacted.

3. **Educate others.** Grantmakers can play a powerful role in helping to educate a community about a policy issue and can even educate policymakers directly in many cases.

4. **Support advocacy organizations.** Organizations that engage in policy advocacy, community organizing, civic engagement, or similar activities are the backbone of policy and systems change work. Providing grants to advocacy organizations allows philanthropists to take advantage of existing expertise and outreach ability.

5. **Support policy implementation.** Once a policy is adopted, the work of implementation begins—and it is where the lion's share of work is contained. National, state, or local policies must be interpreted and put into practice. Sometimes this requires the generation of additional funds and attention.

6. **Legal advocacy.** Most policies are not implemented or enforced flawlessly. Advocacy through the court system is a complementary measure to advance policy goals. One of the most direct ways to support legal advocacy is through legal aid associations that assist marginalized populations in accessing and navigating the court systems.

Remember: The policies that guide our communities did not grow overnight and neither will the changes we wish to see in them. Policy and systems change requires a long-term strategy and a steadfast funding commitment to that strategy. It also offers practically limitless ways for funders to engage in creating change!

Address the Root Cause

No matter what problem you want to tackle, it's important to understand the root causes that led to the problem. That will help you better understand what it will take to create a lasting solution. How do you do this? By strapping on your "root cause goggles," of course! In addition to looking for the systems and policies that helped create or maintain

Transformative Collaboration

While it's increasingly common to find philanthropists supporting policy change, it's still quite uncommon to find them working *together* on a policy issue. Policy is complicated. Figuring out one's view and position on a policy can be tricky. Aligning your policy goals with other funders' goals can be downright impossible. But in California, a loose collaboration of grantmakers did just that.[21]

California's system for funding public schools was convoluted, ineffective, and inequitable. Six different foundations—with diverse priorities for public education—all came together around this problem and worked together to support a better approach to funding. For two years, the Stuart Foundation, Charles and Helen Schwab Foundation, Broad Foundation, Walton Family Foundation, Dirk and Charlene Kabcenell Foundation, and Silver Giving Foundation overcame potentially polarizing differences of opinion to focus on one issue that made sense to everyone: improving the way the state funds public schools.

Together, these six foundations were able to fund projects that informed public discussion, built trust and transparency between the diverse parties engaged in that discussion, helped create consensus, amplified voices of communities most likely to be affected by finance reform, and continually monitored and contributed to the public conversation as the new funding law moved toward passage. *Their collaborative funding helped to completely redefine California's school finance system.*

How did they do it? There were several factors that made their collective work a success:

- They kept things informal and loosely structured. There was no pressure to formally adopt a common agenda or make a financial investment.

(continued)

(*continued*)

- They recognized and accepted a diversity of opinions. While they understood that each had a broader agenda for education, they united around the common goal of finance reform.
- They kept the lines of communication open and shared ideas and updates rather than trying to influence opinions.
- Each member made their own grant decisions about which organizations and what specific activities to fund in this common effort.
- Several of the foundations had flexibility when it came to funding decisions, which made quick responses possible as the process gained momentum.
- The foundations maintained a high level of respect for all grantee organizations and viewed them as equal partners. This led to greater transparency and the trust necessary to move quickly when needed.

the problems you want to address, you can also look for the underlying root causes.

To do this, you can ask yourself questions such as, "How did we get here?" "What are the root causes of this problem?" "What is the context that led to this?" "Why?" and, most important, "Where can we best intervene to make the greatest difference?"

The nonprofit 100Kin10 looked for the root cause of the lack of STEM teachers in the United States. In 2011, 100Kin10 set out to add 100,000 excellent STEM teachers to America's K–12 classrooms in 10 years. But it quickly realized that hiring more teachers wasn't good enough. If it didn't understand and address the underlying reasons that not enough people wanted to become STEM teachers or stay in the classroom, it would accomplish little for future generations.[22] According to 100Kin10's cofounder and CEO Talia Milgrom-Elcott, "Focusing on discrete problems leads to pointed, small fixes. For example, to combat the lack of STEM teachers you might offer incentives to bright young people. But if they leave after a few years, that amounts to little more than a Band-Aid. To move the needle, you have to get at the root causes."[23]

Similarly, the corporate foundation of the world's largest construction equipment manufacturer, Caterpillar, made the leap from funding Band-Aid solutions to funding global poverty by looking at the root causes of poverty in areas of the developing world where Caterpillar operates. This was propelled in part by the foundation's first female president, Michelle Sullivan, taking the helm. "I treat the foundation like a business," said then-president Sullivan in an interview for *Inside Philanthropy*. "When we make an investment, I look to get at the root causes [of a problem] . . . Otherwise you're just addressing the symptoms, and the causes will still be there."[24]

Seek Equitable Solutions

PolicyLink, which has been advocating for equitable policy solutions for decades, defines equity as "Just and fair inclusion into a society in which all can participate, prosper, and reach their full potential. Unlocking the promise of the nation by unleashing the promise in us all."[25]

Here is another way to think about it: Equity is "achieved when you can no longer predict an advantage or disadvantage based on race, ethnicity, gender, gender identity, sexual orientation, or ability. An equity framework is a proactive, strategic approach to improving outcomes that accounts for structural differences in opportunities, burdens, and needs in order to advance targeted solutions that fulfill the promise of true equality for all."[26]

A simple way to think about equitable solutions is in teaching reading. It turns out we don't all learn how to read in the same way. And if you are a kid with dyslexia, chances are standard teaching methods won't help you as much as they'll help the kid who isn't dyslexic. Your classmate is halfway through the Harry Potter series, while you're still slogging your way through the first chapter of the first book. Luckily, there are teaching methodologies designed specifically to teach dyslexic kids to read.

What does this mean? It means we have a choice. We could *equally* provide the exact same reading education to all our students and watch some fail while others thrive. Or we can *equitably* provide kids with reading education suited to their needs and watch them all thrive.

Equity is about providing people and communities with what they need to thrive.

This means looking at the issues and problems you want to tackle through yet another lens: an equity lens. Understanding where and why there are inequities. And then determining solutions that eliminate them.

Let's go back to our reading example. You might be in your second year of funding a campaign to ensure that all students in your local school district are reading by third grade. The data look promising. Aggregate reading scores across the district are going up! But before you take the day off to celebrate, check your data again. When you disaggregate your data by race, gender, disability, income, school, or some other criterion, what do you find? You might find some students' scores are *declining*, while others are skyrocketing.

You didn't notice this when you looked at aggregate reading scores. The skyrocketing kids pulled the aggregate score up. But it turns out your reading campaign isn't providing an intervention that equitably helps *all* students. Or there might be deeper, structural inequities in the lives, classrooms, or communities of some students that you haven't yet accounted for. Applying an equity lens in your grantmaking means investing the time and resources to understand inequities and address them.

Seeking equitable solutions also means taking a hard look at yourself. Yes, you. You as an individual and you as a philanthropist. As funders, we can't just apply an equity lens to our grantmaking. We need to apply it to ourselves too. We need to honestly understand how our beliefs, policies, and practices thwart or advance diversity, inclusion, and equity. Being "equitable" isn't a box to check, but an ongoing journey. I continue to learn, and it hasn't always been easy, but the experience of deeply learning, reflecting, and being challenged has helped me become a better consultant and funder.

Fortunately, there are a tremendous number of resources being developed to help philanthropists advance equitable solutions. One I find particularly helpful is the Annie E. Casey Foundation's *Race Equity and Inclusion Action Guide.*[27]

The guide identifies seven steps to advance and embed race equity and inclusion within your organization. These steps include: establish an understanding of race equity and inclusion principles, engage affected populations and stakeholders, gather and analyze disaggregated data, conduct systems analyses of root causes of inequities, identify strategies and target resources to address root causes of inequities, conduct race equity impact assessments for all policies and decision making, and continuously evaluate effectiveness and adapt strategies.

Rebeccah Bennett and Zach Boyers implore philanthropists to prioritize equity. Together they cochair Forward Through Ferguson, the organization created to help achieve a racially equitable St. Louis following the 2014 shooting death of an unarmed, 18-year-old African American man, Michael Brown, Jr., by a white police officer in Ferguson, Missouri.

"Wherever you are, whatever you fund, I invite you to make equity a priority. That means those people who are most impacted by the problem are seated at the decision-making table. I'm not talking voice, I'm talking choice. Consider how to restructure your work so that they are centered in decision making. Absent that, we will exist in the status quo," explains Bennett.[28]

There are many examples of philanthropists who have taken a hard look at themselves through an equity lens and restructured their work as a result.

The San Francisco Foundation (California) is one of them. The foundation is operationalizing equity internally and throughout its grantmaking. Why? Because it wanted to reimagine the potential for a community foundation to deliver on its mission. That includes working to reverse the trajectory of inequality and build a more equitable, inclusive region.[29]

It started with learning and listening. It engaged its trustees, staff, donors, nonprofit and philanthropic partners, business leaders, grassroots activists, academic experts, and more than 1,000 residents across the region. The foundation conducted strategic planning with an equity lens. This ensured its new strategy focused on advancing equity.[30]

Internally, the foundation now operationalizes equity by seeking to create an organizational culture and workplace that is fair, inclusive, and just. Where staff are recognized for their full selves and their voices are valued. And where the foundation is held accountable to providing equitable access to resources and opportunities. Specifically, they are focused on hiring an increasingly diverse staff whose lived experiences deepen the foundation's understanding of the Bay Area's greatest challenges; adopting more equitable personnel policies and benefits; and contracting with diverse, mission-aligned vendors and consultants.

Externally, the San Francisco Foundation focuses its entire program strategy on racial equity and economic inclusion. This includes a conscious effort to fund grantees that are led by diverse leadership (in 2018, 70% of the organizations funded through its equity grants open cycle featured a majority people-of-color leadership team).[31]

The Structure of Your Grants

If you want your philanthropy to help change the world, you might need to change how your funding is structured. The way you structure your funding should align with the type of impact you wish to see.

For example, if you want to achieve long-term results, provide long-term support. If you seek to strengthen the organizations that are solving problems, provide funding that builds their infrastructure, capacity, and talent. If you expect the organizations you fund to achieve certain outcomes, ensure that they are adequately resourced. If you recognize your grantees must be nimble and adapt to rapidly changing conditions, offer flexible funding and get out of their way.

But you know this already. You know this because it's common sense.

Unfortunately, too few philanthropists heed this advice. They nod their heads in genuine agreement. But then they continue providing funding the way they always have. Small grants, one-year grants, and project-specific grants. Grants with lots of hurdles grantees must jump over. Grants with unrealistic expectations compared to the funds provided. Grants that meet the interests of the funder while forcing the nonprofit to stray from its mission.

Below are six different ways to structure your funding that can help you—and your partners—increase your impact velocity.

Offer Multiple Years of Support

The programs that nonprofits operate and the needs they address aren't one-off occurrences. Why should their funding be? Instead of offering funding for one year, consider offering it for multiple years. There are substantial benefits to multiyear funding. When nonprofits have more stable, predictable streams of support, they can spend less time scrambling for money and more time strengthening their organization and making a difference for your community. Nonprofit leaders' time is freed up to lead. It also allows NGOs the ability to plan and make the best long-term decisions.

The Saint Luke's Foundation's multiyear grant of over $100,000 per year for three years to Policy Matters Ohio allowed their executive director to hire top talent for their new policy initiative. "Knowing I have multiple years of funding changes the way I can recruit candidates," explains Amy Hanauer, executive director of Policy Matters Ohio. "If I'm hiring for a three-year position but only have one year's worth of funding committed, I'm not going to convince the top candidate to leave her secure job and come work for me for a year. What if she has kids and a family to support? She can't take that risk. The result is that I'll end up hiring a less qualified person willing to accept a one-year gig."[32]

Provide General Operating Support

General operating support, also known as flexible, unrestricted, or core operating support, is a grant to advance the grantee's mission rather than for specific projects or programs. It's the working capital non-profits need to sustain their day-to-day operations. General operating support allows organizations to adapt to shifts in need, respond to crises, take advantage of unforeseen opportunities, invest in their own infrastructure, upgrade technology, and further their own staff and leadership development. It also allows them to pay the rent, keep the lights on, and make payroll. It can give an organization the breathing room it needs to develop the next highly effective solution to a community problem.

Similar to multiyear grants, core support funding frees up the time nonprofit leaders spend on fundraising, so they can allocate their time where it's needed most—achieving their mission. It also helps reduce the burnout many nonprofit leaders feel just keeping their organizations afloat. On top of that, it can be a lot easier on the funder. Instead of spending long hours devising complex outcomes and grant requirements, you simply invest in the organizations and leaders you feel will best advance your philanthropic goals.

"Sounds great!" you might be thinking. "What's the downside?" Well, there is no downside. Except that it requires . . . trust. When you give a general support grant, you are trusting the nonprofit will spend your grant in the best way it sees fit. Instead of dictating how they use your funds, you let them decide. We'll discuss the importance of building trust later in this chapter, but I believe lack of trust (and its partner, the fear and unwillingness to relinquish power) is the most important reason philanthropists refrain from offering general operating support.

Although there is widespread recognition among funders of the value of general operating support, not enough funders offer it. According to the National Committee for Responsive Philanthropy (NCRP), the percentage of U.S. domestic funding allocated for general operating support among the largest 1,000 U.S. foundations remained stagnant at 20% between 2003 and 2015 (the most recent year that data are available).[33]

General operating grants are less common outside of the United States, but they are certainly not the purview of U.S. funders.

At the Community Foundation Tyne & Wear and Northumberland in the UK, they constitute a core approach to funding. According to Sandra King, chief philanthropy officer and deputy to the chief executive, "At the Community Foundation, we've made the case for donors supporting core operational costs for a long time. It's not always been easy, but our staff are committed to clearly articulating the importance of 'keeping the lights on' alongside funding one-off projects. But that's only half the work. Traditionally we and other foundations have been seen as project funders. So we've also worked harder to make it clear to applicants that we support core costs. As a result, we've seen our funding for core costs rise year on year and are committed to seeing that rise further."

General operating support is also a way that community philanthropies can claim power. When Tewa, Nepal's first and only women's fund, was created, it required that only locally raised money would be used for local grantmaking. Tewa raises the funds for overhead and program costs (core operating support) from external sources, such as international foundations. With donations from more than 3,000 individual Nepalis, this approach allows them to deliberately model locally owned development and prevent dependence upon international aid.

Recently, some funders have taken the plunge and shifted much or all of their funding to general operating support. Notable examples include the Ford Foundation. In 2015,[34] Ford pledged 40% of its grantmaking budget to general operating support. In 2016, it launched the BUILD initiative to give $1 billion to social justice nonprofits, all using a combination of general operating support and grants designed to strengthen organizations. Ford Foundation CEO Darren Walker, along with the CEOs of the Open Society Foundations, MacArthur

Foundation, William and Flora Hewlett Foundation, and David and Lucile Packard Foundation, also pledged in 2019 to increase funding of overhead costs and encourage other funders to do the same.[35]

Bridgespan Group's analysis of 274 nonprofits funded by two or more of the largest 15 U.S. foundations found that 42% had less than three months' worth of cash on hand, and 23% had less than one week's worth.[36] According to Walker, "We funders like to think that we are fair in our funding in terms of administrative costs, overhead, etc., when in fact we kid ourselves. We're not being honest with ourselves if we think that [paying] 10% of overhead actually covers the true administration of our project grants."[37]

Sustaining Nonprofits with Operating Support and Ongoing Support

It's not surprising that a business leader would intuitively understand the value of both general operating support and multiyear funding. After all, businesses make long-term investments in themselves for research and development, infrastructure, and talent. That's just what Boston real estate mogul Bill Cummings did with his foundation, the Cummings Foundation. With nearly $2 billion in assets, it's one of the largest foundations in New England.

The foundation was well known for making $100,000 general operating support grants every year to 100 Boston-area nonprofits. As if that wasn't enough, it launched the Sustaining Grants Program, which provides a few past grantees with ten years of continuous, general operating support (no additional application required).

Last year, the Cummings Foundation debuted a new initiative, the Sustaining Grants Program, that involved identifying past grantees and giving them steady, ongoing support without requiring new applications year after year. In the initiative's first two years, the foundation awarded 38 decade-long grants.[38]

Strengthen Organizational Capacity and Talent

Just as core operating support is vital to help nonprofits be agile, seize new opportunities, and keep the lights on, capacity-building funding helps them be strong. What is organizational capacity building, and how does a philanthropist support it?

Grantmakers for Effective Organizations, a U.S.-based philanthropy-serving organization that helps foundations strengthen their grantmaking and nonprofit organizations, defines capacity building as providing "the funding and technical assistance necessary to help nonprofits increase specific capabilities to deliver stronger programs, take risks, build connections, innovate, and iterate."[39]

It means strengthening the ability of the entire organization to achieve its mission, as opposed to funding specific programs. What are these capabilities we're talking about? Everything from leadership to strategy, including financial management, governance, evaluation, fund development, program quality, communications, technology, and diversity, equity, and inclusion—the knowledge and skills you need to be an effective organization.

Many leading philanthropy organizations, including the National Committee for Responsive Philanthropy, Grantmakers for Effective Organizations, the Center for Effective Philanthropy, and Fund the People have been beating the drum about the importance of building nonprofit capacity and talent development. But just as with core support funding, many funders agree this type of funding is important, but too few provide it.

The Kresge Foundation, the Community Foundation of the Eastern Shore, and donors Frank and Mitzi Perdue understood the importance of building organizational capacity. In 2000 the Kresge Foundation selected the Community Foundation of the Eastern Shore (based in rural Salisbury, Maryland) as one of six community foundations in the United States to participate in a five-year effort, the Partnership to Raise Community Capital. The Partnership sought to build the capacity of community foundations and 19 competitively selected local nonprofits to raise endowment funds. Endowment funds are highly valuable because they provide nonprofits with operating funds in perpetuity. The principal can continue to grow through investments and contributions while providing annual income distribution to the nonprofit. Endowment funds also signal to potential donors that the nonprofit has made a long-term commitment to its future.

Kresge set out to provide a 1:3 match. If the 19 nonprofits could collectively raise $6 million toward their endowments, it would provide $2 million in matching funds.

Frank and Mitzi Perdue were among the area's most generous philanthropists. Frank Perdue was chairman of Perdue Farms, the company he transformed from a family farm into the country's third-largest chicken processor. Mitzi Perdue is a businesswoman and philanthropist in her own right. She is an author, syndicated columnist, and producer and host of television and radio shows, in addition to growing up in the family that owned the Sheraton Hotels. Frank and Mitzi believed that strengthening their community included strengthening the organizations that served the community. They committed another $4 million to the partnership, turning the 1:3 match into a 1:1 match.

As if $6 million in matching funds wasn't enough, the Kresge Foundation strategically provided technical assistance for the community foundation and nonprofit partners to help them successfully raise and utilize their endowments. This included assistance in fundraising, major gifts, communications, and enlisting the support of board members. "The training provided by the Community Foundation was the first training of this type we have ever received or even had access to in this geographical area. It was outstanding and certainly strengthened our team's skills and expertise," said Peggy Bradford, executive director of MAC, Inc., one of the 19 nonprofit recipients. In just three years, the Partnership raised $12.8 million in endowment funding. More than $10.5 million has been distributed to the nonprofits, and the collective fund balance is over $17 million and growing.[40]

Luckily, you don't need to spend $6 million to build nonprofit capacity. There are all kinds of low-cost and no-cost ways you can help your grantees strengthen their people and operations. You or your team can offer advice if you bring expertise that your grantees need, such as legal advising, governance, or financial management. You can also fund training, coaching, professional development, and consulting support.

According to nonprofit expert Joan Garry, author of *Joan Garry's Guide to Nonprofit Leadership*, the relationship between the nonprofit CEO and board chair is the single most important indicator of nonprofit health.[41] The Community Foundation of Lorain County (Ohio) understood this. They asked their grantees if they'd be interested in participating in a training to strengthen this relationship. Ten pairs of board chairs and CEOs agreed to participate. Together they learned about the appropriate roles and responsibilities, tips for strengthening their relationship, models for effective succession planning, how to handle difficult conversations, and more. The cost? About $5,000 to pay a consultant to deliver the training.

Building Trusting Relationships

I once spoke with a foundation executive who told me that he was an extremely busy man and rarely left his office during the workday. While that may be a great practice if you're day trading, it's a terrible one for philanthropy. Philanthropic investments require face-to-face interactions. It's how donor and grantee build trust in one another. If you want to really understand the needs, the players, and the potential solutions that are at work in your community—and build the trust necessary to tackle them—then get out there!

When it comes right down to it, being an effective philanthropist means establishing trust with the people you wish to help and the partners you'll want and need to work with. It doesn't matter whether that's the sophisticated CEO of a nationwide organization or the hardscrabble leader of a struggling grassroots start-up. As human beings, we depend on levels of trust to guide us into new relationships and to see them through even when the going might get tough. And securing that mutual willingness to see things through in tough times is both the reason to establish trust and the reward for doing so.

It may seem like a complex issue, but establishing trust really isn't that difficult. As an advisor to philanthropists for more than two decades, I wouldn't be able to help my clients if we didn't trust each other—so I've made a point of working to establish trust from the get-go. Here are five key things I've learned along the way:

- **Be yourself.** It's perfectly fine if you are a wealthy, privileged man who doesn't need to work to pay the bills, navigating your way through funding projects to end homelessness. It's also perfectly fine if you are formerly homeless and navigating your way through the privileged world of organized philanthropy. Just as dogs can sense fear, sadness, or joy in their human friends, people sense authenticity. Be your authentic self. Look for and appreciate the authenticity of others.

- **Say what you'll do and do what you say.** Trust and dependability go hand in hand. As a funder, be crystal clear about your role, your level of engagement in the partnership, the dollar range you are willing to fund, your deadlines, expectations, and how you can help beyond simply providing funds. Once you've established what others can expect of you, you'll need to follow through on what you said you would do—or provide immediate, full-disclosure updates about why you can't meet those expectations. Although your failure to deliver may not seem like a big deal, remember the cardinal rule of crisis communications: Tell the truth, tell it all, and tell it first.

- **Be vulnerable.** No one is perfect. Funders who are reluctant to admit when they've made mistakes or don't know answers have a hard time establishing trust. There's a kind of intimacy that comes from admitting weaknesses or failures to others, and a type of honesty that emerges when both funder and grantees explore weaknesses and failures by learning and changing together. Saying, "I don't know. How can we figure it out?" or "That was my fault. How can we learn from it and make things better?" does much more to establish trust than perfection ever will.

- **Be trustworthy in times of crisis.** A therapist once explained to me that you can trust someone after they've proven themselves trustworthy over and over again in times of crisis. It's a high bar. But it's true. "I've got your back" may be the ultimate expression of trust. It's a powerful feeling to know your ally will stand beside you no matter what and will offer protection and assistance when the heat is on. Likewise, being there as a funder during the challenging times—providing consistent funding during a nonprofit's leadership transition, making introductions to other funders during difficult economic times, showing up to the neighborhood center after a tragedy, standing up among your peers to push forward important legislation—that builds trust that goes deep and can weather storm after storm.

- **Be patient.** Building trust takes time. It means finding values and goals that you hold in common, recognizing and acknowledging the power dynamic between funder and grantee, and listening longer and more closely than you perhaps ever have before. Obviously, opening the door and declaring, "Hi, I'm a wealthy philanthropist and I'm here to help" will not engender immediate trust. But being authentic in conversation, dependable in what you promise, vulnerable about your shortcomings, and trustworthy in times of crisis will eventually pay off in ways that will amplify the impact of your philanthropy for years and years.

Engage Diverse Perspectives and Let Go

We all want to give back to society in meaningful ways. But we often delude ourselves by thinking we know more than we do, have the perfect solution, or are in the best position to make key decisions about where to invest in the problems we hope to solve.

Quite frankly, many philanthropists believe that they know best or are better able to learn about and analyze problems and solutions than the people whom they purport to serve.

We all do this sometimes. But I know that's not the type of philanthropist you want to be. Right?

This isn't surprising. Our society tends to equate the accumulation of wealth with superior intellect—or at least with superior know-how.

Yet these same funders are often frustrated by the poor results of their philanthropic investments.

To these funders, I say, "Just give up"—control, that is.

In the world of need, few people have knowledge as deep as those who experience that need daily. Instead of confusing poverty or other forms of need with an inability to innovate or a lack of motivation to improve, funders should seek the answers they desire within the communities they wish to serve. In other words, learn from and give up some of the control you have over your philanthropic funds to those who truly know what it will take to make change.

How do you give up (or at least share) control and still get results—better results than you'll get by keeping a tight rein? Here are four key ways to cede control and improve your funding results:

- **Let the community guide your learning.** As a funder, you may have researched intensively. You may have read every paper and study published on a particular topic. Maybe you've met with some of the leading minds on your issue. Heck, perhaps you've even funded studies yourself. But when it comes to social issues, the people who are most affected can be your most valuable sounding board and your greatest source of insight. Never forget that you don't know what you don't know—but the people you want to help most certainly do. And with a little trust building on your part, they'll probably be happy to enlighten you.

  There are many ways to engage diverse perspectives, ranging from low-touch learning to high involvement in decision making. Low-touch approaches might include creating an advisory committee of community members; soliciting input via focus groups, surveys, and listening sessions; and participating in community convenings. For example, the Stuart Foundation in San Francisco made a point of gathering the perspectives of high school–aged foster care youth and college students who had been in foster care before deciding whether to continue a program for youth transitioning out of the foster care system.

- **Look for homegrown solutions.** As funders with an eye toward solving problems, nothing excites us more than a "big bet" that has shown big impact. Many of us practically drool over an evidence-based practice that we think will work wonders in our own communities. But we should recognize that there are no one-size-fits-all solutions, and even interventions that have a strong base of evidence for effectiveness in one community may completely miss the mark in another. Culture, trusting relationships, and the ability to recognize and build on a community's unique assets are all key components of success. And no one understands a community's culture, relationships, and assets like those who live there. Let those who live the problems inform—or, even better, determine—the solutions.

- *Invest beyond the usual suspects.* Once you've given others the power to inform your understanding and the solutions, it's time to make investments. You'll likely want to turn to your trusted grantees and partners, excited to bring them into the mix as allies who will appreciate your newfound knowledge and new approach. While your long-term grantees may indeed play a valuable role, they may not be the best to implement a strategy or, at least, not best to take the lead. Consider the possibility that the spot might be better filled by an organization that is deeply embedded in and trusted by the community—one that is completely plugged in to the culture, relationships, and assets mentioned in the point above.

  This may very well be an organization that is (or at least appears to be) underdeveloped relative to your usual grantees. Your philanthropic investments may need to include funds for capacity building, professional development, or general operating support to help the organization increase and maximize its own effectiveness. Your timeline for change may need to be longer. But in the end, you'll emerge with a new ally and a stronger community resource that can continue to exert positive influence for years to come.

- *Share control of decision making.* There's a heck of a lot of power in being a philanthropist. You give and others receive. While that power dynamic might not go away anytime soon, there are things you can do to mitigate it. Specifically, sharing or giving up control of decision making. For family foundations, this could mean inviting nonfamily members to serve on the foundation board. Some philanthropists have taken this a few steps further: They've decided to hand over control of grantmaking decisions to community members.

The Springs Close Foundation, headquartered in Fort Mill, South Carolina, did just that. The family foundation recognized that as times changed, they needed to change, too. Family members were moving to communities across the country, their hometown was growing and changing, and needs were emerging that they didn't fully understand.

First, they created community advisory committees for each county that the Foundation served. These committees advised the family on community issues and grant allocations, although the foundation board of directors maintained final decision-making authority. However, the family quickly realized that the community advisory committees were so successful and insightful that they transitioned them to community boards with grantmaking budgets and full decision-making authority. The family members retained a small portion of the foundation's grantmaking budget for their own discretionary grants and gave complete control over the rest of the grants budget to the community boards.

"If you've ever been a parent, you understand that you cannot micromanage your kids to become successful adults. It's the same way in philanthropy," explains Dr. Rahsaan Harris, president and CEO of the Emma Bowen Foundation. "You can't micromanage change. If you want to be transformational, you have to relinquish some control. You and your grantees need to be able to take risks. You need the freedom to try and fail. Philanthropists need to be partners in change, not owners and overseers."

These four points apply to any funder, from the smallest individual donor to the largest global foundation. The scope and size of your work may vary, but one key lesson should always hold true: If you really want to help people, learn from them and give up some control. Ask them what they need to make change, and then give them the means to do it.

Leverage All of Your Assets

You are more than money. This can be challenging to remember when it seems everyone is asking for your money, criticizing you for how you spend your money, or lavishing praise on you for the money you give.

You bring a tremendous amount of nonfinancial assets to the table. You just need to think about how you can use and leverage them to extend the reach and increase the impact of your charitable gifts. This includes intellectual capital, reputational capital (influence), the doors you can open for others, other tangible assets you have (your home, conference room, farm, private jet), your talents and expertise (and that of your employees), and so forth.

Most of us don't even think about—much less deploy—these assets. We're so fixated on the limitations of our grant budgets we forget that we can advance our goals through our unique talents. We're so frequently asked to *give money* we forget our philanthropy is *more than money*.

The CEO of JP Morgan Chase, Jamie Dimon, knows this. In addition to donating $200 million to help revitalize Detroit, Michigan, JP Morgan Chase gave more than money. A lot more. In addition to funding affordable housing, workforce development, and small business development for entrepreneurs of color, they deployed data analytics.

"We use big data and artificial intelligence in running our businesses around the world for risk and credit and marketing. So here [in Detroit], we actually have huge data, too, about how people spend their money," explained Jamie Dimon.[42] For example, they used data analytics to determine where people in Detroit use credit cards, debit cards, and checks at places like stores and restaurants, and how far they had to drive from home to do that. This information was then shared to help entrepreneurs determine the best places to open new businesses and restaurants, and where to put affordable housing. While $200 million in funding is nothing to sneeze at, access to this type of information is almost priceless.

The good news is you don't need to be the billionaire CEO of JP Morgan Chase to deploy your assets. You just need to be you. You need to identify your assets and you need to deploy them.

You also bring a lot of financial assets in addition to your grantmaking dollars, as well as your entire portfolio of investments (and how they might be aligned toward positive social impact). Jed Emerson, editor of *The ImpactAssets Handbook for Investors*, believes investors can align their investments for social good.

"Regardless of how much money you may have to invest, and while specific strategies may differ, it is increasingly possible to achieve positive impact across all one's capital investments," he says.[43] He refers to this practice as Total Portfolio Management. With this approach, all capital—philanthropic, near-market, and market-rate—is managed to optimize financial performance while maximizing the impact potential of each asset class.

Community philanthropy, which is a practice of locally driven development that strengthens community capacity, voice, and decision making, is effective in large part because it taps into and builds on local resources and assets. These assets might include local knowledge, experience, and leadership as well as physical assets, such as natural resources.

The Newmont Ahafo Development Foundation (NADeF), for example, uses its asset of natural resources to advance community change. NADeF is the corporate foundation of a gold-mining company in Ghana. It was established through an agreement between the company and local communities as a mechanism to channel a portion of its profits for long-term community benefit.[44] NADeF has accrued over $24.5 million to fund various development initiatives through the Ahafo Mine's contributions of $1 per ounce of gold produced and 1% annual net profit. "What makes NADeF unique from other corporate foundations is the local ownership and participation in the selection, execution, and management of all projects in the host communities. In effect, the locals decide what their needs are and work through NADeF to achieve them," explained Elizabeth Opoku Darko, NADeF's executive secretary.[45]

Lastly, a way to leverage your charitable giving is to pool it with others. There are countless examples of philanthropic collaboratives and pooled funds. Simply stated, we are better together.

Notes

1. https://etcanada.com/news/502111/lenny-kravitz-helps-the-bahamas-get-back-on-their-feet-after-hurricane-dorian/.

2. https://www.kinaracapital.com/.
3. https://sorensonimpactfoundation.org/what-we-do/.
4. https://www.owla.co.za/academy.
5. https://variety.com/2017/biz/news/oprah-winfrey-leadership-academy-for-girls-10-year-anniversary-1202510605/.
6. https://thesystemsthinker.com/wp-content/uploads/2016/03/Introduction-to-Systems-Thinking-IMS013Epk.pdf.
7. https://www.investopedia.com/slide-show/car-recalls/.
8. P.G. Foster-Fishman, B. Nowell, and H. Yang, "Putting the System Back into Systems Change: A Framework for Understanding and Changing Organizational and Community Systems," *American Journal of Community Psychology* 39 (2007): 197–215, also at https://www.thinknpc.org/resource-hub/systems-change-a-guide-to-what-it-is-and-how-to-do-it/.
9. https://www.alliancemagazine.org/feature/systems-change-in-effect/.
10. https://www.packard.org/wp-content/uploads/2017/02/Global-Seafood-Markets-Strategy-2017-2022-EXTERNAL.pdf
11. https://www.dentaquestpartnership.org/.
12. https://whatsnew.dentaquest.com/preventistry-systems-change-and-oral-health/.
13. https://solidairenetwork.org/wp-content/uploads/2017/06/Movement-Philanthropy.pdf.
14. https://www.innonet.org/media/Exec_Sum-Amplifying_Movement_Knowledge_for_Philanthropy.pdf.
15. https://solidairenetwork.org/wp-content/uploads/2017/06/Movement-Philanthropy.pdf.
16. https://grantcraft.org/content/guides/advocacy-funding/.
17. https://www.lloydsbankfoundation.org.uk/ourimpact/.
18. https://www.lloydsbankfoundation.org.uk/2018%20%20Impact%20Report.pdf.
19. Author's email correspondence with Melissa Schwartz, Joyful Heart Foundation, on October 3, 2019.
20. http://www.joyfulheartfoundation.org/programs/advocacy.
21. https://putnam-consulting.com/wp-content/uploads/Stuart-LCFF-FINAL_12-10-20141.pdf.
22. https://ssir.org/articles/entry/ending_teacher_shortages_with_network_mapping.

23. https://www.inc.com/greg-satell/this-productivity-hack-from-toyota-production-system-can-help-solve-education-everything-else.html.

24. https://www.insidephilanthropy.com/home/2014/10/3/root-causes-the-clarity-of-michele-sullivan-and-the-remaking.html.

25. https://www.policylink.org/about-us/equity-manifesto.

26. From National Committee for Responsive Philanthropy's Power Moves Toolkit, https://www.ncrp.org/initiatives/philamplify/power-moves-philanthropy. They note that this definition combines definitions from OpenSource Leadership Strategies and CHANGE Philanthropy.

27. https://www.aecf.org/resources/race-equity-and-inclusion-action-guide/.

28. Bennet, Rebeccah. "Forging a Path Toward Change." 2019 CONNECT Conference, Exponent Philanthropy, St. Louis, MO.

29. https://sff.org/advancing-equity-reimagining-the-ways-a-community-foundation-delivers-on-its-mission/.

30. https://2ib5hhzq9vn2r0apq17idfk1-wpengine.netdna-ssl.com/wp-content/uploads/2019/05/SFF_EquityReport_Full_Final-1.pdf.

31. https://sff.org/about-us/equity-inclusion-and-diversity/.

32. Author interview with Amy Hanauer.

33. https://www.ncrp.org/2019/01/the-gig-economy-continues-to-hold-back-the-nonprofit-sector.html.

34. https://philanthropynewsdigest.org/news/ford-foundation-to-refocus-grantmaking-on-inequality.

35. https://www.philanthropy.com/article/Foundations-Pledge-to-Pay/247078.

36. https://www.philanthropy.com/article/5-CEOs-of-Big-Foundations/247063.

37. Ibid.

38. https://www.insidephilanthropy.com/home/2018/5/15/cummings-foundation-sustaining-grants-program.

39. https://philanthropynewyork.org/sites/default/files/resources/geo_2016_strengtheningnonprofitcapacity.pdf.

40. Author interview with Erica Joseph, CEO, Community Foundation of the Eastern Shore, September 5, 2019.

41. https://blog.joangarry.com/best-sign-healthy-nonprofit/.

42. https://www.cbsnews.com/news/jamie-dimon-jp-morgan-chase-ceo-makes-data-focused-investment-in-detroit-60-minutes-2019-11-10/.

43. https://www.impactassets.org/files/Handbook-Ch-01-Construction-of-an-Impact-Portfolio.pdf.

44. https://globalfundcommunityfoundations.org/wp-content/uploads/2019/04/NewHorizonsForCommunityLedDevelopment.pdf.

45. https://www.ghanaweb.com/GhanaHomePage/business/Newmont-Ahafo-Development-Foundation-named-Corporate-Foundation-Philanthropist-of-the-year-527915#.

12 You Are Unstoppable

Many things can improve your chances of success—as a solo philanthropist, the head of a small family foundation, or someone who is responsible for tens of millions of dollars in grants to nonprofit partners. In fact, we've already explored many of these things.

But what can you do to make you and your philanthropy *unstoppable*—a powerful force of nature that has the power to change people's lives, entire communities, and the world?

Over the years, I've found five specific strategies that, when applied—in tandem—can make you truly unstoppable.

This, of course, begs the question of whether you can do just one or two of these things and still improve your efficiency and effectiveness. Sure. By engaging in even one of these strategies, you will definitely improve your philanthropy. However, when you pursue them simultaneously—and keep at it over a sustained period of time—you'll find tremendous improvement in the way you do business over the long run.

177

It's important that we continuously stay on the alert for and eliminate steps, bottlenecks, barriers, and other obstacles to doing good because they constantly emerge and find their way into our organizations, our processes, and our mind-sets.

Remember: As you evolve as a philanthropist, what brought you success in the past may not bring you success in the future—what got you here won't necessarily get you there.

But we can't be unstoppable just by eliminating the bad. We have to innovate, adapt to changing circumstances, and be proactive and agile to create new opportunities for learning and growth. Just as you can't build your wealth by only cutting costs, you need to spend and invest in yourself to grow.

Some of the things I talk about in this chapter are strategies many forward-thinking nonprofit and business leaders have already adopted and used to their benefit for some time. That said, none of them require a degree in rocket science. Applying these strategies is actually quite easy. The harder part is turning them into a habit.

Let's take a look at five proven strategies that have the power to make you and your organization unstoppable.

Eliminate Steps

While large bureaucratic organizations rightfully get a lot of grief for ladling lots of extra procedures and red tape onto their grantmaking processes, even small foundations and individual philanthropists may do more than the minimum required to accomplish a task or achieve a goal. Sometimes much more.

Years ago, automobile manufacturer Toyota developed and implemented a process it called the Toyota Production System, which inspired the idea of lean process thinking. Among other things, at its heart was the elimination of *muda*—waste that doesn't add value to the end product.[1] Examples of waste for an automobile manufacturer like Toyota include inefficiencies and non-value-adding activities such as excess inventory, defects, and excess movement of machines and people. Toyota (and the other manufacturers that eventually followed their examples) dramatically increased their profits and the quality of their products by eliminating *muda*.

What do you do that doesn't add value to your philanthropy? What can you do to eliminate it?

Here are sure signs you've got extra steps to eliminate:

- Releasing proposal guidelines that are 14 single-spaced pages long—for grant proposals that cannot exceed eight pages
- Spending four months developing a request for proposals (RFP), but giving applicants only three weeks to prepare their proposal
- Forcing a partner to send 14 follow-up emails and leave four voice messages before responding, regarding a time-sensitive issue that you requested
- Delaying interaction with the outside world (partners, grantees, consultants, in-laws) because you're consumed by an annual three-month budgeting process
- Telling your vendors it will take four weeks to approve a payment when really it takes just four minutes
- Asking grant applicants to answer questions that are interesting to you but don't influence your funding decision
- Requiring site visits for every applicant, even though you only have a handful of people to conduct them and this takes up months of your time

If any of these sound familiar to you, here are three ways you can reduce and eliminate the extra steps that are getting between you and effective philanthropy:

1. **Conduct a bureaucracy-breaker audit.** Take an honest look at the practices and processes you currently use. Where do they begin to lose their effectiveness because they are overcome by complexity or complications? How are the expectations or requests of one thing you do hindering another? What can you do to remove needless requirements, approvals, or other steps to streamline and get to effective outcomes more quickly and simply?

2. **Commit to the 50% principle.** First, identify a single form of red tape that currently clogs up the works in your philanthropy—maybe it takes four months to approve a nonprofit partner for your employee volunteerism program, or you require at least three consultants to submit proposals before you hire the one you already know you should use, or your board docket is two inches thick and no one will ever read it all. Then brainstorm three things you can do to reduce that red tape by half. What would it take to approve the nonprofit in four weeks instead of four months? How about if only one highly qualified consultant must submit a proposal before you can hire her? And what unnecessary information and duplication can you remove to get your 200-page board docket down to 100 pages (or, better yet, 20 pages)?

3. **Think like a two-year-old.** As everyone knows, a two-year-old's go-to question is "Why?" Tap into your inner child and apply this question to everything you do in philanthropy. Are you about to post a job description to hire a communications manager, when you already know the person you'd love to hire? Why? Are you about to send your new grant guidelines to every internal department for review before you publish them? Why? Occasionally the answers to these questions deliver a satisfactory explanation, but what about the practices that have no good explanation? Keep digging and keep asking why.

When I think about eliminating steps, I'm reminded of the words of Michelangelo. He explained how he found the image of his subject in a block of stone by removing what wasn't necessary: "I saw the angel in the marble and carved until I set him free."

Find the angel in your philanthropy and set it free.

Increase Agility

It's no secret that the world is moving faster than ever, mostly driven by rapid advances in technology and the disruptive innovations flowing from it. Organizations and individuals are responding to this rapid pace of change by becoming more agile—quickly responding to changes in their environment.

The most effective people and organizations? They anticipate change and are ready for it when it arrives.

In her book *The Agility Advantage*, my colleague Amanda Setili explains how organizations of all kinds can become more agile—seeing and capitalizing on new opportunities quickly. Agile leaders do this by looking for innovation from any source, acting quickly on new ideas, and remaining flexible. According to Setili, there are three main components of agility:[2]

1. **Market agility.** "Identify potential opportunities that are being created by market change," explains Setili. In philanthropy, you need to worry less about the "competition" and more about the changing environment and how it hurts or helps the issues you support. This could include keeping an eye on what's happening outside your organization, such as changing government policies (e.g., immigration), demographics (e.g., the aging population), emerging issues (e.g., the opioid crisis), and so on to discover new opportunities.

2. **Decision agility.** "Generate creative alternatives for capitalizing on these opportunities, and make fast, fact-based decisions about which alternatives to pursue" is another piece of Setili's advice. Philanthropy often suffers from options paralysis and lacks clarity about who makes what decisions (e.g., board vs. CEO, CEO vs. management team, the donor dad vs. his adult kids who don't feel they have any influence).

   Further, there are rarely criteria for how decisions are made. Think about it. The people working in most organizations don't know how decisions are supposed to be made. There are no criteria. Does everyone on your team know the criteria for how you make decisions? Chances are, they don't. Most people have never even thought about this.

   The most effective organizations have clearly defined, objective approaches for decision making that are informed by data and not on who has the loudest voice or the highest rank.

3. **Execution agility.** "Enlist and inspire your organization to execute the new direction and adjust course as events unfold," shares Setili. Once you decide what new opportunities to pursue, then you need to move quickly to executing them, learning from what goes right—and what goes wrong—and making course corrections along the way. In Chapter 14, "You Do What It Takes," we dive deep into the execution of your strategy.

Over the next decade, a rapidly growing percentage of all grantmaking will focus on solving problems that do not currently exist today or that we aren't yet aware of. Solving these problems will mean using data that has not yet been collected, applying technologies that have not been created or thought about thus far, and engaging a workforce in jobs that do not currently exist.

To be positioned to identify and tackle tomorrow's problems—and to respond to them in an agile way when they arise—I suggest you ask yourself these five questions:

1. Are we continually scanning the field, community, and environment to notice changes and opportunities?
2. In what ways do we regularly expose ourselves to new ideas and thinking, especially outside of philanthropy?
3. Do we routinely review our human capital and leadership and make strategic investments in their development?
4. Do we intentionally stay abreast of technology and identify ways to leverage it?
5. Do we ask ourselves how can we begin, today, to create our future?

We don't need to be able to look into a crystal ball to respond with agility. But it does help to determine what could be likely to happen, what we envision with respect to those anticipated events, and what we can do now to prepare ourselves to respond quickly.

Be Adaptive

In addition to being agile, effective philanthropists must also be adaptive. What's the difference, you ask?

Agile means you see and capitalize on new opportunities quickly. *Adaptive* means you are consistently able to change yourself to accommodate and maximize the benefits of change (change that might be happening around you or within you).[3]

Agility is proactive—you are searching for new opportunities and potential threats, so that you can take advantage or navigate around them. Being adaptive is reactive—when change happens, you can change yourself and your approach in response.

You want to be both.

Everyone relies on standard ways of doing things—from getting kids out the door to school or making the next big grant, we all need processes and systems that help us remember what's next, what's to be expected, and how to move forward. But sometimes things change, and we need to be able to change as well to accommodate a new short-term situation or a new long-term reality.

In 2017, I was working with Community Foundation Sonoma County to revise its business model when tragic and devastating wildfires engulfed the area. The fires burned more than 36,000 acres, destroyed more than 5,300 homes and 126 businesses, caused the deaths of 24 people, and resulted in an estimated $13 billion in damage. After the fire hit, Community Foundation Sonoma County adapted quickly. It set aside its business model project and put its full focus on providing support to the survivors of the conflagration.

Within days, the foundation established the Sonoma County Resilience Fund, specifically designed to address the community's mid- to long-term recovery needs, including helping individuals impacted by the fires, healing the long-term effects of trauma, and providing housing solutions to the community.[4] Within a year, the fund had raised $15 million from more than 7,500 donations.[5]

What impresses me most about the foundation, and its visionary CEO Beth Brown, was not just that it quickly sprang into action in response to a crisis. It also immediately adapted *how* it gave and *how* it operates.

Supporting disaster recovery of this magnitude required bolder, faster, and more innovative grantmaking. It also meant adapting to changing circumstances by creating new partnerships. "Several of our most significant fire recovery grants have been to collaborative organizations that did not exist before the fires and were formed to meet the new needs of our community," explained Brown.[6]

The foundation also recognized that while the fire itself did not discriminate (people from all socioeconomic backgrounds were impacted), the recovery certainly did. For example, the home of Jean Schulz, widow of "Peanuts" creator Charles Schulz and one of the foundation's founders, burned to the ground,[7] as did the homes of undocumented immigrant workers employed by the region's vineyards, hotels, and restaurants. But those who were most vulnerable before the fire have the greatest challenges recovering. People with resources can recover faster, while others are left behind. In fact, research shows that natural disasters increase income inequality by race.[8] The foundation adapted to this reality by applying an equity lens to all its disaster recovery grantmaking.[9]

And remember when I said the foundation was exploring its business model when the fires struck? Part of that exploration included reimagining the role of foundation as a community leader (not just a community grantmaker). Within weeks of the fire, the foundation *became* that community leader. It adapted to its dramatically changed environment by stepping into its new business model—its leadership role—before the model had even been finalized! It did this because it had to. And it did this because the foundation—its leadership, staff, and board—were willing to adapt quickly to meet the needs of its community.

"Our response to the wildfires showed us who we are in a crisis, as well as a glimpse of the type of foundation we can become. We decided to incorporate this experience—of being bigger and bolder in our fundraising, grantmaking, and community leadership—into our business model rather than consider it a one-time experience," explained Brown.[10]

Many philanthropists frequently assume their processes are best and fail to adapt quickly to needs presented by their grantees or communities.

We all fall into this trap. Instead, we should be ready to recognize and adapt when changes are warranted. Ask yourself:

- How can you quickly get money out the door to help a grantee respond to a crisis situation, rather than requiring them to fill out a full proposal and wait for the next quarterly board meeting to approve a grant? Some foundations keep discretionary grant budgets or have expedited approval processes just for this purpose.
- Are you looking under your own hood to identify what is not working, and quickly shedding it so that you can double down your resources on what's most impactful?
- Can you continuously scan your community to identify emerging trends, and then adapt your grantmaking strategies accordingly?

Your immediate answers to these questions could be, "I'm not sure . . . ." But that doesn't mean you don't have it in you to be more adaptive. Imagine a situation that would truly light a fire of adaptability under you. (For many funders in the United States, President Donald Trump's election caused a rapid adaptation into a new world of funding policy advocacy and organizing.)

What would you need to do to adapt to that reality? And what can you do now to bring that adaptability into your current work?

Increase Innovation

As I pointed out in the introduction to this chapter, what got you here won't necessarily get you there. This means that you and your organization need to constantly innovate to continue to achieve your goals.

What I typically see is that funders want to fund innovative projects, but it doesn't occur to them that they can generate their own innovations.

Does this sound familiar?

You want to fund innovative leaders, innovative programs, and innovative ideas. You put the onus for innovation on other people. Especially your grantees. And while that's all well and good, it's not enough. As a philanthropist, you can and should be innovating—regularly generating your own innovative ideas.

Yes, you!

We're all born with the innovation gene. It's something that we can draw on at any time. It's easier than we think, and it gets stronger the more we practice it. Don't just fund innovation, *be* innovative.

The CEO of a private foundation once told me they were looking for "innovative" ideas to fund. It made sense, except for the fact that no one could define what they meant by innovative. Fast-forward 20 years and "innovation" remains a ubiquitous buzzword throughout the global philanthropic sector.

While noble, funders' insistence on funding innovation brings up problems. Few philanthropists have defined what they mean by innovation. And if you haven't defined it, it is difficult to communicate this expectation to grant seekers. The expectation for innovation is almost always on the grantees. Philanthropists rarely expect themselves to be innovative. In many cases, I am sure that thought never crosses their minds. And what's worse is that funders give little to no thought about *how* they expect grantees to be innovative. Most efforts to build nonprofit capacity, for instance, don't include building innovation capacity.

Lacking a clear definition of innovation or an understanding of how to build one's innovation muscle, the implied assumptions are that innovation "just happens." Further, lack of clear definition has come to imply that innovation must be a dramatic, game-changing, disruptive new idea or practice: the iPhone of early childhood education, the Uber of economic development. The expectations for innovation are so high that most people naturally feel intimidated, not realizing that they, too, can create innovations and that innovation is not the exclusive domain of those who are smarter or more creative.

The reality is the opposite. Most people, in a supportive environment and with proper supervision, can generate, vet, test, and implement innovative ideas. You can, too.

One of my favorite thinkers on innovation is Alan Weiss, coauthor of *The Innovation Formula* (with Michael Robert). I appreciate and use Weiss and Robert's definition of innovation simply as "applied creativity."[11] To generate an innovation, you can't just be creative, you need to also apply that creativity in useful ways.

They identified four key conditions that are necessary to support innovation in organizations and a four-step process that leaders can follow to help innovation flourish. These can be applied to any organization or philanthropist. They apply to you, too.

The four key conditions include:

- Top leaders—especially the donor or CEO—serve as champions for innovation.
- The organization believes that everyone (from the billionaire donor to the assistant) can generate innovations.
- The organization is willing to regularly identify, test, pilot, and implement innovative ideas.
- The organization adheres to prudent risk tolerance (not every innovative idea is worth pursuing).

Once these four conditions are in place, there are four steps that any philanthropist—including you—can take to generate innovations. It is critical that these steps not be one-off activities but that they are conducted regularly, over time. The practice of innovation should become a regular way of doing business at your donor-advised fund, corporate giving program, or family office, in much the same way that monthly financial reporting, annual performance reviews, and periodic strategy development are part of the ongoing routine. The four steps are:

1. **Regularly search for innovative ideas.** There are many sources of innovation that you and your team can review and discuss to generate ideas. These could include unexpected successes (outstanding evaluation results from a grantee, a recent policy win), unexpected failures (high school graduation rates declining

despite significant investments to improve them), unexpected events (a natural disaster), process weakness (your grantee survey identified dissatisfaction with your application process), changes in industry (government crackdowns on civil society organizations, digital revolutions), or changes in demographics (influx of migrants into the country, China's shrinking population).

The goal is to search for changes that can produce opportunities. Funders can feed group discussions with questions that help mine opportunities, such as: Have any unanticipated internal or external events occurred recently? Where are others scaling their efforts? What technologies are changing? How are demographics changing in our region?

With the raw material generated from these discussions, funders can then ask themselves: What specific opportunities or ideas can we develop from these changes, challenges, and successes? What new approaches, products, or services can we create to take advantage of these opportunities or to address these needs?

2. **Assess innovative ideas.** Once a funder has identified possibilities for innovation, the next step is to assess them against these four criteria:

   - Cost—What investment will this require in terms of grants, staff, outside expertise, new technology, etc.? What are the potential risks?
   - Benefit—What are the benefits, do they outweigh the risks, and how long until we achieve results?
   - Strategic fit—Does this opportunity fit with and advance our mission and strategy? Or would it take us off course?
   - Implementation—What are the processes and approaches we'll need to make this work?

   Assessing the opportunities against these four criteria will reveal the innovative opportunities with the highest potential to succeed.

3. **Develop the innovation.** Intentionally taking time (in terms of weeks, not years) to develop an innovation can help to prepare your philanthropy to implement it. It can also surface any additional challenges with the innovation idea (or possibly eliminate it from further consideration). This involves evaluating the opportunity,

assessing pros and cons, creating best- and worst-case scenarios—and the critical factors that lead to each—and identifying risks and rewards. If the development process indicates that an innovation is worth pursuing, it's time to move to implementation.

4. **Implement the innovation.** This step involves formulating an implementation plan and beginning to act on it. A funder should identify the factors and actions that will support the implementation, as well as those that will work against it (and what it can do about them). It also involves creating a detailed action plan for implementation, which includes identifying activities, deadlines, and responsible parties.

Innovation can take many forms, depending on the community, the foundation, and the opportunities at hand. But perhaps the most inspiring aspect of innovation is that one innovative action often breeds another, and then another. In fact, the only limits to innovation are the ones we place on ourselves.

Intentionally Learn and Improve

Philanthropists (whether a couple, a giving circle, or a corporate giving program) need to intentionally learn from their experience and make course corrections along the way. It's part and parcel of reducing unnecessary steps while being agile, adaptive, and innovative.

Learning isn't hard to do, but it must be intentional, documented, discussed within your team, and it must lead to decision making. It can't simply exist inside your head. One of our clients asks themselves, "What will make or break this grant?" when deciding whether to recommend a significant grant to their board. They are clear on the risks involved and what needs to happen to make the grant successful. The answer is documented in the staff summary of the grant. Six to nine months later, like clockwork, they revisit the grant during program team meetings to assess progress on that risk and identify ways they can help ensure success. That is intentional learning.

Chances are, you already have many kinds of information available to you that can inform your learning: grantee reports; grantee convenings; evaluations; dashboards; your understanding of changing conditions; and the observations and knowledge of your staff, trustees, consultants, and grantees. You could also seek new insights at minimal cost by conducting an online survey, convening all your stakeholders, soliciting outside perspectives, or simply asking questions.

Here are 12 "learning questions" I share with my clients that you can regularly ask yourselves and your partners:

1. What are the top three things we have learned about our strategy thus far?
2. If we could do it all over again, what would we do differently?
3. What has surprised us? What are we seeing that is different from what we originally expected?
4. What progress are we making on our strategy overall?
5. What progress have we made on each of our short-term and long-term outcomes?
6. What are some of the early accomplishments/wins?
7. What has been the most challenging?
8. Are there areas where we have not yet made much progress? Why?
9. What are the current conditions now compared to when we launched this effort, and what impact has that had (or will it have) on the work?
10. Have we made modifications or improvements to any aspect of our strategy, approach, or funding since this strategy was created (or since we started working at the foundation)? Has that helped?
11. At this time, do we anticipate making any modifications or improvements? If so, what are they? When will we make that decision?
12. What opportunities do we see with this strategy going forward?

The Saint Luke's Foundation in Cleveland followed this approach to update their board and inform strategy development. The board wanted to know what staff had learned in each of three new program areas that had been created three years prior, including what progress had been made and whether they should continue the same course of funding or make course corrections.

Rather than invest significant time and resources in conducting evaluations or environmental scans in each of these areas, they asked themselves the questions above, summarized their key insights, discussed them within their team, and shared them with their board, all within a few months' time. The board was thrilled—it provided them with timely information they needed to make decisions about strategy and direction.

Make a commitment to truly become a learning organization. To become intentional learners, you must:

- Commit to learning as a part of your goals and day-to-day duties.
- Document and share what you learn.
- Discuss what you learn with your entire team.
- Use what you've learned to make decisions.
- Apply what you've learned to your work.

You'll want to incorporate continuous learning into your everyday, ongoing work.

Let me stop you for a moment to emphasize this point. You don't need to retain a consultant or hire a Chief Learning Officer to intentionally learn and improve. You need to do it. And the best way to do it is to embed it in your everyday work. Engaging in intentional learning is incredibly habit forming, and fortunately it's a habit you can easily maintain. Plan for a few simple, ongoing activities, like convening a group of grantees once a quarter.

Let me show you how easy this can be. David Siegel, executive director of the Bee Vradenburg Foundation in Colorado Springs, Colorado, makes it a point to take a city council member to lunch regularly. The lunch meetings have no formal agenda, only to learn from each other. Bill Young, executive director of the Alice Virginia and David W. Fletcher Foundation in Hagerstown, Maryland, took a unique approach. He didn't just meet with local nonprofit leaders to understand his community. He walked every single street throughout his city.

You can also make learning part of your staff's work plans and even have them create their own individual learning agendas, for which you'll hold them accountable.

In addition, it pays to remember that learning should always be a two-way street. You can't expect others to open up and be honest with you if you aren't also forthcoming and open in sharing with them. This doesn't mean you need to air dirty laundry, but it does mean you should be clear that you don't have all the answers, be honest about where you have questions, and be open to where you'd like to improve your own knowledge or capacity.

Learning should not be confined to inside the confines of your philanthropy. Collective learning among philanthropists and across sectors is equally important. The Wellcome Trust, Cloudera Foundation, and Omidyar Network realized this when they collaborated with Nesta, a UK-based innovation foundation, to support collective intelligence. Collective intelligence is "something that is created when people work together, often with the help of technology, to mobilize a wider range of information, ideas and insights to address a challenge."[12] Ideas funded through this collaborative approach include testing whether algorithms modeled on how fish and bees swarm could help create consensus among people in conflict, and how machine learning might translate unstructured online discussions to meaningful policy proposals.

As human beings, we are hardwired to learn. It's in our nature. And as we begin to learn more about and with our communities, apply what we've learned to new solutions, and share what we've learned with others, we'll begin to see deep and lasting changes in our communities and our world.

Notes

1. https://theleanway.net/muda-mura-muri.
2. Amanda Setili, *The Agility Advantage: How to Identify and Act on Opportunities in a Fast-Changing World* (San Francisco: Jossey-Bass, 2014).

3. https://www.linkedin.com/pulse/agile-adaptable-adaptive-which-organisation-do-you-kate-christiansen/.
4. http://www.sonomacf.org/sonoma-county-resilience-fund/.
5. Ibid.
6. Email correspondence with Beth Brown, September 30, 2019.
7. https://www.washingtonpost.com/news/comic-riffs/wp/2017/10/13/peanuts-creator-charles-schulzs-home-burns-down-in-santa-rosa-fire/.
8. https://www.eurekalert.org/pub_releases/2018-08/ru-ndw082018.php.
9. http://www.sonomacf.org/sonoma-county-resilience-fund/.
10. Email correspondence with Beth Brown, September 30, 2019.
11. https://www.amazon.com/Innovation-Formula-Organizations-Opportunity-Strategist/dp/0887304001.
12. https://www.nesta.org.uk/blog/new-500k-collective-intelligence-experimentation-fund/.

13 | You Found Your North Star

I've spoken with thousands of philanthropists just like you, and one thing is for sure: You don't want to dillydally. While you might enjoy a bit of wandering through Europe on vacation, you don't want to wander through your philanthropy. With your giving, you'd like clarity. You want to know what you want to accomplish, and the best way to do it.

To do that, you need a strategy.

Unfortunately, too few philanthropists have one. They don't know their North Star.

The good news is that formulating your strategy is easier than you might think. Having one will bring you clarity, guide your decision making, save you time, help you take risks, and increase your impact. Guess what else? It's your secret weapon for demolishing delusional altruism.

Let's take a close look at strategy, specifically how to most effectively develop it—quickly and with a minimum of friction—and then communicate it to your stakeholders.

What Is Strategy and Why Is It So Important?

So, what exactly is strategy, and why should you care?

As we learned in Chapter 6, "You Are Fooled by Your Own Efforts," *strategy* is a framework within which decisions are made that influence the nature and direction of the enterprise. It's a *tool* that helps you make decisions that are congruent with where you as an individual or you as an organization (for example, family office, donor-advised fund, foundation, or philanthropy association) want your philanthropy to go. It provides the guardrails that will help you decide where to direct your funds and your efforts.

For example, if your strategy is to empower ordinary citizens in India to understand the legal system and stand up for their rights, as journalist, philanthropist, and Giving Pledge signatory Rohini Nilekani's is, you know that developing an online portal that provides reliable information about India's laws using simple language is a great use of funds.[1] Other things a philanthropist could fund, like building schools and increasing access to health care, are not. While important, they don't help you advance your strategy.

There are two parts to strategy: strategy *formulation* (developing your strategy) and strategy *implementation* (executing your strategy). You've got to have both parts for your strategy to succeed. Too often, I've found, philanthropists lump them both into a single, lengthy, cumbersome "strategic planning process." It's far better to separate strategy formulation from its implementation.

Let's dive deeper into the formulation side of the strategy equation.

Strategy Formulation

To formulate your strategy, you first need clarity on a few other things:

- **Mission:** Why you exist. Your reason for being, or raison d'être.
- **Values:** The beliefs that guide organizational thinking and actions and define organizational culture.

- **Vision:** Your picture of the future. This is determined by your mission and values.
- **Culture:** That set of beliefs which govern behavior.

The Need for Shared Values in Family Foundations

Early in my career I didn't understand the value of values. I had seen too many inspirational values statements hung on office walls that everyone ignored. You know, those motivational posters that boldly proclaim "Courage" and feature a lion.

But then I started to see philanthropists who lived by their values. I saw how living and breathing their values transformed their giving and themselves. I also saw how a lack of agreed-upon values could derail philanthropy.

Joanne Florino, vice president of philanthropic services at the Philanthropy Roundtable and a former family foundation executive, believes agreement upon shared values is foundational for effective family foundations. She's seen how lack of shared values can split family foundations apart. "Family members don't always agree with each other or even get along! But if they want to come together around their family philanthropy, they need to have the hard conversations about values. Often, this requires bringing in objective, outside expertise, such as consultants and facilitators."

The role of strategy is to take the present state of your philanthropy and move it to your desired future state, ideally as quickly as possible.

To formulate your strategy, you identify your desired future state (e.g., the change you want to see in your community, the type of philanthropist you want to become). This is informed by your mission, vision, and values. It's also informed by data, such as demographic trends, needs assessments, and the perspectives of those you are seeking to help.

How do you identify your desired future state? You ask yourselves questions such as:

- What is the impact we want to have on our community? The world?
- What are the relationships we want to have with each other and our community?
- What do we want to look like, sound like, feel like, smell like a year from now?
- If we could achieve our ideal outcome, what would it be?

To implement your strategy, you figure out how to get from where you are today (your current state) to where you want to be (your desired future state). This includes aligning your people (e.g., you, your board, staff), your structures (the way people are put together), and your processes (the way people interact). We'll talk more about strategy implementation in Chapter 14, "You Do What It Takes."

If the role of strategy is to move you from your current state to your desired future, it needs to be part of your every day. At every meeting, with every decision, for every employee performance review, strategy should be on the table. It should set the parameters. Remember, strategy is a framework (or a tool) that helps you made decisions congruent with where you want to go.

The Vadon Foundation in Seattle knows about this need for strategy. The foundation started out by giving to a variety of local causes. It was a conventional, responsive grantmaker. But in 2018 it changed.

How?

It formulated a strategy. Its strategy—and the entire purpose of the foundation—is now squarely focused on sustaining healthy, thriving indigenous nations in perpetuity. The foundation looks to "fund programs working to ensure that every successive generation of indigenous people and culture will face an increasingly brighter future of healthy self-determination, autonomy, evolution, and sustainability."[2]

How did this happen? The foundation was created by tech entrepreneur Mark Vadon. Vadon founded online jewelry retailer Blue Nile and cofounded online retailer Zulily. Zulily was acquired by home-shopping giant QVC for $2.4 billion. Vadon started his philanthropic journey like most billionaire entrepreneur-turned-philan-thropists do: He genuinely wanted to give back. So he began supporting local causes as needs presented themselves.

But along the way he learned a lot from his Stanford Business School friend (and now the executive director of the foundation), Dave LaSarte-Meeks. LaSarte-Meeks grew up on the Coeur d'Alene Indian reservation in northwestern Idaho. He returned as a professional, working for tribal nonprofits and legal organizations and running a tribal casino.

Together, Vadon and LaSarte-Meeks realized that very few phil-anthropic dollars are directed to indigenous communities. They also understood the importance of supporting grassroots efforts to train new fluent speakers of native languages.

"We've been talking to communities about a range of issues, whether it's unemployment, high school dropout rates, substance abuse, and vio-lence in communities. A lot of people bring it back to the destruction of their culture, which goes back to U.S. programs to eradicate native languages and force tribes to assimilate. Sure, it's an indirect and oblique approach, and for people outside the community, it feels odd. But a lot of this goes back to families being broken down generationally and tearing at the fabric of communities," explained LaSarte-Meeks in an interview with *Inside Philanthropy*.[3]

Vadon wasn't satisfied reactively writing checks when people approached him for funding. He wanted to use his resources to achieve maximum impact for multiple generations in indigenous communities. To do that, he needed a strategy. And for Vadon, his strategy is rooted in his belief that "developing and supporting visionary changemakers within native communities provides the most proven path for fostering long-term progress."[4]

Strategic Sprint

In my experience, individuals and organizations alike spend far too much time on formulating strategy—up to a year, and sometimes more—when a much shorter process will actually work better in almost every case. I have two approaches for speedy strategy formulation that I use with my own clients. I call these approaches "strategic sprints" because they are specifically designed to move through the process much more quickly—and ultimately more effectively—than many funders are used to.

The strategic sprints are of roughly two different durations:

- Seven-week strategy formulation
- Seven-hour strategy formulation

Yes, that's right. Seven weeks or seven hours. Which one you'll pick depends a lot on the size of your organization, the amount of funds and other support you plan to disburse, how much knowledge you already have about the issues and communities you want to work with, the dynamics of your team, and your own experience in formulating strategy.

Here's a quick summary of how each strategic sprint is laid out:

Seven-Week Strategy Formulation

I have a few different approaches to seven-week strategy formulation that I use with my clients. Here is one that breaks the process into three distinct phases. Keep in mind that you can shorten or lengthen each of these phases to suit your individual requirements—these schedules are not fixed in concrete.

- **Weeks 1–3: Information gathering.** This includes the *what* (e.g., What you want to learn? What information must inform your strategy?), the *how* (What is the best way to learn it? Interviews with board, staff, grantees, experts; reviewing existing data; conducting focus groups), and the *who* (who gathers the information: staff, a consultant, etc.).
- **Weeks 4–5: Summarize and share.** It's here that you'll identify key themes, surface concerns, and opportunities; identify potential scenarios or recommendations; and summarize your findings in a brief document to share with decision makers, along with key materials and an agenda.

- **Weeks 6–7: Strategy retreat and progress check.** The retreat is where you will share themes, establish your plan and gain alignment, identify critical issues, determine top priorities, and assign "accountability champions." A week later, accountability champions give progress updates on critical issues and priorities. The retreat might cover any of these topics (and more!):
  - Values, mission, and vision
  - Review of key findings from research to inform planning
  - Where the philanthropist/organization is aligned and achieving goals
  - Where the philanthropist/organization is misaligned and falling short
  - Driving forces, key issues, and opportunities
  - How you want to be viewed in the next three years
  - Growth options (assets, grantmaking, learning, capacity, talent, etc.)
  - Agreements on core strategic direction
  - Appropriate roles for board and staff in setting and implementing strategy

We always end by identifying critical issues that need to be addressed, determining top implementation priorities, and assigning accountabilities. In advance of a strategy formulation retreat, I send out some homework assignments, usually consisting of four or five questions for people to think about. Here are a few of my favorites:

- What are your biggest opportunities for growth or impact?
- What should be abandoned?
- What do you think is the driving force of your philanthropy/organization/company?

Seven-Hour Strategy Formulation

This approach is much simpler and less complex than the seven-week strategy formulation above, which makes it perfect for the solo philanthropist, team, or small funding organization. It also works well as an annual strategy "refresh" for groups of any size. Depending on your needs and starting point, formulating your strategy in one day might involve asking and answering the following questions:

- What is your philanthropy's driving force?
- What is your ideal future state in terms of impact, grantees, growth, innovation, reputation, governance, talent, operations, and so forth (whichever categories are most important to you)?
- Where are you now in each of these categories?
- What will it take for you to make dramatic progress toward those goals or to sustain where you are? What factors would improve multiples of these (e.g., making dramatic improvement in your talent might also improve operations and reputation)?
- What are your top priorities?
- What critical issues must be resolved (or your strategy will fail)?
- Who has accountability for what and by what deadline?

Flexibility in Your Sprints

I know what you might be thinking. "We're too complex, we could never do this in seven weeks, much less seven hours!" First, give it a whirl. Try it out. Or at least, take whatever amount of time you think it should take, and cut that in half. Think of "seven weeks" as a metaphor for speed if it makes you feel better. Remember, your goal is to increase your speed to impact.

Second, don't get caught up in the number. Does it matter if it takes you seven weeks or seventeen weeks? Seven hours or seven days? No. I simply want to let you know that it's possible to set strategy quickly.

Don't Leave Home without It

Remember: Strategy should be ever present. It's a tool you should utilize every day. It's a framework that should inform every conversation. It is not a set-it-and-forget-it piece of paper to file away in your office drawer. Too often funders forget this!

Recently, for instance, I was speaking to members of a large foundation and I was told that while their board members and executive leaders have been tinkering with a strategic plan for five years, half their staff didn't even know such a plan existed!

For strategy to be a living and breathing thing, you need to refresh it on a regular basis. This builds momentum while ensuring that you're constantly focused on what's most important to you and your organization. There are two key ways to do this:

- **Annual strategy refresh.** In today's ever-changing environment, it's impossible to plan well ten or even five years in advance. Three years ahead can be a challenge, and one year is the most realistic. Unfortunately, philanthropists often find themselves taking close to eighteen months just to create an extensive strategic plan. Rather than doing this every three to five years and making a big hullabaloo out of it, take a few days each year to refresh your strategic plan. This will contribute to your agility and adaptability while helping maintain your momentum.
- **Daily touchpoints.** Strategy should be a part of every meeting, every proposal review, every discussion you have regarding your philanthropy every day of the week. It should be so woven into the fabric of your organization that you naturally refer to it without even thinking.

Strategic Friction

As you can imagine (and as you may have experienced), a variety of obstacles can get in the way, slowing down your efforts at formulating a strategy. These obstacles, impediments, and bumps in the road constitute a kind of strategic friction for you or your organization—slowing you down and perhaps even wearing you out. Some of the sources of this friction can really throw your strategy off course, while others are just minor annoyances along the way. In any case, you'll need to be constantly on the alert and ready to address them when they find their way into your planning efforts.

Here are some of the most common sources of strategic friction no matter what size your organization may be—from solo philanthropist to global operation with offices around the world. As you review each one, take a moment to consider whether it is currently getting in the way of your own strategy formulation and, if so, what you can do to neutralize it. The first step in solving a problem, after all, is recognizing what it is.

Assumptions. You erroneously assume that strategy development is supposed to take a year to do, because it seems to take everyone else a year. In reality, there's nothing that says strategy formulation is supposed to take a year, or six months, or any other fixed amount of time. Put your assumptions aside and try something new. Why not try to set your strategy in a month—or in a week, or even in a day or two? You might be surprised at how quickly you can get the job done when you and your team are fully focused on it.

Excessive data gathering. I find that often, with lengthy strategic planning processes, what's really sucking up a lot of time is lengthy data gathering at the front end. Environmental scans, learning tours, listening sessions, commissioning research, evaluations, focus groups, board self-assessments, and so on. While gathering data, understanding community needs, and identifying best practices is critical, you can't let it get out of hand.

I suggest two things to help ensure that data gathering doesn't slow you down. First, separate "data gathering" from "strategy formulation"—the former should inform the latter. Both don't need to be lumped into one "strategic planning" bucket.

Second, if you are taking the time to continually learn, then you shouldn't have to embark on a one-off data gathering exercise to prepare for strategy formulation. You should be able to quickly and relatively easily gather together information you already have.

Process is the tail that wags the outcome dog. Back to that one-year strategic planning process: You naturally schedule monthly planning meetings that ultimately have little to show for them until you're close to the end—when everything finally comes together in a flurry of activity. Instead of scheduling monthly planning meetings that do little more than fill the space on your calendar for an entire year, why not devote two entire days to the effort? This focused approach is much more efficient than an unfocused approach that extends over a prolonged period of time.

Scheduling. I was once involved in a strategy development process in which the two-day, off-site strategy retreat was postponed for four months simply due to the difficulty of finding a date when all board members, the executive team, and I were able to travel across the country and spend those two days together. This happens—in fact, it's almost expected when you've got the schedules of a lot of busy people to try to coordinate. And it's also why an annual, one-day refresh is better—you can plan for and schedule it a year ahead!

Creating elaborate RFP processes to hire consultants to conduct strategic planning. Let's say you decide that it would be beneficial to hire a consultant to help guide your strategy work. Good idea! But then you spend three months coming up with a detailed RFP that identifies in great detail every single activity you wish the consultant to do (as if you weren't hiring an expert—someone who will bring their own ideas, methodology, and experience to the table). You spend two months obtaining and reviewing proposals, and another month approving the contract. Six months after you started the RFP process, you are finally ready to start developing your strategy. If you had streamlined the process of hiring a consultant in the first place, the whole thing could have been done by then.

Consultants who are paid by the hour. In my experience, the vast majority of consultants are mission-driven, honest, and don't "make work" just to earn higher fees. But it can't be denied that when consultants bill by the hour or day, it's in their own best interest to recommend lengthy, complex processes that ultimately increase billable hours. I know some who do. Be alert to this potential problem, and don't hesitate to talk with your consultant about their chosen approach. Too often people complexify the simple, when we should simplify the complex!

Bells and whistles. There is so much weight put into the idea of a strategic plan that it can be incredibly difficult to muster the courage to pull the trigger and take the first steps toward action. In philanthropy, the strategic plan has become the holy grail of social transformation—we expect compelling and well-written prose, eye-catching infographics, and complex theories of change. In reality, the simpler the plan, the more likely you are to actually get it done—and to succeed in developing strategies that will help you achieve your mission. Don't waste time and money adding all the bells and whistles that look great but don't contribute to the likelihood that you'll actually do what you say you'll do. Leave them on the cutting-room floor.

Even so, there are times when you'll need to go slow to go fast. This includes when you truly have a lot to learn or are just starting out, when you have damage to repair or relationships to rebuild, and when you need a more inclusive process that involves diverse community members and stakeholders in decision making.

In the Vadon Foundation example above, strategic focus on indigenous peoples could not have been developed quickly absent deep knowledge of indigenous communities and ongoing communication with the people they sought to help. You cannot simply declare, "I want to help indigenous peoples," and, with zero understanding of or connection to native communities, formulate a strategy in seven weeks or seven hours! To do so would be irresponsible and likely doom your strategy to failure. But you can certainly declare, "I want to help indigenous communities" and then set yourself on a learning journey to identify the various ways you might do that.

Communicating a New Direction to Your Grantees

After you formulate your strategy, you may find that your priorities have changed—perhaps significantly. Some new grantees may be selected to receive funding and support—bringing exciting new initiatives along with them—while some current grantees may maintain their status for the most part unchanged. However, the strategic planning process may also result in some of your grantees—perhaps some that have been with you for many years—being designated for major funding cuts or let go altogether.

For good reason, there's a phrase that is sure to strike fear in the heart of any grantee: "We're about to start a strategic planning process." A funder undergoing strategic planning often pulls the rug out from under grantees, at least temporarily, while the funder "suspends grant-making" for a few months or even a year to "evaluate priorities and approaches." During that time, grantees might be asked to answer questions about their work, participate in discussion or focus groups, or even (gulp) share their opinions with funders in person. And all the while, the foremost question on a grantee's mind must be, "Will they still continue to fund our organization?"

Although you can do your best to help mitigate grantee angst during a strategic planning process, the work doesn't stop when the final plan is approved. In fact, for grantees that aren't part of your future plan, or that will constitute a much smaller percentage of your grantmaking budget, the work has likely just begun.

For those unlucky grantees that are no longer a priority for you going forward, don't make hearing the bad news an excruciating act akin to ripping a very sticky Band-Aid off your child's arm. Instead, make sure the rollout of your new strategy includes short-term efforts to help your grantees navigate the transition while mitigating the pain. Here are six specific things you can do to help:

> **Communicate your new priorities clearly.** Before sharing your new strategic plan with anyone outside your foundation, be sure to develop a set of clear and consistent messages that communicate and explain these four key points: *Why* you've settled on a new direction, *how* you got there, *when* the change in direction will take effect, and *who* is affected.
>
> **Break the news in person.** Yes, looking a former grantee in the eye and explaining why his organization is no longer a fit for your foundation is uncomfortable, but you are both members of the phil-anthropic community and you owe him that courtesy and respect. This is not a job for email or a text message or (perish the thought) a tweet. If you've created clear messages as I suggested above, your grantee will understand. Not only that but your future strategy may

very well bring them back into the fold, so be sure to treat them with respect—in the same way you would like to be treated yourself.

Spend down gradually. There's no rule that says you have to pull the plug all at once, starting tomorrow. Consider reducing a grantee's allocation incrementally over time—months or a year instead of days—as you simultaneously work to increase your investments elsewhere. This gives outgoing grantees time to plan and prepare, and your new grantees and program staff a chance to grow more intentionally. Remember: Your grantees have bills to pay and mouths to feed too. Be empathetic to their situation.

Provide bridge grants. When I was consulting to the Charles and Helen Schwab Foundation, we used bridge grants—an additional year of core support funding—to help grantees transition to new sources of funding as the foundation drew down its support due to a change in strategic direction. This helped grantees prepare for change mentally and fiscally.

Consider capacity building. If your foundation supported a particular aspect of nonprofit operations, such as leadership development or technology training, consider offering short-term (one-year) grants to help nonprofit staff amp up that capacity internally. Even if you don't have this kind of grant history to build on, consider capacity-building support for fund-development functions—especially since grantees will need the skills to replace the funds they'll no longer receive from you. This has the added bonus of building on your previous investment and building the nonprofit's expertise.

Offer general operating support. General operating support is always welcome and can allow grantees to adjust as they see fit to this new change in their operating environment. Plus, providing operating support with no strings or expectations attached sends the message that, "Even though your work and our strategy no longer align, we still think you're valuable and trust your judgment."

Ending a professional relationship with a grantee can be just as emotionally trying as ending a personal one—sometimes even more so. But using the above strategies can help pave the way for a less painful transition for everyone involved, while smoothing those ruffled feathers that are sure to result when you announce your new direction.

Now that you've formulated your strategy, let's turn our attention to how to implement it.

Notes

1. https://yourstory.com/2016/11/nyaaya.
2. http://vadonfoundation.org/how-to-apply.php.
3. https://www.insidephilanthropy.com/home/2019/3/13/getting-proactive-a-tech-givers-journey-to-more-strategic-giving.
4. http://vadonfoundation.org/how-to-apply.php.

14

You Do What
It Takes

Now that you've formulated your strategy, it's time to implement it. Sounds simple, right? Unfortunately, most philanthropists get stuck in implementation. It turns out that for all the effort that went into developing a strategy, the harder part is getting the darned thing to work!

Implementation problems begin immediately. They show up in the form of unread emails in your inbox, your overscheduled calendar, your old strategy. These problems impede implementation because the worst thing you could do right now, at this very moment, is continue doing everything the way you were doing it before.

Right now, you need to change how you allocate your time, resources, and brainpower to achieve your new strategy. Your new priorities need to bump out your old priorities. And if bumping them doesn't work, you need to give your old priorities a beat down.

Luckily, you are undaunted! When it comes to implementing, you're ready to do what it takes.

I'd like to share with you a process for implementing anything quickly. It starts with only four steps, and it's stunningly simple. You can use it to implement your new organizational strategy or your weight loss goals.

As I share these four steps, I'd like to tell you a story about the Kate B. Reynolds Charitable Trust in Winston-Salem, North Carolina, a private foundation that awards approximately $24 million in grants annually. In 2018, the Trust profoundly changed its strategy to focus on measurable outcomes rather than issues, in order to have a greater impact on the people they serve. "We knew it was time to update our founder's vision into the modern context of rapid change and growing inequities," said Laura Gerald, MD, president of the Trust.[1]

The Trust's staff and leadership immediately began implementing their new strategy. While work was under way on many fronts, these four steps significantly accelerated strategy implementation. I think you will see a lot of yourself in their experience.

Step 1: Identify Your Top Priorities

Your first step in implementing anything is to determine what's most important. What are your top priorities for implementation? It doesn't matter if you are trying to implement a new strategic plan or a kitchen remodel; you need to prioritize. Yet most philanthropists forget this important first step.

Your top priorities are the most important things that need to happen next, in order to implement your strategy. I'm talking about the top priorities for your *entire enterprise* (whether you are a donor-advised fund, a philanthropy association, or a married couple). I do not mean each individual's own priorities. If you don't have clarity about your top *enterprise-wide* implementation priorities, your strategy either won't be achieved or it will take three times as long. It's that simple.

You might think since your entire team was involved in strategic planning, they certainly will know what's most important to do next.

Right? Wrong. Don't assume everyone knows the top enterprise-wide priorities.

Here's a little trick to find out if your team is on the same page:

Ask them.

After I began advising the Kate B. Reynolds Charitable Trust's president, Dr. Laura Gerald, and her leadership team on strategy implementation, one of the first things I did was interview staff members. I simply asked, "What are the top three priorities for implementing the new strategy?"

Guess what? I heard 23 different answers! Not 3, not 5—23!

Don't be surprised. In fact, it is quite common across any type of organization or industry. When your new strategy is a significant departure from your old one, it feels like there are a zillion things to do. Further, we all view strategy through our own lens and how it impacts our work. Naturally, each staff person had their own spin on what seemed "most" important.

But you can't focus on a zillion things at once. You can't even focus on 23 things at once. You need to pick your top implementation priorities. The most important things that need to happen *next*.

If your team isn't all on the same page, how do you determine those top priorities? It depends in part on how you make decisions typically. Does the CEO decide? Do you strive for consensus? It's probably a little bit of both.

There might be a natural leader—the donor, the CEO, the parents—in your philanthropy whose opinion weighs more heavily. When my husband and I had a goal of buying a new house, we identified our top priorities: A house large enough to accommodate our growing family and two home-based businesses, proximity to Lake Erie, and a home that was "move-in ready." My 11-year old stepson, however, had his own priority. He didn't care which house we bought as long as it had a basketball hoop! Every time we visited a potential home, his opinion was decided the moment we pulled in the driveway. "This one's great, it has a basketball hoop!" "No hoop, we can't live here." Needless to say, as the parents who were paying for the house, our priorities were the ones we focused on (although we assured him we could address his priority in the near future).

At the same time, if you want everyone to be involved in *implementing* your top priorities, it's a good idea to involve them in *determining* the priorities. Buy-in is helpful. At the Trust, we brought the implementation team together for the afternoon. We reviewed the list of 23 priorities and agreed it was far too many. Dr. Gerald shared what she felt was most important, and after a facilitated discussion we landed on these initial priorities: revise and clarify strategic thinking in the Trust's two overarching program areas and its two special initiatives; and implement a communications plan, including a new website, messaging, and community events to clearly communicate the new strategic direction.

These weren't the only things that needed to happen. These were the *most important* things that needed to happen *next* to shift this organization 180 degrees from being a grantmaker organized around focus areas to one focused on outcomes.

Once you've identified your top priorities, you need to tell everyone. Every single person at every level of your philanthropy, be it program officers, family members, your wealth advisor, or the receptionist, need to know the top implementation priorities. Write them down and post copies in the conference room, in the hallways, and on the internal web portal. Everyone needs to keep these priorities top of mind, because everyone has a role to play.

The Trust did this. At first, they simply took that same easel paper from our discussion and brought it to their next staff meeting. At that meeting they shared the top implementation priorities with all staff and described why they were important and who was accountable for them. At subsequent staff meetings, the priorities were listed at the top of agendas and in a shared online tool, and progress in achieving them was always discussed. Trust leadership also explained that while certain people were accountable for each priority, everyone in the organization had a role to play in achieving them.

Keep in mind that identifying top priorities is not a one-and-done exercise. The point is to tackle them *first*. Once you do, new priorities will emerge. The Trust did this. As its initial three priorities were handled, new ones emerged. These new priorities were also identified, shared with everyone, and assigned people accountable for them. This ongoing process accelerates momentum and your speed to impact.

In addition to identifying top priorities, funders must also resolve any critical issues they identified while formulating your strategy. As I mentioned in Chapter 13, "You Found Your North Star," critical issues are simply any issue that must be resolved or your strategy will fail.

Step 2: Hold Everyone Accountable

Now that everyone knows your top implementation priorities, step two is to hold people accountable for achieving them. To do this, you must assign "priority champions." For each priority, pick a person who will be accountable for achieving it. This person does not need to do everything, but they need to make sure a specific priority is achieved, and they need to be held accountable.

Ask priority champions to create a list of the top 5–10 most important things that need to happen next for their priority. For each item, add a deadline. Keep it simple. You don't need a full-blown work plan or Gantt chart! In fact, at this stage such a complex plan would be unrealistic and slow things down. You want a list of the most important activities and a deadline for each.

For example, if your strategy involves increasing girls' access to education in Africa, your top 5–10 activities might include:

1. Identify other funders who are funding girls' access to education in Africa, to learn from them. Start with reviewing members of the Africa Grantmakers Affinity Group. (1 week)
2. Schedule calls to talk with each funder to better understand the funding landscape. (2 weeks)
3. Spend one month researching this topic to understand needs and best practices. (4 weeks)
4. Identify and talk with potential intermediary organizations that can facilitate international grantmaking. (4 weeks)

5. Determine if and how to narrow our focus, such as by focusing on certain regions or countries, types of educational needs, or grade levels. (8 weeks)
6. Create a list of potential grantees. (8 weeks)
7. Determine an annual grantmaking budget. (12 weeks)
8. Develop funding guidelines. (14 weeks)

Priority champions don't need to do all these things, but they need to make sure they get done. Remember when I said everyone has a role to play? Now is the time to identify others who can help the priority champion tackle this to-do list. For example, your financial advisor can forecast funding. A program associate can assist with research. Someone else might develop communications messages to convey your new funding priority, and your receptionist can be trained to convey them.

Nora Ferrell, the Kate B. Reynolds Charitable Trust's director of communications and the leader tasked with overseeing and accelerating strategy implementation, identified 11 different "work streams" that needed to be accomplished within the priorities. These were things like "Organize community engagement events" and "Change the grantmaking process and timeline." She worked with the priority champions to identify the lead person for each work stream, appropriate staff to join the teams, and goals for each work stream. She also met with each lead and tasked them with convening their teams to come up with action plans to get the work done.

This organization of work streams and staff proved critical. The magnitude of change involved in shifting an organization's strategy 180 degrees cannot be understated! There were a tremendous number of programmatic, operational, evaluation, and communications issues that needed to be understood, tackled, and implemented by staff. They also needed to be coordinated across departments to eliminate silos.

Step 2 is also a good time to identify supporters and resisters. Strategy implementation involves change. Some on your team will enthusiastically embrace the change. Harness their enthusiasm and engage their leadership. Some will resist. Help them see how it's in their self-interest to get on board. Sometimes your strongest resisters can become your staunchest allies.

Next, ask priority champions to regularly share progress with everyone. I suggest that this occur at least biweekly to start, perhaps monthly after implementation is in full swing. If you have employees, staff meetings are a great place to do this. If it's you and your wife, schedule times when you can sit down together and share updates. Put these dates on your calendar. Priority champions should bring their Top 10 lists and update everyone on progress. That holds them accountable and lets your team troubleshoot and solve problems together. As some activities are accomplished, add new ones to the list.

Step 3: Change Your Ways

You've accomplished a lot in your life. Today you are in the marvelous position to help others, either by giving your own financial resources or as a professional grantmaker, stewarding the resources of other philanthropists. However, the skills, experience, talent, and smart thinking that got you here might not be what you need to reach your desired future. As best-selling author and world-renowned executive coach Marshall Goldsmith succinctly states, "What got you here won't get you there."

In my experience, there are three things you will need to change to achieve whatever goals you've set for yourself: How you spend your time, your people, and your systems and processes. All of them need to be aligned to implement your strategy.

Your Time

Your new top priorities should be reflected in your schedule and how you spend your time. Block out time in your calendar to work on them, even if it's only an hour a day to start. It may seem simple and obvious, but if you don't make this change in how you spend your time, you will fail at implementation.

Let's assume you are the priority champion for determining how your family office will evaluate the impact of your philanthropy. You've identified the most important 5–10 activities you need to do next. Those activities should show up in your calendar! And even if you aren't sure what those activities are, block out time over the next few months and call it "Work on top priority." During the first block of time, pick one of your activities and make progress on it.

Guess what else you have to do? Get rid of all that other stuff that's sucking up your time! Before you developed your new strategy, your calendar was rapidly filling up with a whole bunch of other stuff. Perhaps they were activities to implement your old strategy. But chances are it's just a lot of stuff. Grantee events you felt obligated to attend, conferences that sounded interesting when you signed up last year, and people who want to meet with you to "catch up." Chances are, 75% of what's scheduled in the coming months has nothing to do with your new implementation priorities. You need to change that, immediately.

You do this by printing out your calendar for the next 3–6 months. Review every call, meeting, and scheduled activity and ruthlessly ask yourself: Will this help me implement my strategy? Will it help me achieve my top priorities? If the answer is "No," circle it.

Then take all those circled activities and determine whether they are otherwise mandatory (e.g., tax audit), are important personal priorities (e.g., attending your son's hip-hop dance performance), or whether canceling them will cause more problems than it solves (e.g., dinner with your board chair and her spouse). If so, mark an X through them (they stay on your calendar). What should remain circled are all the calendar activities that are not advancing your top strategic priorities, are not mandatory, are not personal priorities, and that won't cause you more headaches if you eliminated them.

Now, eliminate, delegate, or dramatically shorten these remaining items. For example, you've been attending meetings for a new funding collaborative to reduce lead poisoning, but now that you've decided on a strategy to increase the pipeline of leaders of color in the nonprofit sector, you can politely stop attending those meetings (eliminate). You've enjoyed updating your website, but now that strategic communications are a top priority to implement your strategy, it's time to retain a communications firm (delegate). And just about any meeting on your calendar could be shortened by half (shorten).

About six months into strategy implementation at the Kate B. Reynolds Charitable Trust, the president's emerging priority was recruiting top talent to meet new leadership needs. I suggested a significant amount of her time and the Trust's resources should be devoted to talent over the next few months. With the support of an HR consultant, the result was a revamped organizational chart, a professional review of all human resources practices, refreshed job descriptions for all existing staff, plans to promote several staff, identification of new senior positions and job descriptions, and a plan to recruit and retain them.

Your People

Successful strategy implementation might call for a parting of ways. Sometimes the new strategy is simply not the right fit for members of your team. There might be people who can't or don't want to get on board. This happened at Facebook when a longtime senior executive and friend of Mark Zuckerberg stepped down because he disagreed with Zuckerberg's shift in strategy to focus on private messaging.

Anticipating this in advance and acknowledging it openly with everyone can help mitigate awkwardness and pain down the road.

However, you might not work in a philanthropic organization with employees. You might be building your philanthropic future alone, with a partner, or through a donor-advised fund. It's important at this stage to honestly reflect on the people you surround yourself with. Do they support you in achieving your goals, or do they hold you back? This includes anyone: family members, friends, and neighbors. It includes the people you interact with as a volunteer, on boards of directors, and events you attend. It includes professional advisors, such as your accountant, attorney, and agent.

While you can't get rid of your family, you can choose how and when you spend time with them. Other people you can simply avoid, and you can end professional relationships. You want to reduce or eliminate time spent with people who are holding you back from your philanthropic vision. At the same time, increase the time you spend with those who support you, including those who challenge you (in a helpful way) to do better. Find new friends, join philanthropy-serving organizations, attend new events or conferences. Ask your wealth advisor or family office to introduce you to other like-minded clients. Many estate planners, multifamily offices, and donor-advised fund sponsoring organizations offer philanthropy-related networking and learning events for their ultra-high-net-worth clients and donor-advised fund holders.

You also may need to bring in new talent or expertise. This could include employees, but it also could include consultants, board members, partners, experts, a community advisory board, evaluators, a virtual assistant, or a fractional CFO. Be open to a variety of ways you can obtain the expertise and support your needs. The Trust revamped their Advisory Councils to bring in additional expertise from around the state and began meeting more regularly with Council members to gather ongoing input and ideas on their work and outcomes.

Your Systems and Processes

It's not just your people and your time that need to align with your strategic vision. How those people are structured and the way they interact need to align, too. I'm talking about your systems, processes, and structures. Everything should be in alignment, thereby reducing friction and increasing your speed to impact. Here are a few examples:

- **Grants:** To meet your new goals, you might need to change the structure of your grants. This could include grant size, multiyear grants, provision of general operating support, funding of policy advocacy, and more. Don't assume bigger is better. When the startup Headwaters Foundation realized it needed to quickly infuse funding into rural communities to achieve its strategy, it created "GO! Grants." GO! Grants provide small grants up to $5,000 for general operating support with a simple, online application process that can be completed in 10 minutes. The foundation allocated 78 of these grants in its first year.

At the Kate B. Reynolds Charitable Trust, shifting to being a more outcomes-focused grantmaker required a complete overhaul of their grantmaking. Just about everything had to change. For example, instead of each program officer recommending individual grants for Trustee approval (old, responsive approach), program officers recommended bodies of work summarizing what the Trust was trying to accomplish with each funding opportunity (new, strategic approach). These included goals tied to the overall strategy, metrics for tracking progress and outcomes, and a portfolio of grantees.

- **Operations:** How you operate might need to shift to align with your new strategy, including everything from how you manage human resources and how you code and track grants to your financial and grants management systems. The Reynolds Trust changed its coding system, since it no longer needed to track grants by focus area such as "diabetes." Staff meetings shifted from staff updates to working sessions where staff collectively work through issues, provide feedback, and develop solutions to implementation challenges.

- **Your role as a funder:** Rather than passively reviewing proposals from your kitchen table or office, you might need to change how you interact in your community, by, for example, joining local funding collaboratives or advocating for policy change with state legislators. When the Char and Chuck Fowler Foundation wanted to support a new initiative to expand arts education in Cleveland, trustee Chann Fowler-Spellman joined the leadership council and the planning team. She rolled up her sleeves with local arts leaders, teachers, principals, and parents in monthly meetings and planning retreats to brainstorm and develop a new arts education plan.

- **Your assets:** Your financial assets can also align with your giving strategy. "Impact investment" or "mission-related investing" simply means making financial investments that also produce significant social or environmental benefits.[2] If you haven't already done so, you should talk with your financial advisor, asset manager, or investment committee about impact investing.

Funders can also think about all the nonfinancial "assets" they can deploy to implement their strategies: Offering their knowledge and expertise (or that of their employees), introductions to business leaders and politicians, and space (e.g., conference rooms or their home) are just a few ways philanthropists like you bring their whole selves to their giving. You are more than money. The Kate B. Reynolds Charitable Trust knows this. In addition to offering grant funding, their staff's expertise in early childhood education, the Affordable Care Act, Medicaid expansion, and value-based care helps inform local and state policy work.

- **Philanthropic vehicles:** Today there are increasing types of funding "vehicles" or entities: foundations, donor-advised funds, limited liability corporations (LLCs), charitable remainder trusts, and family offices. As your goals change, the entity you use to allocate funds might need to change as well. One woman started a family foundation with her husband. After he passed away, she wanted to continue her philanthropic journey but didn't want the hassle of managing a foundation. She decided to convert it to a donor-advised fund. This allowed her to make funding decisions while the fund manager handled all the administrative and tax issues.

  Another donor's strategy was to increase women's access to reproductive health care. When she realized the organization managing her donor-advised fund prohibited her from making a grant to her chosen organization, she chose to move her fund to another donor-advised fund sponsor. This allowed her to align her funding to her values.

Step 4: Maintain Momentum

Speed is your friend in implementation. The quicker you can begin implementing your strategic plan, the more momentum you will gain. The more momentum you gain, the faster everyone gets on board (including the resisters) and the quicker you achieve results. Consulting guru Alan Weiss advises thinking of implementation as a series of short sprints rather than a marathon. You want to quickly start meeting milestones and celebrating accomplishments. That's why I advise priority champions to immediately create punch lists of 5–10 activities that need to happen next, rather than elaborate work plans. You want to quickly get moving on your top priorities and create opportunities for everyone to see progress.

When I spoke with Nora Ferrell about the status of strategy implementation, I was blown away by all that Kate B. Reynolds Charitable Trust had accomplished in just a few months. We knew if everyone on staff realized the magnitude of foundation-wide progress, they would be energized. Collective success would propel them forward. We agreed that at their next staff meeting, she'd facilitate a session for all staff to brainstorm every accomplishment they could think of, big or small. They identified a list of 26 accomplishments! This included developing goals and strategies for new bodies of work, revamping their advisory council, launching new funding opportunities, successfully communicating their new strategy to grantees, and installing new technology tools to support staff collaboration.

You also want to celebrate successes as they occur. These can be big accomplishments (we created our first communications plan!), wonky wins (we recoded our grants management system!), and tiny victories (we identified potential grantees!). Everyone will appreciate being appreciated. The Trust's President Laura Gerald makes a point at staff meetings to congratulate staff who have made substantial progress, highlights examples of teams working effectively across departments, and emphasizes the significance of implementation milestones.

The results? After less than a year implementing its new strategy, the Kate B. Reynolds Charitable Trust—and its impact on North Carolina—has changed significantly.

"The proof is in the pudding," says Gerald. "We're far more clear about what our vision is and how we interpret the founder's mission. We have a clear description of our values, our strategic grantmaking processes, how we do our work. It's hard to describe the magnitude of not only documenting our vision and strategy but having our staff, new trustee representatives, and advisory councils completely understand it all. At the end of the day, this will help us meet our mission."[3]

These four steps I've outlined by no means describe every activity necessary to implement your strategy. There is a lot of devil in those details! But these steps point you in the right direction, help you stay focused and accountable, and accelerate your speed of implementation.

Notes

1. Author interview with Laura Gerald, MD, October 23, 2019.
2. https://ssir.org/articles/entry/unpacking_the_impact_in_impact_ investing.
3. Author interview with Laura Gerald, MD, October 23, 2019.

15 | Get Moving: Transform Your Giving and Change the World!

Delusional altruism is a problem, and too many philanthropists are under its spell.

Are you?

I would guess by now you've identified at least a few ways you, too, are delusional in your altruism. How you've gotten in your own way without realizing it. How you've slowed yourself down on the road to impact. How you've been mired in tactics when a clear strategy would set you free. How a scarcity mentality has held your genius hostage.

As a philanthropy adviser, speaker, and writer, I have seen far too many philanthropists—individuals and organizations of all sizes—fall under the spell of delusional altruism. The result has been a tremendous loss of efficiency and effectiveness. A dramatic reduction in impact. Unleveraged assets. Money that never created change because the entrepreneur or the celebrity never started that foundation or opened that donor-advised fund. It seemed to risky. They were overcome by fear.

While I can't put an exact number on the impact reduction caused by delusional altruism, I estimate it's easily in the hundreds of millions—and probably billions—of dollars lost. When you factor in a $68 trillion intergenerational transfer of wealth in the next three decades, you can see how the damage of delusional altruism could grow exponentially.

Pure and simple, delusional altruism prevents philanthropists from being as fabulous, catalytic, and impactful as they can be.

But I know you. You don't want to be delusional in your altruism. You want to ask questions that bring you clarity. You want to embrace an abundance mind-set, not just in your philanthropy but throughout your life. You want to understand the root causes of problems so that you can develop equitable, lasting solutions. You want to learn from others and understand the context that brought us here. You aren't just satisfied with agility and speed, you want aerodynamic philanthropy.

You want to be transformational.

Now is the time to take a deep look within yourself and your organization to see if the seeds of delusional altruism have begun to sprout. If they have, do something about it. Do everything in your power to avoid the pitfalls of delusional altruism and achieve your vision for changing the world. When you shine a light on this condition and recognize it for what it is, you do have the power to defeat it. This book gives you all the tools you need to win the fight against delusional altruism, and then ensure it never takes root again.

The key is to act—and act *now*.

Seven Steps You Can Take Today

As Albert Einstein is widely quoted as saying, "Insanity is doing the same thing over and over again and expecting different results." Whether or not he actually said these words, it's true that you can't change things for the better if you continue to do the same things over and over.

Here are seven steps you can take right now to defeat delusional altruism, transform your giving, and to be the change you want to see in the world.

1. **Pick one change you want to make and run with it.** I'll bet you've already identified a list of improvements you want to make in the way you deliver your philanthropy, but you've felt overwhelmed by the sheer magnitude of what awaits you. The problem is that, if you try to make five or ten improvements at the same time, you likely won't make much progress on *any* of them. In my experience, it's best to focus on one improvement, complete it, and then work on the next. As you start completing your improvements, one after another, you'll build the kind of momentum that will drive you and your organization forward.

   So, which delusion should you banish? Which improvement should you focus on? There's honestly no "right" way to decide. My suggestion is that you pick whichever one you and your team are most excited about, that most aligns with your goals or strategy, or that represents the 20% of effort that will drive the 80% of the results. You can also gather your colleagues to read this book and then meet to discuss how you can put what you've learned into practice. Don't overthink—just do it!

2. **Schedule time on your calendar to make it happen.** There's an old saying, "What gets planned gets done." It's one thing to declare that you want to address the root causes of the problem, and it's of course another thing altogether to do something about it. One particularly effective way to ensure you do something about it is to schedule an appointment with yourself on your calendar.

   For example, let's say you've decided to do a better job involving the people you want to help in the design and decision making of your next funding initiative. Make a daily or weekly one-hour appointment on your calendar to do it. And when the time arrives and your computer or smartphone chime to get your attention, sit down and work on it.

3. **Be rapid and dramatic.** Think in terms of speed and dramatic impact. For example, if you want to refresh your strategy, what would it take to get it done in half the normal time? If you want to explore

new funding areas, who are the top experts in the world you should talk to? What kind of change could you make immediately? Allow yourself an opportunity to make dramatic change quickly.

Once you have an idea of what you can accomplish quickly, list three concrete action steps that will get you there. If there are other people you need to involve—a colleague, board member, grantee, or community member—write their names down. If there are any internal deadlines that could motivate your work, such as an upcoming board meeting, document that as well.

4. **Learn from your grantees.** Few people can recognize delusional altruism better than the nonprofits on the receiving end of your philanthropy. Ask your grantees for candid feedback on how you do business. Is your application process fair? Do you communicate and interact with them in helpful ways? More specifically, ask them to list three things that your team could do better that would in turn help them become more productive and effective. Once you've considered grantee feedback, let them know how you plan to address problem areas they've identified.

5. **Don't go it alone.** One of the things I most appreciate about philanthropy is that there is an abundance of people who are willing to share their experiences and offer guidance. Many philanthropy-serving organizations and media outlets provide a cornucopia of resources for free or minimal charge. Take advantage! Recognize also that you can benefit from objective and trusted advising and coaching, a confidential sounding board to discuss anything related to your charitable giving. Someone to help you navigate your philanthropic journey and hold you accountable to your goals. This can help you achieve results much faster and avoid mistakes.

6. **Continue the conversation.** Freeing a philanthropist from delusional altruism isn't a one-time exercise. It requires ongoing vigilance and attention. It's easy to fall back into old habits or allow new ones to grow while we are busily attending to our day-to-day work. Find ways to keep the conversation fresh and present. If your organization is large enough, consider establishing a Delusional Altruism Task Force among your staff to maintain watch. Have different departments or units within your foundation provide friendly critiques of

potential delusional behavior in other departments. Allow staff to choose "delusion buddies" to check their own thinking at regular intervals. Create channels for grantees and partners to provide anonymous input on your actions and culture as a grantmaker. The possibilities are endless, as long as you have the discipline to keep the conversation going. No one intends to create bureaucracy, cause delays, or be disrespectful. But to have great impact and transform issues, communities, and neighborhoods, we need to look closely at the mirror and transform ourselves, too.

7. **Visit DelusionalAltruism.com for more ideas, tools, and resources.** It's full of helpful tools and resources for you to view or download wherever you are, 24/7—all for free. Please take a look and see what's waiting there for you.

One more thing: Have fun with this book. I coined the term "delusional altruism" because it makes me laugh. In a field (philanthropy) where everyone is nice and polite to each other, and in a world where those with money are treated with great reverence, I chuckle when I refer to philanthropists as delusional.

When I started talking about delusional altruism with clients, colleagues, and other philanthropists, their reaction was either to laugh and say, "I love it," or ask me to tell them more. I knew I was onto something! I'm onto something because delusional altruism happens to all of us. You, me, the philanthropist down the hall from you, and the one halfway around the globe. We all want to make a difference and we all get in our own way. The good news is that, since we are the ones getting in our own way, we have the power to get out of it!

I hope you'll contact me with your own success stories—I would love to hear them. And if I can ever be of help to you, please don't hesitate to ask. Feel free to email me directly at kris@putnam-consulting.com. You can learn more about what I do and how I have helped philanthropists of all kinds at http://putnam-consulting.com.

Now, go out and change the world!

Acknowledgments

This book would not have been written without the encouragement, advice, and talent of many people. In particular I'm indebted to Alan Weiss, for encouraging me to write this book and providing the insight, tools, and community to help me do it. To Mark Levy, for being the world's most amazing writing coach—you made this book far more interesting, helped me find my voice, and improved my writing, all while making me laugh every week for six months. To Pamela Norley, for generously writing the foreword to this book and for the integrity with which you lead Fidelity Charitable. To Lauren Janus, for just-in-time book research; Mary VanClay, for expert copywriting assistance; Kristine McAfee and the team at Jennasis & Associates, for creative book promotion; Lori Jolliffe and Jane Wise for helping manage my schedule; and to Kelly Talbot, Brian Neill, Vicki Adang, Mike Isralewitz, Alyssa Benigno, Sharmila Srinivasan, and the entire team at Wiley for their fabulous partnership, encouragement, and editing to ensure this book will help philanthropists transform themselves and the world.

I'd also like to thank the following people who generously shared ideas, insights, and examples that informed this book: Melinda K. Abrams (Commonwealth Fund); Tanya Acker (CBS's *Hot Bench*); Don Akkermans (De Dikke Blauwe); Judy Belk (The California Wellness Foundation); Benjamin Bellegy (Worldwide Initiatives for Grantmaker Support); Henry Berman (Exponent Philanthropy); Elizabeth Brown (Community Foundation Sonoma County); Evelyn Burnett

232 Acknowledgments

(ThirdSpace Action Lab); Sam Caplan (Walton Family Foundation); Andy Carroll (Exponent Philanthropy); Ashley Carson (Atlantic Capital Bank); Melissa Daar Carvajal (Silicon Valley Community Foundation); Guy Cave (Guy Cave Consulting); Maria Chertok (Charities Aid Foundation Russia); Melvin Chibole (Kenya Community Development Foundation); Aaron Dorfman (Lippman Kanfer Foundation for Living Torah); Aaron Dorfman (National Committee for Responsive Philanthropy); Lee Draper (Draper Consulting Group); Jon Eesley (Windsor Advisory Group); Nora Ferrell (Kate B. Reynolds Charitable Trust); Joanne Florino (The Philanthropy Roundtable); Chann Fowler-Spellman (The Char and Chuck Fowler Family Foundation); Simone Foxman (Bloomberg News); Brian Frederick (Brian Frederick & Associates); Susan Fulford (Dynamic Legacy); Tamara Fynan (The J.M. Smucker Company); Laura Gerald (Kate B. Reynolds Charitable Trust); Deanna Gomby (The Heising-Simons Foundation); Carolina Gomez (Filantropía Transformadora); Lisa Hamilton (Annie E. Casey Foundation); Amy Hanauer (Policy Matters Ohio); Carly Hare (CHANGE Philanthropy); Rahsaan Harris (Emma Bowen Foundation); Carter Hatch (Windsor Advisory Group); Jenny Hodgson (Global Fund for Community Foundations); Erica Joseph (Community Foundation of the Eastern Shore); Lara Kalafatis (Cleveland Clinic Foundation); Charles Keidan (Alliance Magazine); Vidya Krishnamurthy (William and Flora Hewlett Foundation); Kathy LeMay (social change strategist); Lindsay Louie (William and Flora Hewlett Foundation); Glen Macdonald (Wealth & Giving Forum); Elaine Martin (Fidelity Charitable); Janet Naumi Mawiyoo (Kenya Community Development Foundation); Tim McCarthy (The Business of Good); Angela McCrae (The Springs Close Foundation); Andrew McCracken (Community Foundation for Northern Ireland); Lisa Earle McLeod (McLeod & More); John Meyers (Meyers Global + Associates); Talia Milgrom-Elcott (100Kin10); Becky Morphis (Fidelity Charitable); Adrienne Mundorf (Sisters of Charity Foundation); Ganesh Natarajan (Social Venture Partners India); Tamir Novotny; Heather Peeler (ACT for Alexandria); Jill Penrose (The J.M. Smucker Company); Mitzi

Perdue (Win This Fight! Combatting Human Trafficking); Betsey Russell (Last Word LLC); Gerry Salole (European Foundation Centre); Jenny Santi (Saint Partners Philanthropy Services); Melissa Schwartz (The Joyful Heart Foundation); Meredith T. Shields (Sorenson Impact Foundation); Paul Shoemaker (Social Venture Partners International); Brenda Solorzano (Headwaters Foundation); Jesse Spector (Thousand Currents); Rusty Stahl (Fund the People); Mamie Kanfer Stewart (Lippman Kanfer Family Philanthropies); Gina Stilp (Zilber Family Foundation); Mia St. John (Mia St. John Foundation); Leslie Strnisha (William J. and Dorothy K. O'Neill Foundation); Nonet T. Sykes (Atlanta BeltLine); Stephanie Teleki (California Health Care Foundation); Emma Turner (Barclays Private Bank); Edwin Venema (De Kopijmeester); Deb Vesy (Deaconess Foundation); Max von Abendroth (DAFNE—Donors and Foundations Networks in Europe); Charles Way (Purple Bridge Management); and Abe Wellington (Opal Group).

Lastly, I'd like to thank my youngest children, Isabella and Austin, for your patience and understanding when I had to escape the house so many mornings to write all day. I'm glad you still recognize me! I hope someday you read and appreciate this book. I love you so much.

About the Author

Kris Putnam-Walkerly is a trusted advisor to the world's leading philanthropists. For over 20 years, ultra-high-net-worth donors, foundations, Fortune 500 companies, celebrity activists, and wealth advisors have sought and benefited from her advice to transform their giving and catapult their impact. As a philanthropy advisor, speaker, and award-winning author, she's helped over 100 philanthropists strategically allocate over half a billion dollars in grants and gifts. Kris's clients include the Robert Wood Johnson Foundation, J.M. Smucker Company, Charles and Helen Schwab Foundation, Heising-Simons Foundation, Annie E. Casey Foundation, David and Lucile Packard Foundation, Kate B. Reynolds Charitable Trust, National Center for Family Philanthropy, Blue Shield of California, and Avery Dennison Foundation, among many others.

A thought leader in transformational giving®, Kris was named one of America's Top 25 Philanthropy Speakers. She is the author of the award-winning book *Confident Giving®: Sage Advice for Funders*, a Forbes.com contributor on philanthropy, a global philanthropy content partner to *Alliance Magazine*, and the U.S. philanthropy expert to the leading Dutch philanthropy media outlet De Dikke Blauwe. Kris is also a frequent contributor to publications of leading philanthropy organizations and has provided expert commentary about philanthropy to the *Wall Street Journal, Washington Post*, Entepreneur.com, NPR's

Marketplace Morning Report, *Philanthropy News Digest*, and *Chronicle of Philanthropy*.

Prior to forming Putnam Consulting Group, Inc., Kris was a grant-maker at the David and Lucile Packard Foundation and an evaluator at the highly esteemed Stanford University School of Medicine. She holds a master's degree in social work from San Francisco State University and a bachelor's degree from Indiana University. She and her husband have five children and reside near Cleveland, Ohio. Learn more at putnam-consulting.com.

Index

50% principle, commitment, 180
80/20 rule (Pareto Principle), anticipation, 134
100Kin10 (nonprofit organization), 154–155
1772 Foundation, 114
2018 Grantmaker Salary and Benefits Report,
    47–48

Abundance
    action, 109
    mind-set, 111–115
        adjustment, 109
        embracing, knowledge, 120–121
Accidental Genius (Levy), 75
Accomplishment, direction (understanding),
    62–64
Accountability, 215–217
    champions, assignation, 201
Activist donors, impact, 33
Activities
    identification, 189
    ranking, 215–216
Adaptive actions, 182–185
Adaptive, meaning, 183
Administrative burden, reduction, 46
Advisory Councils, change, 220
Advocacy
    definition, 150
    legal advocacy, 152
    organizations, support, 152
Advocacy Funding (GrantCraft), 150
Advocates for Children and Youth (ACY), 118
Aerodynamic funding, creation, 136–139
Africa Grantmakers Affinity Group, 215
Agile, meaning, 183

Agility
    components, 181–182
    decision agility, 181
    execution agility, 182
    market agility, 181
    thinking, 180–182
Agility Advantage, The (Setili), 181
Alice Virginia and David W. Fletcher
    Foundation, 191
Al-Maamal Foundation, 94
America Mentors, support, 56
Annie E. Casey Foundation, 118, 119
    Race Equity and Inclusion Action Guide, 127,
        149, 157
Annual grantmaking budget, determination, 216
Annual performance reviews, 187
Annual strategy refresh, 203
Anthony, Mary, 114
ASAP connect, 91
Asociación Femenina para el Desarrollo de
    Sacatepéquez (AFEDES), movement, 148
Assets, 201
    changes, 221–222
    leveraging, 170–172
    unleveraged assets, 225
    usage, 109

Back-office management, provision, 116
Back-to-back calls, usage, 61
Back-to-back meetings, scheduling, 55
Bass, Andy, 38
BBB Wise Giving, 16
Bee Vradenburg Foundation, 191
Behavior Gap, The (Richards), 55

Beliefs, change, 18
Benefit, innovation criteria, 188
Bennett, Rebeccah, 157
Best-in-class questions, usage, 101
Best information/ideas/technology/talent,
     deserving, 113–114
Best practices, initiation, 96–97
Bill and Melinda Gates Foundation, 49–50
Black Foundation Executives, 117
Blue Nile, 198
Blue Shield of California
   funding decisions, streamlining, 134
   grantmaking program creation, 119
Board of directors, 24
   diversification, 84
   meetings, holding (cost), 133
   members
      involvement, 228
      succession plan, 32
   relationship, 113–114
Bookkeeping, importance, 12
Boyers, Zach, 157
Bradford, Peggy, 164
Brainstorming, usage, 76, 99, 125
Bridge grants, provision, 208
Bridgespan Group, nonprofit analysis, 162
Broad Foundation, 153
Brown, Beth, 183
Brunet, Ariane, 100
Bully, role, 69
Bureaucracy
   activity, 40
   breaker audit, conducting, 179
   creation, avoidance, 41
Bureaucratic bloat, development, 39–41
Business of Good Foundation, 55
Busyness, confusion, 62

California State Department of Education, 92
Callahan, David, 31
Calls, scheduling, 215
Campaign management, importance, 88
Capacity, 201
   addition, impact, 121
   building, consideration, 208
   investment, 115
      absence, 13–17
   organizational capacity, 116
   self-limitation, 7–8
Capital, types, 171

Carazzone, Carola, 16
Case, Jean, 34
Cause, support
   coming out, fear, 22–23
   discovery, overwhelming, 53
Celebrity foundation, work, 96
Center for Effective Philanthropy, 163
Central Square Foundation, 146
Change. See Systems change
   creation, 142
   encouragement, 132
   impact, 53–54
   usage, 227
CHANGE Philanthropy, 113
Char and Chuck Fowler Foundation, 221
Charitable lead trusts (CLTs), cash flow
     (provision), 36
Charitable remainder trusts, 222
Charity Navigator, 16
Charles and Helen Schwab Foundation, 94, 153
Chief executive officer (CEO), 52
   resignation, 62, 103
   role, 53–54
Child Liberation Foundation, 114
China Foundation Forum, 120
Choices, impact, 53
Citrin, Richard, 113
Client deadlines, 126
Climate change, 52–53
Cloudera Foundation, 192
Coalition building, 136
Collaborative funding, participation, 97
Collective impact, 83
Collective success, impact, 223
College scholarships, offering, 75
Colorblind people, 30
Columbine High School massacre, 23
Coming out, fear, 22–23
Commonwealth Fund Fellowship in Minority
     Health Policy, 135–136
Communication
   importance, 88
   lines, openness, 154
   plan
      development, 65
      implementation, 214
      investment, 32–33
   problem, 99
Communities
   changes/opportunities, 182

disaster/violence, experience, 58
foundations, grantmaking public charities, 22
government investment, increase, 85
guidance, 168
initiatives, design, 63
members
    advisory committee, creation, 168
    engagement, 94
    involvement, 228
    need, meeting, 67–68
    philanthropy, 172
    scanning, 185
Community Advisory Committee, connections, 95
Community Foundation of Lorain County (Ohio), 165
Community Foundation of the Eastern Shore, 163
Community Foundation Sonoma County, 183
Community Foundation Tyne & Wear and Northumberland, 161
Competition, support, 119
Con Alma Health Foundation, 95
Constituent relationship management (CRM) systems, 117
Consultants
    hiring, 205
    hourly payment, 205
    interaction, delay, 179
Continuous improvement, encouragement, 132
Conversation, continuation, 228–229
Coordination, problem, 99
Corner, Julian, 149
Corporate foundation, initiation, 86
Corporate giving program, 187
Corporate philanthropy, power player (corporate leader placement), 12
Corporate socially irresponsible role, 69
Cost, innovation criteria, 188
Courage, 112
Creativity
    asset, 109
    stifling, 75
Criminal, role, 69
Crisis
    situation, grantee response (assistance), 185
    trustworthiness, importance, 166–167
Cross-cutting themes, 53
Crowdfunding, 83

Culture
    addressing, 145
    strategy formulation, 197
Cummings, Bill, 162
Cummings Foundation, Sustaining Grants Program, 162
Cybersecurity, 117

Dagger-through-the-heart funder, 69
Daily touchpoints, 203
Data gathering, 114
    excess, 204
David and Lucile Packard Foundation, 32, 147, 162
Decision agility, 181
Decision making
    control, sharing, 169–170
    criteria, 72
    deceleration, 46
    mistrust, 6–7
Delusional altruism, 6, 30, 225–226
    defeat, steps, 227–229
    website, usage, 229
Delusional Altruism Task Force, establishment, 228–229
Delusion buddies, staff selection, 229
DentaQuest Partnership for Oral Health Advancement, focus, 147
Deserving, disbelief, 8–9
Desjardins, Simon, 15
Destructive frugality, 4
Detractors, question, 93
Dhawan, Ashish, 146
Difference, making (disbelief), 9–10
Dimon, Jamie, 171
Dirk and Charlene Kabcenell Foundation, 153
Disappointments, fear, 27–28
Disaster recovery, support, 183–184
Discomfort, impact, 17
Discretionary brant budgets, usage, 185
Disruptions, decrease, 128–129
Diversity, importance, 84
Does this bring me joy? (question), 104–106
Donor
    activist donors, impact, 33
    advice, 6
    circles, joining, 49
    data collection, 37
    donor-advised funds

Donor (*continued*)
  solution, 29
  sponsors, 18
  legacy, control (loss), 32
  relations, importance, 88
  social conscience, 70
  strategy, 222
  tactics, focus, 74
  ultra-high-net-worth, 29–30
Donor-advised funds (DAFs)
  business, 187
  checks, issuance, 49
  contribution requirements, 36
  opening, 225
  prohibitions, 222
  sponsor, 116
Donor distraction disorder, 66–68
Drama, 227–228
Driving forces, 201
Drucker, Peter, 124

Education, 152
Efforts, fooling, 61
Ego-driven role, 69
Einstein, Albert, 226
Elton John AIDS Foundation, 82
Emerson, Jed, 171
Emma Bowen Foundation, 170
Emotional intelligence, 83
Employee volunteerism programs, 93–94
Endeavor, success (importance), 18
Enterprise
  enterprise-wide implementation principles, 212
  nature/direction, 63
Environment
  change, 182, 203
  opportunities, 182
Equitable solutions, seeking, 155–158
Equity
  achievement, 155
  impact, 155–156
Evaluation expert, involvement, 96
Evaluators, finding, 45
Event planners, usage, 57
Execution agility, 182
Executive coach, hiring (justification), 32–33
Experts, identification, 93
Exposure, fear, 23–25
External sources, location, 95

Failure, 103
  fear, 25
  risk, 102
Family foundation
  direction, example, 26
  shared values, requirement, 197
  trustee, chaos, 56
Fear, 225
  fear-based questions, usage, 26–27
  guilt, comparison, 32–33
  hostage situation, avoidance, 34
  justification, 33
Fearfulness, 21
Feedback, elicitation, 101
Ferrell, Nora, 216, 222
Fidelity Charitable, 36
Financial loss, 102
Financial risks, 103
Financing, decisions, 93
First hour (workday), attention, 125
Florino, Joanne, 197
Focus group participants, feedback (elicitation), 101
Follow-up emails, sending, 179
Ford Foundation, 161
Forward Through Ferguson, 157
Foundations
  collective work, success (factors), 153–154
  discretionary grant budgets, 185
  initiation, 28
  management, 52
  self-imposed restrictions, 36
  starting, 84
    alternative, 29
  transparency, 45
Fowler-Spellman, Chann, 221
Frugality, impact, 4
Full Cost Project, creation, 15
Fund development, 88
Funders
  collaboration, 47
  identification, 215
  learning, 28
  philanthropic stewardship, role, 25–26
  role, changes, 221
Funding
  aerodynamic funding, creation, 136–139
  allocation, delay, 46
  collaborative, 218–219
  guidelines, development, 216

initiatives
  brainstorming, 125
  capacity, addition (impact), 121
  development, 96
nonprofit leaders, relationship, 31
organization, relationship, 103
prevention, 43
solution, impossibility, 17
Fundraising events, attendance, 61

Gantt charts, usage, 39, 215
Garry, Joan, 165
General operating support, 161–162
  offering, 208
    absence, 31
  provision, 160
Generosity, proactive approach, 111–112
Gerald, Laura, 212–214, 223
Givers, The (Callahan), 31
Giving
  focus, clarification, 93
  joy/frustration, 105
  transformation, 225
  transformational giving, 142
Giving Pledge, 196
Giving Tuesday campaign, creation, 84
Global Anti-Trafficking Auction, creation, 115
Global Fund for Community Foundations, 94
Global South, 30
Goals
  achievement, changes (requirements), 217–219
  clarity, 74
  prioritization, 57
GOJO Industries, 83
Goldman, Richard/Rhonda, 33
Goldsmith, Marshall, 217
Gomby, Deanna, 116
Government investment, increase, 85
GrantCraft, 150
Grantees
  direction, change (communication), 206–209
  effectiveness, increase, 121
  empathy, 208
  final reports, 131
  finding, 65
  impact, increase, 98
  infrastructure, investment, 119
  interaction, delay, 179

investment, 3, 115
involvement, 228
learning, 228
list, creation, 216
questions, 131
response, assistance, 185
support, 118–119
trusting relationship, building, 118
Grantmakers, education, 152
Grantmakers for Effective Organizations, assistance, 163
Grantmaking, 201
  annual budget, determination, 216
  changes, 221
  program, Blue Shield creation, 119
  public charities, 22
  steps, elimination, 178–180
  strategies
    adaptation, 185
    implications, 96
Grants
  amount, increase, 75
  bridge grants, provision, 208
  budget, 114
  changes, 220–221
  employee, signing, 131
  expectations, 159
  guidelines, 180
  management, 117
    software, usage, 61
  program, continuation (debate), 132–133
  structuring, 158–172
  usage, 31
Grassroots efforts, support, 199
Great Work (Stuart), 81
Growth
  courage, 112
  options, 201
GuideStar, 16
Guilt, fear (comparison), 32–33

Hanauer, Amy, 159
Handlers, impact, 48–49
Hare, Carly, 113
Hargitay, Mariska (activism), 151
Harris, Rahsaan, 170
Headwaters Health Foundation of Western Montana, 133–134, 221
Heising-Simons Foundation, growth preparation, 116

Henderson, Naomi, 101
Hewlett, Bill, 32
Homework assignments, 201
Hootsuite, 106
How can I do this in half the time? (question), 126
How can we speed this up? (question), 99–100
Human capital, review, 182
Hutchison, Paul, 114

Ideas, exposure, 182
Impact Assets Handbook for Investors, The (Emerson), 171
Impact investment, 221–222
  advisors, usage, 116
Implementation
  halt, 46
  innovation criteria, 188
  problems, 211
Implicit biases, understanding, 84
Inclusion, embracing, 113
Income inequality, 52–53
Indigenous peoples, strategic focus, 206
Information
  gathering, 200
  increase, 6–7
Informing, meaning, 93–94
Infrastructure investment, regularity (absence), 17
In-house staff, usage, 116
Inner focus group moderator, channeling, 101
Innovation
  development, 188–189
  implementation, 189
  increase, 185–189
  organizational generation, 187
  possibilities, identification, 188
  support, conditions, 187
Innovation Formula, The (Weiss/Robert), 187
Innovative ideas, 185
  assessment, 188
  implementation, 187
  search, 187–188
In-person meetings, accomplishment, 126
Intellectual capital, 171
Intentional learners, objectives, 191
Intentional learning, focus, 117
Intentional learning/improvement, 189–192
Intermediary organizations
  donor search, 139

identification/interaction, 215
Internal best practices, usage, 95–97
Interruptions, prevention, 128–129
Investment, 169
  absence, 10–17
  determination, 77
  impact investment advisors, usage, 116
  team meeting, involvement, 103
Issue, selection, 91

Joan Garry's Guide to Nonprofit Leadership (Garry), 165
Joyful Heart Foundation, 151
JP Morgan Chase, 171
Junk, impact, 37–38

Kanfer, 83
Kate B. Reynolds Charitable Trust, 212–213, 216, 221
  grantmaking, changes, 221
  strategy implementation, 219
Keidan, Charles, 26
Kim, Daniel H., 144
Kinara Capital, 142
King, J., Martin Luther, 82
Knowledge, asset, 109
Kravitz, Lenny, 142
Kresge Foundation, 163–164

Lankelly Chase Foundation, impact, 146–147, 149
LaSarte-Meeks, Dave, 199
Leaders, identification, 93
Leadership
  funding, 185–186
  review, 182
  role, 184
    exit, 87
Leading with Noble Purpose (McLeod), 12
Learning, 117–118, 201
  commitment/discussion, 191
  community, guidance, 168
  documentation/sharing, 191
  ease, 189
  intentional learning, 189–192
  organization, becoming (commitment), 191
  questions, 190
  usage/application, 191

Legacy, control (loss). *See* Donor
Legal advocacy, 152
Lemma, Solomé, 148
Let Love Rule Foundation, 142
Levy, Mark, 75
Limited liability corporation (LLC), 222
    creation, 94
Lippman Kanfer Family Foundation, 82–83
Lives, transformation, 141
Lloyds Bank Foundation of England and Wales,
    151
Long-term planning, investment, 119
Lopez, Rafael, 119
Loss, fear, 30–32

MacArthur Foundation, 161–162
Market agility, 181
McLeod, Lisa, 12
Mechanics, behavior (imitation), 130–132
Meetings, double-booking, 55
MentorcliQ technology, usage, 56–57
Messaging, 214
Michael & Susan Dell Foundation, 146
Milgrom-Elcott, Talia, 154–155
Millennials (reaching), social media (usage), 74
Mind-set. *See* Abundance; Scarcity mind-set
Mission, 201
    achievement, 160
    fulfillment, 14
    mission-related investing, 221–222
    strategy formulation, 196
    value delivery, 111
Mistakes, avoidance, 18
Momentum
    acceleration, 215
    building, 203, 227
    maintenance, 222–224
Money
    raising, belief, 17
    reduction, steps excess (impact),
        47–48
    saving, problems, 3
    spending, 109
Movement
    definition, 148
    ecosystem, 149
Movement building, 67
Muda, elimination, 178–179
Multiyear commitment, 121
Musabekova, Dinara, 17

Narada Foundation, 120
National Committee for Responsive
    Philanthropy (NCRP), 160, 163
National Summer Learning Association, 91
Newmont Ahafo Development Foundation
    (NADeF), 172
Nilekani, Rohini, 196
Nonfinancial assets, funder perception, 222
Nongovernmental organizations (NGOs)
    ability, 159
    application, 26
    board, service, 27
    management, 12–13
    number, estimation, 53
Nonprofit Finance Fund, creation, 15
Nonprofits
capacity, building, 164–165
    funding opportunities, notification, 66
    overhead, spending, 3–4
    support, 159
    sustaining, operating support/ongoing
        support (usage), 162
    talent/capacity, investment (absence), 13–17
North Star, 67
    location, 195

Occam's Razor, principle, 38–39
O'Donnell, Rosie, 23
Omidyar Network, 192
Ongoing support, usage, 162
Open Society Foundations, 33, 161
Operating support
    offering, 160–162, 208
        absence, 31
    usage, 162
Operations, changes, 221
Opinions, diversity (recognition/acceptance),
    154
Opoku Darko, Elizabeth, 172
Oprah Winfrey Leadership Academy for Girls,
    142–143
Oracheva, Oksana, 13
Organizational capacity, 116
    investment, 119
    strengthening, 163–165
Organizations
    acceleration, 130–136
    funding, relationship, 103
    intermediary organizations,
        identification/interaction, 215

244

Index

Organizations (*continued*)
  involvement, 92
  vision, 9–10
Outcomes
  change, 98
  outcomes-focused grantmaker, 221
Outside expertise, retention (absence), 31–32
Outsized impact, achievement, 9
Overwhelm
  contributors, 58
  impact, 54
  occurrence, 51

Packard Foundation, 92
Pareto Principle. *See* 80/20 rule
Participation, elevation, 145
Partners
  interaction, delay, 179
  investment, 118–119
  leveraging, 121
  question, 93
Partnership for Children and Youth, 91
Partnership to Raise Community Capital,
  163–164
Peace Corps, joining, 30
Peng, Yanni, 120
People
  abundance/presence, impact, 228
  changes, 219–220
  investment, 11
   absence, 57
Perdue, Frank, 163, 164
Perdue, Mitzi, 114–115, 163, 164
Periodic strategy development, 187
Personnel cost, payment (absence),
  14–15
Perspectives, engagement, 167–170
Philanthropic capital, usage, 31
Philanthropic vehicles, usage, 222
Philanthropists
  exposure, fear, 23
  research, conducting, 112
Philanthropists, overwhelming, 52–54
  badge of honor, wearing, 55
  change, impact, 53–54
  choices, impact, 53
  expectations, setting (problems), 55
  feeling
   contribution, 54–58
   normalcy, 57–58

  people, investment (absence), 57
  self-care, absence, 57
  strategy/plan, absence, 55–56
  systems, placement (absence), 56
  technology, investment (absence),
   56–57
  time, impact, 54
Philanthropy
  accomplishment
   direction, understanding, 62–64
   question, 74–76
  advisor, usage, 116
  approach, question, 74–76
  behavior, problems (examples), 68–70
  bully, role, 69
  corporate irresponsible, role, 69
  criminal, 69
  dagger-through-the-heart funder, 69
  driving force, 202
  ego-driven, role, 69
  expectations, setting (problems), 55
  goals, reaching, 31–32
  infrastructure, investment, 119–120
  instinct, usage, 139
  journey, navigation, 18
  mean, role, 69
  money, spending, 109
  people
   involvement, determination, 92
   presence, 10
  perspectives, diversity, 167–170
  plan, absence, 55–56
  power tripper, 70
  question, 72–74, 86
  renegade, 69
  services, provision, 31–32
  shape-shifter, role, 69
  solutions, complicating, 38–39
  spotlight seeker, 69
  steps, problems, 51
  system, junk (impact), 37–38
  tax-benefit grabber, 70
  time wasters, 68
  toxic role, 69
  value, addition, 179
Philanthropy Roundtable, 197
Philanthropy, steps (excess), 43
  impact, 46–49
  meaning, 44–46
  reasons, 49–50

Philanthropy strategy
  absence, 55–56
  achivement, difficulty, 64–66
  annual strategy refresh, 203
  defining/importation, 196
  development, 218
  formulation, 196–199
    retreat, questions (usage), 201
  framework, 63
  implementation, 63, 196, 211
    leader assumption, 64
  initiation, question, 76–77
  presence, 202–203
  retreat, 201
  setting/implementation, board/staff roles, 201
Policies
  advocacy
    avoidance, 150–151
    grant, nonprofit request, 4–5
    support, 14, 151–152
  change, 134–135, 150–152
  implementation, support, 152
Policies, addressing, 145
PolicyLink, 155
Policy Matters Ohio, 159
Power tripper, 70
Printed calendar, usage, 129
Priorities, 217
  attention, 124–125
  calendar, comparison, 54
  communication, 207
  identification, 212–215
  ranking, 202
  simplicity, 65
  time allocation, 125–126
Private foundation
  creation, 94
  strategy refresh, 38
Problems, learning (fear), 28–30
Problem solving
  assumptions, 204
  data gathering, excess, 204
  process, impact, 204–205
  scheduling, usage, 205
  skills, 52
Procedures/practices, addressing, 145
Process
  changes, 220–222
  importance, 204

Productivity
  busyness, confusion, 62
Productivity propensity, identification, 129
Program expansion, 5
Program team, support, 96
Progress check, usage, 201
Project
  assignation, 129–130
  vetting, 133
Proposal. *See* Request for proposal
  guidelines, release, 179
  review, 45, 61, 63, 66
Prudent risk, determination, 104
Purple Bridge Management, 29

Quality
  abundance, 112
  impact, 17
  reduction, steps excess (impact), 47
Questions
  asking, 71, 92–93
    cessation, 131
  does this bring me joy, 104–106
  how can i do this in half the time, 126
  initiation, 81
  problems, 77–78
  strategic questions, usage, 73
  tactical questions, usage, 73
  thinking, 180
  what, 84–86
  what are all the ways we can do this, 97–98
  what are our best practices internally, 95–97
  what do I know already, 86–88
  what don't I know, 88–89
  what's the risk, 102–104
  what would best-in-class look like, 101–102
  what would you do differently, 98–99
  who else needs to be involved, 89–95
  why, 82–84

Race Equity and Inclusion Action Guide (Annie E. Casey Foundation), 127, 149, 157
Rawa, community member engagement, 94
Red tape, 44–45
  origination, 49
Relationships
  asset, 109
  building, 18, 139
  leveraging, 121
  strain, 102

Relationships (*continued*)
  trusting relationships, 169
    building, 165–167
Renegade, role, 69
Reputational capital, 171
Reputation, damage, 102, 103
Request
  negation, 127
  steps, meeting, 44
Request for proposal (RFP)
  development, 7, 179
  issuance, 45
  processes, 136
    creation, 205
  receiving, 47
Research, conducting, 152
Resilience, 112–113
Resilience Advantage, The (Citrin), 113
Resources
  abundance, 112
  investment, 191
  stewards, role, 40–41
Response
  acceleration, commitment, 41
  slowness, 35, 44
Retreat. *See* Strategy
Richards, Carl, 55
Risk, 159
  assessment, 77
  elimination, 103
  potential, 103
  prudent risk, determination, 104
  taking, 115
  tolerance, 187
R.J. McElroy Trust, 137
Robert, Michael, 187
Robert Sterling Clark Foundation, 131, 137
Robert Wood Johnson Foundation, grants,
  138
Rockefeller Brothers Fund, funding, 94
Rockefeller Foundation, 147
Root cause, 8
  addressing, 152–155

Saint Luke's Foundation, 159
San Francisco Foundation, 157–158
Scarcity mentality, 6–10
  analysis, 110–111
  obliviousness, 110
Scarcity-minded donors, impact, 5–6

Scarcity mind-set, 5, 7
  causes, 19
  knowledge, 17–19
  quiz, 17
Schink, Margaret, 100
Schulz, Jean/Charles, 184
Self-care, absence, 57
Self-change, 149
Self-dealing, 104
Self-development, courage, 112
Self-investment, 116–118
Self-limitation, 7–8
Selleck, Tom, 23
Setili, Amanda, 181–182
Seven-hour strategy formulation, 200–202
Seven-week strategy formulation,
  200–201
Shape-shifter, role, 69
Shaw, Julie, 100
Sheep dipping, 38
Sheraton Hotels, 164
Shields, Meredith, 25
Siegel, David, 191
Silver Giving Foundation, 153
Sinek, Simon, 82
Site visits, requirement, 179
Small thinking, impact, 102
Smucker, Mark, 90
Social change, frugality (impact), 4
Social conscience, 70
Social media
  impact, 23
  usage, 74
Solidaire, 149
Solutions, seeking, 155–158, 168–169
Sorenson Impact Foundation, 25, 142
Speaking engagements, 126
Speech writers, impact, 57
Speed, 134–136, 222, 227–228
  acceleration, 220
  approach, 139–140
  impact, 17
  increase, 76–77, 123
Spotlight seeker, 69
Springs Close Foundation, 170
Sprint. *See* Strategic sprint
Staff
  hiring, 139
  productivity, 5
Staff, organization, 216

Stakeholders, experiences/outcomes
(improvement), 145
Start with Why (Sinek), 82
Stewardship, inadequacy (fear),
25–27
Strategic fit, innovation criteria, 188
Strategic friction, 203–206
Strategic planning
bucket, 204
conducting, 205
Strategic questions, usage, 73
Strategic sprint, 199–200
durations, 200
flexibility, 202
Strategy. *See* Philanthropy strategy
Strategy Transition Year, 66
Strengths-based approach, 146
Stuart, David, 81
Stuart Foundation, 153, 168
Success
chances, improvement, 177
collective success, impact, 223
Sullivan, Michelle, 155
Summarizing, action, 200
Summer Matters, 91–92
Sustaining Grants Program (Cummings
Foundation), 162
Sykes, Nonet, 127
Systems
definition, 144
elements, 145
Systems change, 144–149, 220–222
definition, 145
initiation, 145–147
movements, support, 147–149

Tactical questions, usage, 73
Tactics, impact, 73
Talent, 116–117, 201
hiring, 12
strengthening, 163–165
Talent, investment, 14–15, 115
absence, 10–13
regularity, absence, 17
Tax-benefit grabber, 70
Tax documents, filing, 100
Taxes, preparation, 57
Team
acceleration, 130–136
building, importance, 15

grantmaking strategies, implications, 96
improvements, 131
Technology
investment, 117
absence, 56–57
knowledge, 182
Tewa (fund), 161
Thinking big, 114–115
Thinking, exposure, 182
Thousand Currents, 148
Time
allocation, 125–126
asset, 109
cost assessment, 132–134
investment, 191
management practices, 96
recouping, 123–130
saving, 18
scheduling, 217–219, 227
Time wasters, role, 68
Total Portfolio Management, 172
Touchpoints. *See* Daily touchpoints
Transformational giving, impact, 142
Transformative collaboration, 153
Trauma-informed care, 83
Trends, identification, 185
Trustees, impact, 116
Trust, establishment, 166–167
Trusting relationships, 169
building, 165–167
Turner, Emma, 70

UNICEF, 146
Unleveraged assets, 225
Urgent Action Fund for Women's Human
Rights, launching, 100

Vadon Foundation, 46, 198–199, 206
Values, 201
clarity, 74
delivery, 111
strategy formulation, 196
Vendors, payment approval time, 179
Virtual administrative assistants, 57
Vision, 201
establishment, 151
strategy formulation, 197
Voice messages, leaving, 179
Voices, elevation, 145
Vulnerability, 166

Walker, Darren, 161–162
Walton Family Foundation, 147, 153
Way, Charles, 28–29
Wealth
  creation, 84
  intergenerational transfer, 226
Weiss, Alan, 128, 187, 223
Wellcome Trust, 192
What are all the ways we can do this?
    (question), 97–98
What are our best practices internally?
    (question), 95–97
What do I know already? (question), 86–88
What don't I know? (question), 88–89
What, question, 84–86
WhatsApp chats, 124
What's the risk? (question), 102–104
What would best-in-class look like (question),
    101–102
What would you do differently? (question),
    98–99
Who else needs to be involved? (question),
    89–95
Why (question), 82–84
William and Flora Hewlett Foundation, 162
  grantmaking practice changes, 136

Williams, Rick, 94
Winfrey, Oprah, 142–143
Work
  importance, 123
  streams, organization, 216
  workplace culture valuation, 17
Workday
  completion, proportion, 127–128
  first hour, usage, 125
  interruptions, prevention,
    128–129
  priorities, attention, 124–125
  productivity propensity, identification,
    129
  project, assignation, 129–130
  request, negation, 127
  time, allocation, 125–126
Workshop, participation, 30
World
  change, 225
  problems, impact, 52–53
Worldwide Initiatives for Grantmaker Support
    (WINGS), 120

Zuckerberg, Mark, 219
Zulily (retailer), 198–199